THE NEXT 100 YEARS

THE

NEXT

100

YEARS

A FORECAST FOR THE 21ST CENTURY

GEORGE FRIEDMAN

First published in Great Britain in 2009 by
Allison & Busby Limited
13 Charlotte Mews
London W1T 4EJ
www.allisonandbusby.com

First published in the United States in 2009 by Double Day,
an imprint of The Doubleday Publishing Group,
a division of Random House, Inc., New York.

All maps created by Stratfor.
Book design by Elizabeth Rendfleisch.

A CIP catalogue record for this book is available from
the British Library.

10 9 8 7 6 5 4 3 2 1

13-ISBN 978-0-7490-0762-1 (Hardback)
13-ISBN 978-0-7490-0752-2 (Trade Paperback)

Paper used in this publication is from sustainably managed sources.
All of the wood used is procured from legal sources and is fully traceable.
The producing mill uses schemes such as ISO 14001
to monitor environmental impact.

Printed and bound in the UK by
CPI Mackays, Chatham ME5 8TD

For Meredith, muse and taskmaster

To him who looks upon the world rationally, the world in turn presents a rational aspect. The relation is mutual.

—George W. F. Hegel

CONTENTS

LIST OF ILLUSTRATIONS

AUTHOR'S NOTE

I have no crystal ball. I do, however, have a method that has served me well, imperfect though it might be, in understanding the past and anticipating the future. Underneath the disorder of history, my task is to try to see the order—and to anticipate what events, trends, and technology that order will bring forth. Forecasting a hundred years ahead may appear to be a frivolous activity, but, as I hope you will see, it is a rational, feasible process, and it is hardly frivolous. I will have grandchildren in the not-distant future, and some of them will surely be alive in the twenty-second century. That thought makes all of this very real.

In this book, I am trying to transmit a sense of the future. I will, of course, get many details wrong. But the goal is to identify the major tendencies—geopolitical, technological, demographic, cultural, military—in their broadest sense, and to define the major events that might take place. I will be satisfied if I explain something about how the world works today, and how that, in turn, defines how it will work in the future. And I will be delighted if my grandchildren, glancing at this book in 2100, have reason to say, "Not half bad."

THE NEXT 100 YEARS

OVERTURE

An Introduction to the American Age

Imagine that you were alive in the summer of 1900, living in London, then the capital of the world. Europe ruled the Eastern Hemisphere. There was hardly a place that, if not ruled directly, was not indirectly controlled from a European capital. Europe was at peace and enjoying unprecedented prosperity. Indeed, European interdependence due to trade and investment was so great that serious people were claiming that war had become impossible—and if not impossible, would end within weeks of beginning—because global financial markets couldn't withstand the strain. The future seemed fixed: a peaceful, prosperous Europe would rule the world.

Imagine yourself now in the summer of 1920. Europe had been torn apart by an agonizing war. The continent was in tatters. The Austro-Hungarian, Russian, German, and Ottoman empires were gone and millions had died in a war that lasted for years. The war ended when an American army of a million men intervened—an army that came and then just as quickly left. Communism dominated Russia, but it was not clear that it could survive. Countries that had been on the periphery of European power, like the United States and Japan, suddenly emerged as great powers. But one thing was certain—the peace treaty that had been imposed on Germany guaranteed that it would not soon reemerge.

Imagine the summer of 1940. Germany had not only reemerged but conquered France and dominated Europe. Communism had survived and the Soviet Union now was allied with Nazi Germany. Great Britain alone stood against Germany, and from the point of view of most reasonable people, the war was over. If there was not to be a thousand-year Reich, then certainly Europe's fate had been decided for a century. Germany would dominate Europe and inherit its empire.

Imagine now the summer of 1960. Germany had been crushed in the war, defeated less than five years later. Europe was occupied, split down the middle by the United States and the Soviet Union. The European empires were collapsing, and the United States and Soviet Union were competing over who would be their heir. The United States had the Soviet Union surrounded and, with an overwhelming arsenal of nuclear weapons, could annihilate it in hours. The United States had emerged as the global superpower. It dominated all of the world's oceans, and with its nuclear force could dictate terms to anyone in the world. Stalemate was the best the Soviets could hope for—unless the Soviets invaded Germany and conquered Europe. That was the war everyone was preparing for. And in the back of everyone's mind, the Maoist Chinese, seen as fanatical, were the other danger.

Now imagine the summer of 1980. The United States had been defeated in a seven-year war—not by the Soviet Union, but by communist North Vietnam. The nation was seen, and saw itself, as being in retreat. Expelled from Vietnam, it was then expelled from Iran as well, where the oil fields, which it no longer controlled, seemed about to fall into the hands of the Soviet Union. To contain the Soviet Union, the United States had formed an alliance with Maoist China—the American president and the Chinese chairman holding an amiable meeting in Beijing. Only this alliance seemed able to contain the powerful Soviet Union, which appeared to be surging.

Imagine now the summer of 2000. The Soviet Union had completely collapsed. China was still communist in name but had become capitalist in practice. NATO had advanced into Eastern Europe and even into the former Soviet Union. The world was prosperous and peaceful. Everyone knew that geopolitical considerations had become secondary to economic considerations, and the only problems were regional ones in basket cases like Haiti or Kosovo.

Then came September 11, 2001, and the world turned on its head again.

At a certain level, when it comes to the future, the only thing one can be sure of is that common sense will be wrong. There is no magic twenty-year cycle; there is no simplistic force governing this pattern. It is simply that the things that appear to be so permanent and dominant at any given moment in history can change with stunning rapidity. Eras come and go. In international relations, the way the world looks right now is not at all how it will look in twenty years . . . or even less. The fall of the Soviet Union was hard to imagine, and that is exactly the point. Conventional political analysis suffers from a profound failure of imagination. It imagines passing clouds to be permanent and is blind to powerful, long-term shifts taking place in full view of the world.

If we were at the beginning of the twentieth century, it would be impossible to forecast the particular events I've just listed. But there are some things that could have been—and, in fact, were—forecast. For example, it was obvious that Germany, having united in 1871, was a major power in an insecure position (trapped between Russia and France) and wanted to redefine the European and global systems. Most of the conflicts in the first half of the twentieth century were about Germany's status in Europe. While the times and places of wars couldn't be forecast, the probability that there *would* be a war could be and *was* forecast by many Europeans.

The harder part of this equation would be forecasting that the wars would be so devastating and that after the first and second world wars were over, Europe would lose its empire. But there were those, particularly after the invention of dynamite, who predicted that war would now be catastrophic. If the forecasting on technology had been combined with the forecasting on geopolitics, the shattering of Europe might well have been predicted. Certainly the rise of the United States and Russia was predicted in the nineteenth century. Both Alexis de Tocqueville and Friedrich Nietzsche forecast the preeminence of these two countries. So, standing at the beginning of the twentieth century, it would have been possible to forecast its general outlines, with discipline and some luck.

THE TWENTY-FIRST CENTURY

Standing at the beginning of the twenty-first century, we need to identify the single pivotal event for this century, the equivalent of German unification for the twentieth century. After the debris of the European empire is cleared away, as well as what's left of the Soviet Union, one power remains standing and overwhelmingly powerful. That power is the United States. Certainly, as is usually the case, the United States currently appears to be making a mess of things around the world. But it's important not to be confused by the passing chaos. The United States is economically, militarily, and politically the most powerful country in the world, and there is no real challenger to that power. Like the Spanish-American War, a hundred years from now the war between the United States and the radical Islamists will be little remembered regardless of the prevailing sentiment of this time.

Ever since the Civil War, the United States has been on an extraordinary economic surge. It has turned from a marginal developing nation into an economy bigger than the next four countries combined. Militarily, it has gone from being an insignificant force to dominating the globe. Politically, the United States touches virtually everything, sometimes intentionally and sometimes simply because of its presence. As you read this book, it will seem that it is America-centric, written from an American point of view. That may be true, but the argument I'm making is that the world does, in fact, pivot around the United States.

This is not only due to American power. It also has to do with a fundamental shift in the way the world works. For the past five hundred years, Europe was the center of the international system, its empires creating a single global system for the first time in human history. The main highway to Europe was the North Atlantic. Whoever controlled the North Atlantic controlled access to Europe—and Europe's access to the world. The basic geography of global politics was locked into place.

Then, in the early 1980s, something remarkable happened. For the first time in history, transpacific trade equaled transatlantic trade. With Europe reduced to a collection of secondary powers after World War II, and the shift in trade patterns, the North Atlantic was no longer the single key to anything. Now whatever country controlled both the North Atlantic and the Pacific could control, if it wished, the world's trading system, and therefore the global economy. In the twenty-first century, any nation located on both oceans has a tremendous advantage.

Given the cost of building naval power and the huge cost of deploying it around the world, the power native to both oceans became the preeminent actor in the international system for the same reason that Britain dominated the nineteenth century: it lived on the sea it had to control. In this way, North America has replaced Europe as the center of gravity in the world, and whoever dominates North America is virtually assured of being the dominant global power. For the twenty-first century at least, that will be the United States.

The inherent power of the United States coupled with its geographic position makes the United States the pivotal actor of the twenty-first century. That certainly doesn't make it loved. On the contrary, its power makes it feared. The history of the twenty-first century, therefore, particularly the first half, will revolve around two opposing struggles. One will be secondary powers forming coalitions to try to contain and control the United States. The second will be the United States acting preemptively to prevent an effective coalition from forming.

If we view the beginning of the twenty-first century as the dawn of the American Age (superseding the European Age), we see that it began with a group of Muslims seeking to re-create the Caliphate—the great Islamic empire that once ran from the Atlantic to the Pacific. Inevitably, they had to strike at the United States in an attempt to draw the world's primary power into war, trying to demonstrate its weakness in order to trigger an Islamic uprising. The United States responded by invading the Islamic world. But its goal wasn't victory. It wasn't even clear what victory would mean. Its goal was simply to disrupt the Islamic world and set it against itself, so that an Islamic empire could not emerge.

The United States doesn't need to win wars. It needs to simply disrupt things so the other side can't build up sufficient strength to challenge it. On one level, the twenty-first century will see a series of confrontations involving lesser powers trying to build coalitions to control American behavior and the United States' mounting military operations to disrupt them. The twenty-first century will see even more war than the twentieth century, but the wars will be much less catastrophic, because of both technological changes and the nature of the geopolitical challenge.

As we've seen, the changes that lead to the next era are always shockingly unexpected, and the first twenty years of this new century will be no exception. The U.S.–Islamist war is already ending and the next conflict is in sight. Russia is re-creating its old sphere of influence, and that sphere of influence will inevitably challenge the United States. The Russians will be moving westward on the great northern European plain. As Russia reconstructs its power, it will encounter the U.S.-dominated NATO in the three Baltic countries—Estonia, Latvia, and Lithuania—as well as in Poland. There will be other points of friction in the early twenty-first century, but this new cold war will supply the flash points after the U.S.–Islamist war dies down.

The Russians can't avoid trying to reassert power, and the United States can't avoid trying to resist. But in the end Russia can't win. Its deep internal problems, massively declining population, and poor infrastructure ultimately make Russia's long-term survival prospects bleak. And the second cold war, less frightening and much less global than the first, will end as the first did, with the collapse of Russia.

There are many who predict that China is the next challenger to the United States, not Russia. I don't agree with that view for three reasons. First, when you look at a map of China closely, you see that it is really a very isolated country physically. With Siberia in the north, the Himalayas and jungles to the south, and most of China's population in the eastern part of the country, the Chinese aren't going to easily expand. Second, China has not been a major naval power for centuries, and building a navy requires a long time not only to build ships but to create well-trained and experienced sailors.

Third, there is a deeper reason for not worrying about China. China is inherently unstable. Whenever it opens its borders to the outside world, the coastal region becomes prosperous, but the vast majority of Chinese in the interior remain impoverished. This leads to tension, conflict, and instability. It also leads to economic decisions made for political reasons, resulting in inefficiency and corruption. This is not the first time that China has opened itself to foreign trade, and it will not be the last time that it becomes unstable as a result. Nor will it be the last time that a figure like Mao emerges to close the country off from the outside, equalize the wealth—or poverty—and begin the cycle anew. There are some who believe that the trends of the last thirty years will continue indefinitely. I believe the Chinese cycle will move to its next and inevitable phase in the coming decade. Far from being a challenger, China is a country the United States will be trying to bolster and hold together as a counterweight to the Russians. Current Chinese economic dynamism does not translate into long-term success.

In the middle of the century, other powers will emerge, countries that aren't thought of as great powers today, but that I expect will become more powerful and assertive over the next few decades. Three stand out in particular. The first is Japan. It's the second-largest economy in the world and the most vulnerable, being highly dependent on the importation of raw materials, since it has almost none of its own. With a history of militarism, Japan will not remain the marginal pacifistic power it has been. It cannot. Its own deep population problems and abhorrence of large-scale immigration will force it to look for new workers in other countries. Japan's vulnerabilities, which I've written about in the past and which the Japanese have managed better than I've expected up until this point, in the end will force a shift in policy.

Then there is Turkey, currently the seventeenth-largest economy in the world. Historically, when a major Islamic empire has emerged, it has been dominated by the Turks. The Ottomans collapsed at the end of World War I, leaving modern Turkey in its wake. But Turkey is a stable platform in the midst of chaos. The Balkans, the Caucasus, and the Arab world to the south are all unstable. As Turkey's power grows—and its economy and military are already the most powerful in the region—so will Turkish influence.

Finally there is Poland. Poland hasn't been a great power since the sixteenth century. But it once was—and, I think, will be again. Two factors make this possible. First will be the decline of Germany. Its economy is large and still growing, but it has lost the dynamism it has had for two centuries. In addition, its population is going to fall dramatically in the next fifty years, further undermining its economic power. Second, as the Russians press on the Poles from the east, the Germans won't have an appetite for a third war with Russia. The United States, however, will back Poland, providing it with massive economic and technical support. Wars—when your country isn't destroyed—stimulate economic growth, and Poland will become the leading power in a coalition of states facing the Russians.

Japan, Turkey, and Poland will each be facing a United States even more confident than it was after the second fall of the Soviet Union. That will be an explosive situation. As we will see during the course of this book, the relationships among these four countries will greatly affect the twenty-first century, leading, ultimately, to the next global war. This war will be fought differently from any in history—with weapons that are today in the realm of science fiction. But as I will try to outline, this mid-twenty-first century conflict will grow out of the dynamic forces born in the early part of the new century.

Tremendous technical advances will come out of this war, as they did out of World War II, and one of them will be especially critical. All sides will be looking for new forms of energy to substitute for hydrocarbons, for many obvious reasons. Solar power is theoretically the most efficient energy source on earth, but solar power requires massive arrays of receivers. Those receivers take up a lot of space on the earth's surface and have many negative environmental impacts—not to mention being subject to the disruptive cycles of night and day. During the coming global war, however, concepts developed prior to the war for space-based electrical generation, beamed to earth in the form of microwave radiation, will be rapidly translated from prototype to reality. Getting a free ride on the back of military space launch capability, the new energy source will be underwritten in much the same way as the Internet or the railroads were, by government support. And that will kick off a massive economic boom.

But underlying all of this will be the single most important fact of the twenty-first century: the end of the population explosion. By 2050, advanced industrial countries will be losing population at a dramatic rate. By 2100, even the most underdeveloped countries will have reached birthrates that will stabilize their populations. The entire global system has been built since 1750 on the expectation of continually expanding populations. More workers, more consumers, more soldiers—this was always the expectation. In the twenty-first century, however, that will cease to be true. The entire system of production will shift. The shift will force the world into a greater dependence on technology—particularly robots that will substitute for human labor, and intensified genetic research (not so much for the purpose of extending life but to make people productive longer).

What will be the more immediate result of a shrinking world population? Quite simply, in the first half of the century, the population bust will create a major labor shortage in advanced industrial countries. Today, developed countries see the problem as keeping immigrants out. Later in the first half of the twenty-first century, the problem will be persuading them to come. Countries will go so far as to pay people to move there. This will include the United States, which will be competing for increasingly scarce immigrants and will be doing everything it can to induce Mexicans to come to the United States—an ironic but inevitable shift.

These changes will lead to the final crisis of the twenty-first century. Mexico currently is the fifteenth-largest economy in the world. As the Europeans slip out, the Mexicans, like the Turks, will rise in the rankings until by the late twenty-first century they will be one of the major economic powers in the world. During the great migration north encouraged by the United States, the population balance in the old Mexican Cession (that is, the areas of the United States taken from Mexico in the nineteenth century) will shift dramatically until much of the region is predominantly Mexican.

The social reality will be viewed by the Mexican government simply as rectification of historical defeats. By 2080 I expect there to be a serious confrontation between the United States and an increasingly powerful and assertive Mexico. That confrontation may well have unforeseen consequences for the United States, and will likely not end by 2100.

Much of what I've said here may seem pretty hard to fathom. The idea that the twenty-first century will culminate in a confrontation between Mexico and the United States is certainly hard to imagine in 2009, as is a powerful Turkey or Poland. But go back to the beginning of this chapter, when I described how the world looked at twenty-year intervals during the twentieth century, and you can see what I'm driving at: common sense is the one thing that will certainly be wrong.

Obviously, the more granular the description, the less reliable it gets. It is impossible to forecast precise details of a coming century—apart from the fact that I'll be long dead by then and won't know what mistakes I made.

But it's my contention that it is indeed possible to see the broad outlines of what is going to happen, and to try to give it some definition, however speculative that definition might be. That's what this book is about.

FORECASTING A HUNDRED YEARS AHEAD

Before I delve into any details of global wars, population trends, or technological shifts, it is important that I address my method—that is, precisely *how* I can forecast what I do. I don't intend to be taken seriously on the details of the war in 2050 that I forecast. But I do want to be taken seriously in terms of how wars will be fought then, about the centrality of American power, about the likelihood of other countries challenging that power, and about some of the countries I think will—and won't—challenge that power. And doing that takes some justification. The idea of a U.S.–Mexican confrontation and even war will leave most reasonable people dubious, but I would like to demonstrate why and how these assertions can be made.

One point I've already made is that reasonable people are incapable of anticipating the future. The old New Left slogan "Be Practical, Demand the Impossible" needs to be changed: "Be Practical, Expect the Impossible." This idea is at the heart of my method. From another, more substantial perspective, this is called geopolitics.

Geopolitics is not simply a pretentious way of saying "international relations." It is a method for thinking about the world and forecasting what will happen down the road. Economists talk about an invisible hand, in which the self-interested, short-term activities of people lead to what Adam Smith called "the wealth of nations." Geopolitics applies the concept of the invisible hand to the behavior of nations and other international actors. The pursuit of short-term self-interest by nations and by their leaders leads, if not to the wealth of nations, then at least to predictable behavior and, therefore, the ability to forecast the shape of the future international system.

Geopolitics and economics both assume that the players are rational, at least in the sense of knowing their own short-term self-interest. As rational actors, reality provides them with limited choices. It is assumed that, on the whole, people and nations will pursue their self-interest, if not flawlessly, then at least not randomly. Think of a chess game. On the surface, it appears that each player has twenty potential opening moves. In fact, there are many fewer because most of these moves are so bad that they quickly lead to defeat. The better you are at chess, the more clearly you see your options, and the fewer moves there actually are available. The better the player, the more predictable the moves. The grandmaster plays with absolute predictable precision—until that one brilliant, unexpected stroke.

Nations behave the same way. The millions or hundreds of millions of people who make up a nation are constrained by reality. They generate leaders who would not become leaders if they were irrational. Climbing to the top of millions of people is not something fools often do. Leaders understand their menu of next moves and execute them, if not flawlessly, then at least pretty well. An occasional master will come along with a stunningly unexpected and successful move, but for the most part, the act of governance is simply executing the necessary and logical next step. When politicians run a country's foreign policy, they operate the same way. If a leader dies and is replaced, another emerges and more likely than not continues what the first one was doing.

I am not arguing that political leaders are geniuses, scholars, or even gentlemen and ladies. Simply, political leaders know how to be leaders or they wouldn't have emerged as such. It is the delight of all societies to belittle their political leaders, and leaders surely do make mistakes. But the mistakes they make, when carefully examined, are rarely stupid. More likely, mistakes are forced on them by circumstance. We would all like to believe that we— or our favorite candidate—would never have acted so stupidly. It is rarely true. Geopolitics therefore does not take the individual leader very seriously, any more than economics takes the individual businessman too seriously. Both are players who know how to manage a process but are not free to break the very rigid rules of their professions.

Politicians are therefore rarely free actors. Their actions are determined by circumstances, and public policy is a response to reality. Within narrow margins, political decisions can matter. But the most brilliant leader of Iceland will never turn it into a world power, while the stupidest leader of Rome at its height could not undermine Rome's fundamental power. Geopolitics is not about the right and wrong of things, it is not about the virtues or vices of politicians, and it is not about foreign policy debates. Geopolitics is about broad impersonal forces that constrain nations and human beings and compel them to act in certain ways.

The key to understanding economics is accepting that there are always unintended consequences. Actions people take for their own good reasons have results they don't envision or intend. The same is true with geopolitics. It is doubtful that the village of Rome, when it started its expansion in the seventh century BC, had a master plan for conquering the Mediterranean world five hundred years later. But the first action its inhabitants took against neighboring villages set in motion a process that was both constrained by reality and filled with unintended consequences. Rome wasn't planned, and neither did it just happen.

Geopolitical forecasting, therefore, doesn't assume that everything is predetermined. It does mean that what people think they are doing, what they hope to achieve, and what the final outcome is are not the same things. Nations and politicians pursue their immediate ends, as constrained by reality as a grandmaster is constrained by the chessboard, the pieces, and the rules. Sometimes they increase the power of the nation. Sometimes they lead the nation to catastrophe. It is rare that the final outcome will be what they initially intended to achieve.

Geopolitics assumes two things. First, it assumes that humans organize themselves into units larger than families, and that by doing this, they must engage in politics. It also assumes that humans have a natural loyalty to the things they were born into, the people and the places. Loyalty to a tribe, a city, or a nation is natural to people. In our time, national identity matters a great deal. Geopolitics teaches that the relationship between these nations is a vital dimension of human life, and that means that war is ubiquitous.

Second, geopolitics assumes that the character of a nation is determined to a great extent by geography, as is the relationship between nations. We use the term *geography* broadly. It includes the physical characteristics of a location, but it goes beyond that to look at the effects of a place on individuals and communities. In antiquity, the difference between Sparta and Athens was the difference between a landlocked city and a maritime empire. Athens was wealthy and cosmopolitan, while Sparta was poor, provincial, and very tough. A Spartan was very different from an Athenian in both culture and politics.

If you understand those assumptions, then it is possible to think about large numbers of human beings, linked together through natural human bonds, constrained by geography, acting in certain ways. The United States is the United States and therefore must behave in a certain way. The same goes for Japan or Turkey or Mexico. When you drill down and see the forces that are shaping nations, you can see that the menu from which they choose is limited.

The twenty-first century will be like all other centuries. There will be wars, there will be poverty, there will be triumphs and defeats. There will be tragedy and good luck. People will go to work, make money, have children, fall in love, and come to hate. That is the one thing that is not cyclical. It is the permanent human condition. But the twenty-first century will be extraordinary in two senses: it will be the beginning of a new age, and it will see a new global power astride the world. That doesn't happen very often.

We are now in an America-centric age. To understand this age, we must understand the United States, not only because it is so powerful but because its culture will permeate the world and define it. Just as French culture and British culture were definitive during their times of power, so American culture, as young and barbaric as it is, will define the way the world thinks and lives. So studying the twenty-first century means studying the United States.

If there were only one argument I could make about the twenty-first century, it would be that the European Age has ended and that the North American Age has begun, and that North America will be dominated by the United States for the next hundred years. The events of the twenty-first century will pivot around the United States. That doesn't guarantee that the United States is necessarily a just or moral regime. It certainly does not mean that America has yet developed a mature civilization. It does mean that in many ways the history of the United States will be the history of the twenty-first century.

CHAPTER 1

THE DAWN OF THE AMERICAN AGE

There is a deep-seated belief in America that the United States is approaching the eve of its destruction. Read letters to the editor, peruse the Web, and listen to public discourse. Disastrous wars, uncontrolled deficits, high gasoline prices, shootings at universities, corruption in business and government, and an endless litany of other shortcomings—all of them quite real—create a sense that the American dream has been shattered and that America is past its prime. If that doesn't convince you, listen to Europeans. They will assure you that America's best day is behind it.

The odd thing is that all of this foreboding was present during the presidency of Richard Nixon, together with many of the same issues. There is a continual fear that American power and prosperity are illusory, and that disaster is just around the corner. The sense transcends ideology. Environmentalists and Christian conservatives are both delivering the same message. Unless we repent of our ways, we will pay the price—and it may be too late already.

It's interesting to note that the nation that believes in its manifest destiny has not only a sense of impending disaster but a nagging feeling that the country simply isn't what it used to be. We have a deep sense of nostalgia for the 1950s as a "simpler" time. This is quite a strange belief. With the Korean War and McCarthy at one end, Little Rock in the middle, and *Sputnik* and Berlin at the other end, and the very real threat of nuclear war throughout, the 1950s was actually a time of intense anxiety and foreboding. A widely read book published in the 1950s was entitled *The Age of Anxiety.* In the 1950s, they looked back nostalgically at an earlier America, just as we look back nostalgically at the 1950s.

American culture is the manic combination of exultant hubris and profound gloom. The net result is a sense of confidence constantly undermined by the fear that we may be drowned by melting ice caps caused by global warming or smitten dead by a wrathful God for gay marriage, both outcomes being our personal responsibility. American mood swings make it hard to develop a real sense of the United States at the beginning of the twenty-first century. But the fact is that the United States is stunningly powerful. It may be that it is heading for a catastrophe, but it is hard to see one when you look at the basic facts.

Let's consider some illuminating figures. Americans constitute about 4 percent of the world's population but produce about 26 percent of all goods and services. In 2007 U.S. gross domestic product was about $14 trillion, compared to the world's GDP of $54 trillion—about 26 percent of the world's economic activity takes place in the United States. The next largest economy in the world is Japan's, with a GDP of about $4.4 trillion—about a third the size of ours. The American economy is so huge that it is larger than the economies of the next four countries combined: Japan, Germany, China, and the United Kingdom.

Many people point at the declining auto and steel industries, which a generation ago were the mainstays of the American economy, as examples of a current deindustrialization of the United States. Certainly, a lot of industry has moved overseas. That has left the United States with industrial production of only $2.8 trillion (in 2006): the largest in the world, more than twice the size of the next largest industrial power, Japan, and larger than Japan's and China's industries combined.

There is talk of oil shortages, which certainly seem to exist and will undoubtedly increase. However, it is important to realize that the United States produced 8.3 million barrels of oil every day in 2006. Compare that with

9.7 million for Russia and 10.7 million for Saudi Arabia. U.S. oil production is 85 percent that of Saudi Arabia. The United States produces more oil than Iran, Kuwait, or the United Arab Emirates. Imports of oil into the country are vast, but given its industrial production, that's understandable. Comparing natural gas production in 2006, Russia was in first place with 22.4 trillion cubic feet and the United States was second with 18.7 trillion cubic feet. U.S. natural gas production is greater than that of the next five producers combined. In other words, although there is great concern that the United States is wholly dependent on foreign energy, it is actually one of the world's largest energy producers.

Given the vast size of the American economy, it is interesting to note that the United States is still underpopulated by global standards. Measured in inhabitants per square kilometer, the world's average population density is 49. Japan's is 338, Germany's is 230, and America's is only 31. If we exclude Alaska, which is largely uninhabitable, U.S. population density rises to 34. Compared to Japan or Germany, or the rest of Europe, the United States is hugely underpopulated. Even when we simply compare population in proportion to arable land—land that is suitable for agriculture—America has five times as much land per person as Asia, almost twice as much as Europe, and three times as much as the global average. An economy consists of land, labor, and capital. In the case of the United States, these numbers show that the nation can still grow—it has plenty of room to increase all three.

There are many answers to the question of why the U.S. economy is so powerful, but the simplest answer is military power. The United States completely dominates a continent that is invulnerable to invasion and occupation and in which its military overwhelms those of its neighbors. Virtually every other industrial power in the world has experienced devastating warfare in the twentieth century. The United States waged war, but America itself never experienced it. Military power and geographical reality created an economic reality. Other countries have lost time recovering from wars. The United States has not. It has actually grown because of them.

Consider this simple fact that I'll be returning to many times. The United States Navy controls all of the oceans of the world. Whether it's a junk in the South China Sea, a dhow off the African coast, a tanker in the

Persian Gulf, or a cabin cruiser in the Caribbean, every ship in the world moves under the eyes of American satellites in space and its movement is guaranteed—or denied—at will by the U.S. Navy. The combined naval force of the rest of the world doesn't come close to equaling that of the U.S. Navy.

This has never happened before in human history, even with Britain. There have been regionally dominant navies, but never one that was globally and overwhelmingly dominant. This has meant that the United States could invade other countries—but never be invaded. It has meant that in the final analysis the United States controls international trade. It has become the foundation of American security and American wealth. Control of the seas emerged after World War II, solidified during the final phase of the European Age, and is now the flip side of American economic power, the basis of its military power.

Whatever passing problems exist for the United States, the most important factor in world affairs is the tremendous imbalance of economic, military, and political power. Any attempt to forecast the twenty-first century that does not begin with the recognition of the extraordinary nature of American power is out of touch with reality. But I am making a broader, more unexpected claim, too: the United States is only at the beginning of its power. The twenty-first century will be the American century.

That assertion rests on a deeper point. For the past five hundred years, the global system has rested on the power of Atlantic Europe, the European countries that bordered on the Atlantic Ocean: Portugal, Spain, France, England, and to a lesser extent the Netherlands. These countries transformed the world, creating the first global political and economic system in human history. As we know, European power collapsed during the twentieth century, along with the European empires. This created a vacuum that was filled by the United States, the dominant power in North America, and the only great power bordering both the Atlantic and Pacific oceans. North America has assumed the place that Europe occupied for five hundred years, between Columbus's voyage in 1492 and the fall of the Soviet Union in 1991. It has become the center of gravity of the international system.

Why? In order to understand the twenty-first century, it is important to understand the fundamental structural shifts that took place late in the twentieth century, setting the stage for a new century that will be radically different in form and substance, just as the United States is so different from Europe. My argument is not only that something extraordinary has happened but that the United States has had very little choice in it. This isn't about policy. It is about the way in which impersonal geopolitical forces work.

EUROPE

Until the fifteenth century, humans lived in self-enclosed, sequestered worlds. Humanity did not know itself as consisting of a single fabric. The Chinese didn't know of the Aztecs, and the Mayas didn't know of the Zulus. The Europeans may have heard of the Japanese, but they didn't really know them—and they certainly didn't interact with them. The Tower of Babel had done more than make it impossible for people to speak to each other. It made civilizations oblivious to each other.

Europeans living on the eastern rim of the Atlantic Ocean shattered the barriers between these sequestered regions and turned the world into a single entity in which all of the parts interacted with each other. What happened to Australian aborigines was intimately connected to the British relationship with Ireland and the need to find penal colonies for British prisoners overseas. What happened to Inca kings was tied to the relationship between Spain and Portugal. The imperialism of Atlantic Europe created a single world.

Atlantic Europe became the center of gravity of the global system (see map, page 20). What happened in Europe defined much of what happened elsewhere in the world. Other nations and regions did everything with one eye on Europe. From the sixteenth to the twentieth century hardly any part of the world escaped European influence and power. Everything, for good or evil, revolved around it. And the pivot of Europe was the North Atlantic. Whoever controlled that stretch of water controlled the highway to the world.

Europe was neither the most civilized nor the most advanced region in the world. So what made it the center? Europe really was a technical and

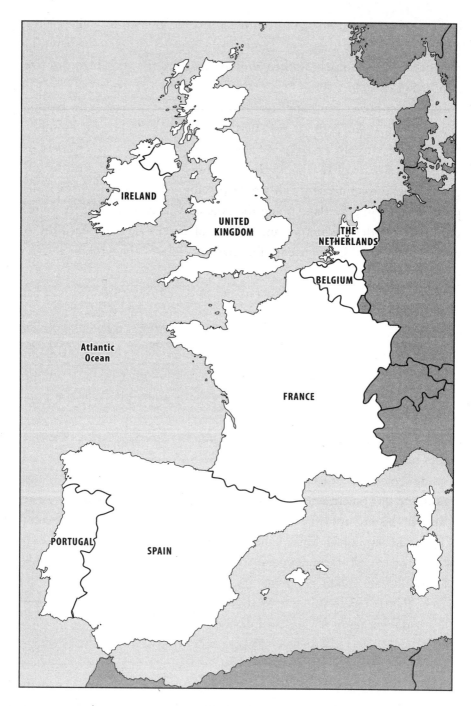

Atlantic Europe

intellectual backwater in the fifteenth century as opposed to China or the Islamic world. Why these small, out-of-the-way countries? And why did they begin their domination then and not five hundred years before or five hundred years later?

European power was about two things: money and geography. Europe depended on imports from Asia, particularly India. Pepper, for example, was not simply a cooking spice but also a meat preservative; its importation was a critical part of the European economy. Asia was filled with luxury goods that Europe needed, and would pay for, and historically Asian imports would come overland along the famous Silk Road and other routes until reaching the Mediterranean. The rise of Turkey—about which much more will be heard in the twenty-first century—closed these routes and increased the cost of imports.

European traders were desperate to find a way around the Turks. Spaniards and Portuguese—the Iberians—chose the nonmilitary alternative: they sought another route to India. The Iberians knew of only one route to India that avoided Turkey, down the length of the African coast and up into the Indian Ocean. They theorized about another route, assuming that the world was round, a route that would take them to India by going west.

This was a unique moment. At other points in history Atlantic Europe would have only fallen even deeper into backwardness and poverty. But the economic pain was real and the Turks were very dangerous, so there was pressure to do something. It was also a crucial psychological moment. The Spaniards, having just expelled the Muslims from Spain, were at the height of their barbaric hubris. Finally, the means for carrying out such exploration was at hand as well. Technology existed that, if properly used, might provide a solution to the Turkey problem.

The Iberians had a ship, the caravel, that could handle deep-sea voyages. They had an array of navigational devices, from the compass to the astrolabe. Finally they had guns, particularly cannons. All of these might have been borrowed from other cultures, but the Iberians integrated them into an effective economic and military system. They could now sail to distant places. When they arrived they were able to fight—and win. People who heard a cannon fire and saw a building explode tended to be more flexible in negotiations. When the Iberians reached their destinations, they could kick in the door and take over. Over the next several centuries, European ships, guns, and money dominated the world and created the first global system, the European Age.

Here is the irony: Europe dominated the world, but it failed to dominate itself. For five hundred years Europe tore itself apart in civil wars, and as a result there was never a European empire—there was instead a British empire, a Spanish empire, a French empire, a Portuguese empire, and so on. The European nations exhausted themselves in endless wars with each other while they invaded, subjugated, and eventually ruled much of the world.

There were many reasons for the inability of the Europeans to unite, but in the end it came down to a simple feature of geography: the English Channel. First the Spanish, then the French, and finally the Germans managed to dominate the European continent, but none of them could cross the Channel. Because no one could defeat Britain, conqueror after conqueror failed to hold Europe as a whole. Periods of peace were simply temporary truces. Europe was exhausted by the advent of World War I, in which over ten million men died—a good part of a generation. The European economy was shattered, and European confidence broken. Europe emerged as a demographic, economic, and cultural shadow of its former self. And then things got even worse.

THE FINAL BATTLE OF AN OLD AGE

The United States emerged from World War I as a global power. That power was clearly in its infancy, however. Geopolitically, the Europeans had another fight in them, and psychologically the Americans were not yet ready for a permanent place on the global stage. But two things did happen. In World War I the United States announced its presence with resounding authority. And the United States left a ticking time bomb in Europe that would guarantee America's power after the next war. That time bomb was the Treaty of Versailles, which ended World War I—but left unresolved the core conflicts over which the war had been fought. Versailles guaranteed another round of war.

And the war did resume in 1939, twenty-one years after the last one ended. Germany again attacked first, this time conquering France in six weeks. The United States stayed out of the war for a time, but made sure that the war didn't end in a German victory. Britain stayed in the war, and the United States kept it there with Lend-Lease. We all remember the Lend part—where the United States provided Britain with destroyers and other matériel to fight the Germans—but the Lease part is usually forgotten. The Lease part was where the British turned over almost all their naval facilities in the Western Hemisphere to the United States. Between control of those facilities and the role the U.S. Navy played in patrolling the Atlantic, the British were forced to hand the Americans the keys to the North Atlantic, which was, after all, Europe's highway to the world.

A reasonable estimate of World War II's cost to the world was about fifty million dead (military and civilian deaths combined). Europe had torn itself to shreds in this war, and nations were devastated. In contrast, the United States lost around half a million military dead and had almost no civilian casualties. At the end of the war, the American industrial plant was much stronger than before the war; the United States was the only combatant nation for which that was the case. No American cities were bombed (excepting Pearl Harbor), no U.S. territory was occupied (except two small islands in the Aleutians), and the United States suffered less than 1 percent of the war's casualties.

For that price, the United States emerged from World War II not only controlling the North Atlantic but ruling all of the world's oceans. It also occupied Western Europe, shaping the destinies of countries like France, the Netherlands, Belgium, Italy, and indeed Great Britain itself. The United States simultaneously conquered and occupied Japan, almost as an afterthought to the European campaigns.

Thus did the Europeans lose their empire—partly out of exhaustion, partly from being unable to bear the cost of holding it, and partly because the United States simply did not want them to continue to hold it. The empire melted away over the next twenty years, with only desultory resistance by the Europeans. The geopolitical reality (that could first be seen in Spain's dilemma centuries before) had played itself out to a catastrophic finish.

Here's a question: Was the United States' clear emergence in 1945 as the decisive global power a brilliant Machiavellian play? The Americans achieved global preeminence at the cost of 500,000 dead, in a war where fifty million others perished. Was Franklin Roosevelt brilliantly unscrupulous, or did becoming a superpower just happen in the course of his pursuing the "four freedoms" and the UN Charter? In the end, it doesn't matter. In geopolitics, the unintended consequences are the most important ones.

The U.S.–Soviet confrontation—known as the Cold War—was a truly global conflict. It was basically a competition over who would inherit Europe's tattered global empire. Although there was vast military strength on both sides, the United States had an inherent advantage. The Soviet Union was enormous but essentially landlocked. America was almost as vast but had easy access to the world's oceans. While the Soviets could not contain the Americans, the Americans could certainly contain the Soviets. And that was the American strategy: to contain and thereby strangle the Soviets. From the North Cape of Norway to Turkey to the Aleutian Islands, the United States created a massive belt of allied nations, all bordering on the Soviet Union—a belt that after 1970 included China itself. At every point where the Soviets had a port, they found themselves blocked by geography and the United States Navy.

Geopolitics has two basic competing views of geography and power. One view, held by an Englishman, Halford John Mackinder, argues that control of Eurasia means the control of the world. As he put it: "Who rules East Europe [Russian Europe] commands the Heartland. Who rules the Heartland commands the World-Island [Eurasia]. Who rules the World-Island commands the world." This thinking dominated British strategy and, indeed, U.S. strategy in the Cold War, as it fought to contain and strangle European Russia. Another view is held by an American, Admiral Alfred Thayer Mahan, considered the greatest American geopolitical thinker. In his book *The Influence of Sea Power on History*, Mahan makes the counterargument to Mackinder, arguing that control of the sea equals command of the world.

History confirmed that both were right, in a sense. Mackinder was correct in emphasizing the significance of a powerful and united Russia. The collapse of the Soviet Union elevated the United States to the level of sole global power. But it was Mahan, the American, who understood two crucial factors. The collapse of the Soviet Union originated in American sea power and also opened the door for U.S. naval power to dominate the world. Additionally, Mahan was correct when he argued that it is always cheaper to ship goods by sea than by any other means. As far back as the fifth century BC, the Athenians were wealthier than the Spartans because Athens had a port, a maritime fleet, and a navy to protect it. Maritime powers are always wealthier than nonmaritime neighbors, all other things being equal. With the advent of globalization in the fifteenth century, this truth became as near to absolute as one can get in geopolitics.

U.S. control of the sea meant that the United States was able not only to engage in but to define global maritime trade. It could make the rules, or at least block anyone else's rules, by denying other nations entry to the world's trade routes. In general, the United States shaped the international trading system more subtly, by using access to the vast American market as a lever to shape the behavior of other nations. It was not surprising, then, that in ad-

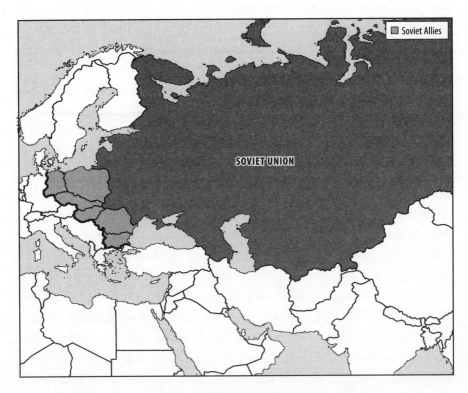

The Soviet Empire

dition to its natural endowments, the United States became enormously prosperous from its sea power and that the Soviet Union couldn't possibly compete, being landlocked.

Second, having control of the seas gave the United States a huge political advantage as well. America could not be invaded, but it could invade other countries—whenever and however it chose. From 1945 onward, the United States could wage wars without fear of having its lines of supply cut. No outside power could wage war on the continent of North America. In fact, no other nation could mount amphibious operations without American acquiescence. When the British went to war with Argentina over the Falklands in 1982, for example, it was possible only because the United States didn't prevent it. When the British, French, and Israelis invaded Egypt in 1956 against U.S. wishes, they had to withdraw.

Throughout the Cold War, an alliance with the United States was always more profitable than an alliance with the Soviet Union. The Soviets could offer arms, political support, some technology, and a host of other things. But the Americans could offer access to their international trading system and the right to sell into the American economy. This dwarfed everything else in importance. Exclusion from the system meant impoverishment; inclusion in the system meant wealth. Consider, as an example, the different fates of North and South Korea, West and East Germany.

It is interesting to note that throughout the Cold War, the United States was on the defensive psychologically. Korea, McCarthyism, Cuba, Vietnam, *Sputnik*, left-wing terrorism in the 1970s and 1980s, and harsh criticism of Reagan by European allies all created a constant sense of gloom and uncertainty in America. Atmospherics gave the United States the continual sense that its advantage in the Cold War was slipping away. Yet underneath the hood, in the objective reality of power relations, the Russians never had a chance. This disjuncture between the American psyche and geopolitical reality is important to remember for two reasons. First, it reveals the immaturity of American power. Second, it reveals a tremendous strength. Because the United States was insecure, it generated a level of effort and energy that was overwhelming. There was nothing casual or confident in the way the Americans—from political leaders to engineers to military and intelligence officers—waged the Cold War.

That is one of the primary reasons the United States was surprised when it won the Cold War. The United States and its alliance had the Soviet Union surrounded. The Soviets could not afford to challenge the Americans at sea and had instead to devote their budget to building armies and missiles, and they could not match American economic growth rates or entice their allies with economic benefits. The Soviet Union fell further and further behind. And then it collapsed.

The fall of the Soviet Union in 1991, 499 years after Columbus's expedition, ended an entire age in history. For the first time in half a millennium, power no longer resided in Europe, nor was Europe the focal point of international competition. After 1991, the sole global power in the world was the United States, which had become the center of the international system.

We have examined how the United States came to power in the twentieth century. There is one additional accompanying fact—a little-studied statistic that I mentioned earlier and that speaks volumes. In 1980, as the U.S.–Soviet duel was moving to its climax, transpacific trade rose to equal transatlantic trade for the first time in history. A mere ten years later, as the Soviet Union was collapsing, transpacific trade had soared to a level 50 percent greater than transatlantic trade. The entire geometry of international trade, and therefore of the global system, was undergoing an unparalleled shift.

How did this affect the rest of the world? Quite simply, the cost of sea lane control is enormous. Most trading countries can't bear the cost of controlling sea lanes and therefore depend on nations that do have the resources to do so. Naval powers therefore acquire enormous political leverage, and other nations don't want to challenge them. The cost of controlling an adjacent body of water is expensive. The cost of controlling a body of water thousands of miles away is overwhelming. Historically, there have been only a handful of nations that have been able to bear that expense—and it's no easier or cheaper today. Take a look at the U.S. defense budget and the amount spent on the navy and on related space systems. The cost of maintaining carrier battle groups in the Persian Gulf is a greater outlay than the total defense budgets of most countries. Controlling the Atlantic or the Pacific without a shoreline on both would be beyond the economic capability of just about any nation.

North America alone can house a transcontinental nation capable of projecting power simultaneously into the Atlantic and the Pacific. Therefore North America is the center of gravity of the international system. At the dawn of the American age, the United States is far and away the dominant power in North America. It is a country that simultaneously invaded Europe and Japan in 1944–45. It took military control of both bodies of water and retains it to this day. This is why it is in a position to preside over the new age.

But it is important to recall that Spain once dominated Europe and presided over the opening century of the European Age. While I expect that North America will be the center of gravity of the global system for the next few centuries, I also expect the United States to dominate North America for at least a century. But as with Spain, the assertion that North America is the center of gravity does not guarantee that the United States will always dominate North America. Many things can happen—from civil war to defeat in a foreign war to other states emerging on its borders over the centuries.

For the short term, however—and by that I mean the next hundred years—I will argue that the United States' power is so extraordinarily overwhelming, and so deeply rooted in economic, technological, and cultural realities, that the country will continue to surge through the twenty-first century, buffeted though it will be by wars and crises.

This isn't incompatible with American self-doubt. Psychologically, the United States is a bizarre mixture of overconfidence and insecurity. Interestingly, this is the precise description of the adolescent mind, and that is exactly the American condition in the twenty-first century. The world's leading power is having an extended adolescent identity crisis, complete with incredible new strength and irrational mood swings. Historically, the United States is an extraordinarily young and therefore immature society. So at this time we should expect nothing less from America than bravado and despair. How else should an adolescent feel about itself and its place in the world?

But if we think of the United States as an adolescent, early in its overall history, then we also know that, regardless of its self-image, adulthood lies ahead. Adults tend to be more stable and more powerful than adolescents. Therefore, it is logical to conclude that America is in the earliest phase of its power. It is not fully civilized. America, like Europe in the sixteenth century, is still barbaric (a description, not a moral judgment). Its culture is unformed. Its will is powerful. Its emotions drive it in different and contradictory directions.

Cultures live in one of three states. The first state is barbarism. Barbarians believe that the customs of their village are the laws of nature and that anyone who doesn't live the way they live is beneath contempt and requiring redemption or destruction. The third state is decadence. Decadents cynically believe that nothing is better than anything else. If they hold anyone in contempt, it is those who believe in anything. Nothing is worth fighting for.

Civilization is the second and most rare state. Civilized people are able to balance two contradictory thoughts in their minds. They believe that there are truths and that their cultures approximate those truths. At the same time, they hold open in their mind the possibility that they are in error. The combination of belief and skepticism is inherently unstable. Cultures pass through barbarism to civilization and then to decadence, as skepticism undermines self-certainty. Civilized people fight selectively but effectively. Obviously all cultures contain people who are barbaric, civilized, or decadent, but each culture is dominated at different times by one principle.

Europe was barbaric in the sixteenth century, as the self-certainty of Christianity fueled the first conquests. Europe passed into civilization in the eighteenth and nineteenth centuries and then collapsed into decadence in the course of the twentieth century. The United States is just beginning its cultural and historical journey. Until now it has not been sufficiently coherent to have a definitive culture. As it becomes the center of gravity of the world, it is developing that culture, which is inevitably barbaric. America is a place where the right wing despises Muslims for their faith and the left wing despises them for their treatment of women. Such seemingly different perspectives are tied together in the certainty that their own values are self-evidently best. And as with all barbaric cultures, Americans are ready to fight for their self-evident truths.

This is not meant as criticism, any more than an adolescent can be criticized for being an adolescent. It is a necessary and inevitable state of development. But the United States is a young culture and as such it is clumsy, direct, at times brutal, and frequently torn by deep internal dissension—its dissidents being united only in the certainty that their values are best. The United States is all of these things, but as with Europe in the sixteenth century, the United States will, for all of its apparent bumbling, be remarkably effective.

CHAPTER 2

EARTHQUAKE

THE U.S.–JIHADIST WAR

The American Age began in December 1991, when the Soviet Union collapsed, leaving the United States as the only global power in the world. But the twenty-first century truly began on September 11, 2001, ten years later, when planes slammed into the World Trade Center and the Pentagon. This was the first real test of the American Age. It is debatable whether the United States has actually won the U.S.–jihadist war— but it has certainly achieved its strategic goals. And it is also clear that the war is, as all wars do, moving toward an end of sorts.

People talk about "the long war," and the idea that the United States and Muslims will be fighting for a century. As is usually the case, what appears permanent is only a passing phase. Consider the twenty-year perspective we have been using. Conflict may continue, but the strategic challenge to American power is coming to an end. Al Qaeda has failed in its goals. The United States has succeeded, not so much in winning the war as in preventing the Islamists from winning, and, from a geopolitical perspective, that is good enough. The twenty-first century has begun with an American success that on the surface looks like not only a defeat but a deep political and moral embarrassment.

Al Qaeda's goal in 2001 was not simply to conduct an attack on the United States. Its goal was to conduct an attack that would demonstrate America's weakness and al Qaeda's strength. Revealing America's weakness, al Qaeda believed, would undermine governments in the Islamic world that relied on their relationship with the United States to stabilize their regimes, in countries like Egypt, Saudi Arabia, Pakistan, and Indonesia. Al Qaeda wanted to overthrow these governments because it knew that it could not achieve its goals unless it had control of a nation-state other than Afghanistan, which was too weak and isolated to serve as more than a temporary base.

The collapse of the Soviet Union obviously had massive effects on the international system. One was particularly surprising. A powerful Soviet Union and a powerful United States had actually stabilized the international system, creating a balance between superpowers. This was particularly true along the frontier of the Soviet empire, where both sides were poised for war. Europe, for example, was frozen into place by the Cold War. The slightest movement could have led to war, so neither the Soviets nor the Americans permitted such movement. The most interesting features of the Cold War, in fact, were all the wars that didn't happen. There was no invasion of Germany by the Soviets. There was no thrust to the Persian Gulf. Above all, there was no nuclear holocaust.

It is important to scrutinize the last twenty years. They are the foundation of what's to come in the next hundred years—and that is why I'll spend more time in this chapter talking about the past instead of the future. Think of the Soviet collapse as a giant tug-of-war in which one side suddenly weakened and let go of the rope. The side still holding the rope won, but lost its balance, and therefore the triumph was mixed with massive confusion and disruption. The rope, which had been locked into place by the two sides, came loose and started behaving in unpredictable ways. This was particularly true along the boundaries of the two blocs.

Some changes were peaceful. Germany reunited and the Baltic states reemerged, as did Ukraine and Belarus. Czechoslovakia had its velvet divorce, splitting into the Czech Republic and Slovakia. Other changes were more violent. Romania underwent a tumultuous internal revolution, and Yugoslavia went completely to pieces.

Indeed, of all the countries along the border of the former Soviet Union, Yugoslavia was the most artificial. It was not a nation-state, but a region of hostile and diverse nations, ethnicities, and religions. Invented by the victors of World War I, Yugoslavia was like a cage for some of the most vicious rivalries in Europe. The victors theorized that in order to avert a war in the Balkans, an entity should be created that made them all part of a single country. It was an interesting theory. But Yugoslavia was an archaeological dig of fossilized nations left over from ancient conquests, still clinging to their distinct identities.

Historically, the Balkans had been a flash point in Europe. This was the Romans' road to the Middle East, and the Turks' road into Europe. World War I started in the Balkans. Each conqueror left behind a nation or a religion, and each one of these detested the other. Each warring group had committed atrocities of monumental proportions against the others, and every one of these atrocities was remembered as if it had happened yesterday. This is not a forgive-and-forget region.

Yugoslavia shattered during World War II, with Croats siding with Germany and Serbs with the Allies. It was subsequently pulled together by the

Yugoslavia and the Balkans

Communist League under Joseph Broz Tito. Yugoslavia was Marxist but anti-Soviet. It didn't want to become a Soviet satellite, and actually cooperated with the Americans. Caught in the force field between NATO and the Warsaw Pact, Yugoslavia hung together, however precariously.

In 1991, when the force field disintegrated, the pieces that made up Yugoslavia blew apart. It was as if a geological fault had caused a massive earthquake. The ancient but submerged and frozen nationalities suddenly found themselves free to maneuver. Names that hadn't been heard since before World War I suddenly came to life: Serbia, Croatia, Montenegro, Bosnia-Herzegovina, Macedonia, Slovenia. Within each of these nations, other ethnic minorities from neighboring nations also came alive, usually demanding secession. All hell broke loose—and this moment would be an important one in the early framing of the twenty-first century.

The Yugoslavian war has been misunderstood as simply a local phenomenon, an idiosyncratic event. It was much more than that. It was first and foremost a response to the collapse of the Soviet Union. Passions that had been kept in check for almost fifty years abruptly reignited. Frozen boundaries became fluid. It was a local phenomenon made possible—and inevitable—by a global shift.

Moreover, war in Yugoslavia was not a singular phenomenon. This was just the first fault line to give—the northern extension of a line that ran all the way to the Hindu Kush, the mountains that dominate northern Afghanistan and Pakistan. The Yugoslavian explosion was the prelude to an even bigger earthquake that began as the Soviet Union collapsed.

THE ISLAMIC EARTHQUAKE

The U.S.–Soviet confrontation spanned the periphery of the Soviet Union. At the end of the Cold War, there were three sections to this border. There was the European section, running from Norway to the German–Czech frontier. There was the Asian section, running from the Aleutians through Japan and into China. And there was the third section, running from northern Afghanistan to Yugoslavia. When the Soviet Union collapsed, this last section was the most heavily affected. Yugoslavia collapsed first, but the

Earthquake Zone

chaos eventually ran the entire length of the sector and engulfed even countries not adjacent to the front line.

The region from Yugoslavia to Afghanistan and Pakistan had largely been locked into place during the Cold War. There was isolated movement, such as when Iran moved from being pro-American to being both anti-Soviet and anti-American, or when the Russians invaded Afghanistan, or the Iran–Iraq war. But in a strange way, the region was stabilized by the Cold War. No matter how many internal conflicts there were, they never grew into full-blown, cross-border crises.

With the Soviets gone, the region destabilized dramatically. This is primarily a Muslim region—one of three major Muslim regions in the world. There is North Africa, there is the Muslim region in Southeast Asia, and then there is this vast, multinational, highly divergent region that runs from Yugoslavia to Afghanistan, and south into the Arabian Peninsula (see map, page 36). This is certainly not a single region in many senses, but we are treating it as such because it was the southern front of the Soviet encirclement.

It's important to remember that the demarcation line of the Cold War ran straight through this Muslim region. Azerbaijan, Uzbekistan, Turkmenistan, Kyrgyzstan, and Kazakhstan were all predominantly Muslim republics that were part of the Soviet Union. There were Muslim parts of the Russian Federation as well, such as Chechnya.

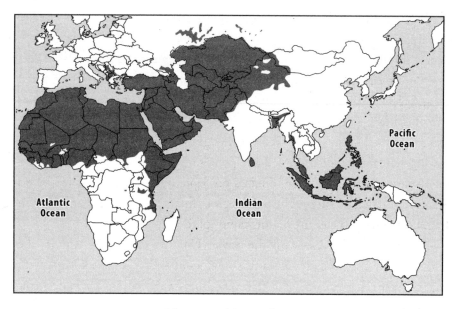

Islamic World—Modern

This entire region is historically unstable. Traversing the region are the great trade and invasion routes used by conquerors from Alexander the Great to the British. The region has always been a geopolitical flash point, but the end of the Cold War truly ignited a powder keg. When the Soviet Union fell, its six Muslim republics suddenly became independent. Arab countries to the south either lost their patron (Iraq and Syria) or lost their enemy (the Saudis and other Gulf states). India lost its patron, and Pakistan suddenly felt liberated from the Indian threat—at least temporarily. The entire system of international relations was thrown up in the air. What little was solid dissolved.

The Soviets withdrew from the Caucasus and Central Asia in 1992. Like a tide receding, this revealed nations that hadn't been free for a century or more, that had no tradition of self-government and, in some cases, no functioning economy. At the same time, American interest in the region declined. After Operation Desert Storm in 1991, American focus on places like Afghanistan seemed useless. The Cold War was over. There was no longer a strategic threat to American interests, and the region was free to evolve on its own.

A detailed description of how the region, and Afghanistan in particular, destabilized is not critical here, any more than a blow by blow of what happened in Yugoslavia would be illuminating. It can be summarized as follows: From the late seventies until the fall of the Soviet Union, the United States helped create forces in Afghanistan that could resist the Soviet Union—and these forces turned on the United States once the Soviet Union collapsed. Trained in the covert arts, knowledgeable about the processes of U.S. intelligence, these men mounted an operation against the United States that involved many stages and culminated on September 11, 2001. The United States responded by surging into the region, first in Afghanistan and then in Iraq, and quickly the entire region came apart.

As had been the case with the Soviet Union after World War II, the United States used the jihadists for its own ends and then had to cope with the monster it had created. But that was the lesser problem. The more dangerous dilemma was that the collapse of the Soviet Union disrupted the system of relationships that kept the region in some sort of order. With or without al Qaeda, the Muslim entities within the former Soviet Union and to its south were going to become unstable, and as in Yugoslavia, that instability was going to draw in the only global power, the United States, one way or another. It was a perfect storm. From the Austrian border to the Hindu Kush, the region shuddered and the United States moved to bring it under control, with mixed results, to say the least.

There is another aspect of this that is noteworthy, especially in light of the demographic trends we will discuss in the next chapter. There was tremendous internal unrest in the Muslim world. The resistance of Islamic traditionalists to shifts in custom, particularly concerning the status of women and driven by demographic change, was one of the driving forces behind the region's instability. The struggle between traditionalists and secularizers upended the region's societies, and the United States was held responsible for the growing calls for secularization. This seems like an obvious and superficial reading of the situation, but as we will see, it has deeper and broader significance than might be apparent at first glance. Changes in the family structure, resistance to those changes, and September 11 were closely linked.

From the broadest geopolitical perspective, September 11 ended the interregnum between the end of the Cold War and the beginning of the next era: the U.S.–jihadist war. The jihadists could not win, if by winning we mean the re-creation of the Caliphate, an Islamic empire. Divisions in the Islamic world were too powerful to overcome, and the United States was too powerful to simply be defeated. The chaos could never have congealed into a jihadist victory.

This era is actually less a coherent movement than a regional spasm, the result of a force field being removed. Ethnic and religious divisions in the Islamic world mean that even if the United States is expelled from the region, no stable political base will emerge. The Islamic world has been divided and unstable for over a thousand years, and hardly looks to become more united anytime soon. At the same time, even an American defeat in the region would not undermine basic American global power. Like the Vietnam War, it would be merely a transitory event.

At the moment, the U.S.–jihadist conflict appears so powerful and of such overwhelming importance that it is difficult to imagine it simply fading away. Serious people talk about a century of such conflict dominating the world, but under the twenty-year perspective outlined in the early pages of this book, the prospect of a world still transfixed by a U.S.–jihadist war in 2020 is the least likely outcome. In fact, what is happening in the Islamic world ultimately will not matter a great deal. If we assume that the upward trajectory of U.S. power remains intact, then 2020 should find the United States facing very different challenges.

AMERICAN GRAND STRATEGY AND
THE ISLAMIC WARS

There is one more element of the American dynamic that we must cover: the grand strategy that drives American foreign policy. The American response to 9/11 seemed to make no sense, and on the surface it didn't. It looked chaotic and it looked random, but underneath, it was to be expected. When one steps back and takes stock, the seemingly random actions of the United States actually make a good deal of sense.

Grand strategy starts where policy making ends. Let's assume for a moment that Franklin Roosevelt had not run for a third term in 1940. Would

Japan and Germany have behaved differently? Could the United States have acquiesced to Japanese domination of the western Pacific? Would the United States have accepted the defeat of Britain and its fleet at German hands? The details might have changed, but it is hard to imagine the United States not getting into the war or the war not ending in an Allied victory. A thousand details might have changed, but the broadest outlines of this conflict as determined by grand strategy would have remained the same.

Could there have been an American strategy during the Cold War other than containment of the Soviet Union? The United States couldn't invade Eastern Europe. The Soviet army was simply too large and too strong. On the other hand, the United States couldn't allow the Soviet Union to seize Western Europe because if the Soviet Union controlled Western Europe's industrial plant, it would overwhelm the United States in the long run. Containment was not an optional policy; it was the only possible American response to the Soviet Union.

All nations have grand strategies, though this does not mean all nations can achieve their strategic goals. Lithuania's goal is to be free of foreign occupation. But its economy, demography, and geography make it unlikely that Lithuania will ever achieve its goal more than occasionally and temporarily. The United States, unlike most other countries in the world, has achieved most of its strategic goals, which I will outline in a moment. Its economy and society are both geared toward this effort.

A country's grand strategy is so deeply embedded in that nation's DNA, and appears so natural and obvious, that politicians and generals are not always aware of it. Their logic is so constrained by it that it is an almost unconscious reality. But from a geopolitical perspective, both the grand strategy of a country and the logic driving a country's leaders become obvious.

Grand strategy is not always about war. It is about all of the processes that constitute national power. But in the case of the United States, perhaps more than for other countries, grand strategy *is* about war, and the interaction between war and economic life. The United States is, historically, a warlike country.

The United States has been at war for about 10 percent of its existence. This statistic includes only major wars—the War of 1812, the Mexican-American War, the Civil War, World Wars I and II, the Korean War, Vietnam. It does not include minor conflicts like the Spanish-American War or Desert Storm. During the twentieth century, the United States was at war 15 percent of the time. In the second half of the twentieth century, it was at war 22 percent of the time. And since the beginning of the twenty-first century, in 2001, the United States has been constantly at war. War is central to the American experience, and its frequency is constantly increasing. It is built into American culture and deeply rooted in American geopolitics. Its purpose must be clearly understood.

America was born out of war and has continued to fight to this day at an ever increasing pace. Norway's grand strategy might be more about economics than warfare, but U.S. strategic goals, and U.S. grand strategy, originate in fear. The same is true of many nations. Rome did not set out to conquer the world. It set out to defend itself, and in the course of that effort it became an empire. The United States would have been quite content at first not to have been attacked and defeated by the British, as it was in the War of 1812. Each fear, however, once alleviated, creates new vulnerabilities and new fears. Nations are driven by fear of losing what they have. Consider the following in terms of this fear.

The United States has five geopolitical goals that drive its grand strategy. Note that these goals increase in magnitude, ambition, and difficulty as you go down the list.

I: THE COMPLETE DOMINATION OF NORTH AMERICA BY THE UNITED STATES ARMY

Had the United States remained a nation of discrete states existing between the Atlantic coast and the Allegheny mountains, it is extremely unlikely that it would have survived. It not only had to unite but had to spread into the vast territory between the Alleghenies and the Rocky Mountains. This gave the United States not only strategic depth but also some of the richest agricultural land in the world. Even more important, it was land with a superb system of navigable rivers that allowed the country's agricultural surplus to be shipped to world markets, creating a class of businessmen-farmers that is unique in history.

The Louisiana Purchase of 1803 gave the United States title to this land. But it was the Battle of New Orleans in 1814, in which Andrew Jackson defeated the British, that gave the nation real control of the region, since New Orleans was the single choke point of the entire river system. If Yorktown founded the nation, the Battle of New Orleans founded its economy. And what secured this in turn was the Battle of San Jacinto, a few hundred miles west of New Orleans, where the Mexican army was defeated by Texans and thus could never pose a threat to the Mississippi River basin again. The defeat of the Mexican army was not inevitable. Mexico was in many ways a more developed and powerful country than the United States. Its defeat made the U.S. Army the dominant power in North America and secured the continent for the United States—a vast and rich country that no one could challenge.

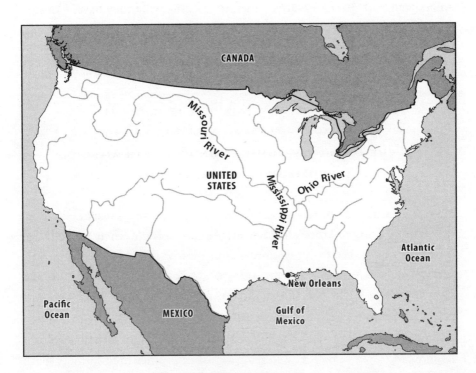

U.S. River System

2: THE ELIMINATION OF ANY THREAT
TO THE UNITED STATES BY ANY POWER IN
THE WESTERN HEMISPHERE

With North America secured, the only other immediate threat came from Latin America. In reality, North and South America are islands, not really connected: Panama and Central America are impassable by large armies. South America's unification into a single entity is remote. When you look at a map of South America, leaving out impassable terrain, you see that there can be no transcontinental power: the continent is sliced in two (see map, page 43). So there is no chance of a native threat to the United States emerging from South America.

The major threats in the hemisphere came from European powers with naval bases in South and Central America and the Caribbean, as well as land forces in Mexico. That is what the Monroe Doctrine was about—long before the United States had the ability to stop the Europeans from having bases there, it made blocking the Europeans a strategic imperative. The only time the United States really worries about Latin America is when a foreign power has bases there.

3: COMPLETE CONTROL OF THE MARITIME
APPROACHES TO THE UNITED STATES BY
THE NAVY IN ORDER TO PRECLUDE ANY
POSSIBILITY OF INVASION

In 1812, the British navy sailed up the Chesapeake and burned Washington. Throughout the nineteenth century, the United States was terrified that the British, using their overwhelming control of the North Atlantic, would shut off its access to the ocean, strangling the United States. It was not always a paranoid fear: the British did consider this on more than one occasion. This general problem was, in other contexts, the origin of the American obsession with Cuba, from the Spanish-American War through the Cold War.

Having secured the hemisphere in the late nineteenth century, the

South America: Impassable Terrain

United States has an interest in keeping the sea lanes approaching its borders free of foreign naval power. The United States secured its Pacific approaches first. During the Civil War it acquired Alaska. In 1898 it annexed Hawaii. Those two actions taken together closed off the threat of any enemy fleet being able to approach the continent from the west, by eliminating any anchorage for supplying a fleet. The United States secured the Atlantic by using World War II to take advantage of British weakness, driving it from near the U.S. coast, and by the end of World War II had created a fleet of such enormous power that the British were unable to operate in the Atlantic without U.S. approval. This made the United States effectively invulnerable to invasion.

4: COMPLETE DOMINATION OF THE WORLD'S OCEANS TO FURTHER SECURE U.S. PHYSICAL SAFETY AND GUARANTEE CONTROL OVER THE INTERNATIONAL TRADING SYSTEM

The fact that the United States emerged from World War II not only with the world's largest navy but also with naval bases scattered around the world changed the way the world worked. As I mentioned previously, any seagoing vessel—commercial or military, from the Persian Gulf to the South China Sea to the Caribbean—could be monitored by the United States Navy, who could choose to watch it, stop it, or sink it. From the end of World War II onward, the combined weight of all of the world's existing fleets was insignificant compared to American naval power.

This highlights the single most important geopolitical fact in the world: the United States controls all of the oceans. No other power in history has been able to do this. And that control is not only the foundation of America's security but also the foundation of its ability to shape the international system. No one goes anywhere on the seas if the United States doesn't approve. At the end of the day, maintaining its control of the world's oceans is the single most important goal for the United States geopolitically.

5: THE PREVENTION OF ANY OTHER NATION FROM
CHALLENGING U.S. GLOBAL NAVAL POWER

Having achieved the unprecedented feat of dominating all of the world's oceans, the United States obviously wanted to continue to hold them. The simplest way to do this was to prevent other nations from building navies, and this could be done by making certain that no one was motivated to build navies—or had the resources to do so. One strategy, "the carrot," is to make sure that everyone has access to the sea without needing to build a navy. The other strategy, "the stick," is to tie down potential enemies in land-based confrontations so that they are forced to exhaust their military dollars on troops and tanks, with little left over for navies.

The United States emerged from the Cold War with both an ongoing interest and a fixed strategy. The ongoing interest was preventing any Eurasian power from becoming sufficiently secure to divert resources to navy building. Since there was no longer a single threat of Eurasian hegemony, the United States focused on the emergence of secondary, regional hegemons who might develop enough regional security to allow them to begin probing out to sea. The United States therefore worked to create a continually shifting series of alliances designed to tie down any potential regional hegemon.

The United States had to be prepared for regular and unpredictable interventions throughout the Eurasian landmass. After the fall of the Soviet Union, it did engage in a series of operations designed to maintain the regional balance and block the emergence of a regional power. The first major intervention was in Kuwait, where the United States blocked Iraqi ambitions after the Soviets were dead but not yet buried. The next was in Yugoslavia, with the goal of blocking the emergence of Serbian hegemony over the Balkans. The third series of interventions was in the Islamic world, designed to block al Qaeda's (or anyone else's) desire to create a secure Islamic empire. The interventions in Afghanistan and Iraq were both a part of this effort.

For all the noise and fuss, these were minor affairs. In Iraq, the largest operation, the United States has used fewer than 200,000 troops and suffered fewer than 5,000 killed. This is about 6 to 8 percent of the casualties suffered in Vietnam, and about 1 percent of the casualties in World War II.

For a country of over a quarter billion people, an occupation force of this size is trivial. The tendency of the United States to overdramatize minor interventions derives from its relative immaturity as a nation (and I say this as a parent of someone who served two tours in Iraq).

The foregoing allows us to understand the American response to the Islamist attacks and much else that has happened. Having systematically achieved its strategic goals, the United States had the ultimate aim of preventing the emergence of any major power in Eurasia. The paradox, however, is as follows: the goal of these interventions was never to achieve something—whatever the political rhetoric might have said—but to prevent something. The United States wanted to prevent stability in areas where another power might emerge. Its goal was not to stabilize, but to destabilize. And that explains how the United States responded to the Islamic earthquake—it wanted to prevent a large, powerful Islamic state from emerging.

Rhetoric aside, the United States has no overriding interest in peace in Eurasia. The United States also has no interest in winning a war outright. As with Vietnam or Korea, the purpose of these conflicts is simply to block a power or destabilize the region, not to impose order. In due course, even outright American defeat is acceptable. However, the principle of using minimum force, when absolutely necessary, to maintain the Eurasian balance of power is—and will remain—the driving force of U.S. foreign policy throughout the twenty-first century. There will be numerous Kosovos and Iraqs in unanticipated places at unexpected times. U.S. actions will appear irrational, and would be if the primary goal is to stabilize the Balkans or the Middle East. But since the primary goal will more likely be simply to block or destabilize Serbia or al Qaeda, the interventions will be quite rational. They will never appear to really yield anything nearing a "solution," and will always be done with insufficient force to be decisive.

AFTER THE AFTERSHOCKS

The international system is now badly out of balance. The United States is so powerful that it is almost impossible for the rest of the world to control

American behavior. The natural tendency of the international system is to move to equilibrium. In an unbalanced world, smaller powers are at risk from larger, unchecked powers. They therefore tend to form coalitions with other countries to match the larger power in strength. After the United States was defeated in Vietnam, it joined with China to control the Soviets, who appeared to be getting too strong.

Creating coalitions to contain the United States in the twenty-first century will be extremely difficult. Weaker countries find it easier to reach an accommodation with the Americans than to join an anti-U.S. coalition—building a coalition and holding it together is an onerous task. And if the coalition falls apart, as coalitions tend to do, the United States can be an unforgiving giant.

As a result, we see this contradiction: on the one hand, the United States is deeply resented and feared; on the other hand, individual nations still try to find a way to get along with the United States. This disequilibrium will dominate the twenty-first century, as will efforts to contain the United States. It will be a dangerous century, particularly for the rest of the world.

In geopolitics there is a key measure known as the "margin of error." It predicts how much room a country has for making mistakes. The margin of error consists of two parts: the types of danger faced by a nation and the amount of power it possesses. Some countries have very small margins of error. They tend to obsess over the smallest detail of foreign policy, aware that the slightest misstep can be catastrophic. Israel and Palestine do not have massive margins of error, because of their small size and their location. Iceland, on the other hand, has a lot of room for mistakes. It is small but lives in a roomy neighborhood.

The United States has a huge margin of error. It is safe in North America and has tremendous power. The United States therefore tends to be careless in how it exercises its power globally. It's not stupid. It simply doesn't need to be more careful—in fact, being more careful could often reduce its efficiency. Like a banker prepared to make bad loans in the expectation that he will do well in the long run, the United States has a policy of making moves that other countries see as reckless. The results would be painful or even devastating for other countries. The United States moves on and flourishes.

We saw this in Vietnam and we see it in Iraq as well. These conflicts are merely isolated episodes in U.S. history, of little lasting importance—except to Vietnamese and Iraqis. The United States is a young and barbaric country. It becomes emotional quickly and lacks a sense of historical perspective. This actually adds to American power by giving the country the emotional resources to overcome adversity. The United States always overreacts. What seems colossally catastrophic at one moment motivates Americans to solve problems decisively. An emerging power overreacts. A mature power finds balance. A declining power loses the ability to recover its balance.

The United States is a very young nation, and is even newer at being a dominant global power. Like a young and powerful adolescent, it tends to become disproportionately emotional about events that are barely remembered a few years later. Lebanon, Panama, Kuwait, Somalia, Haiti, Bosnia, and Kosovo all seemed at the time to be extraordinarily important and even decisive. The reality is that few people remember them—and when they do, they cannot clearly define what drew the United States into the conflict in the first place. The emotionalism of the moment exhausts itself rapidly.

The crucial flip side to this phenomenon is that the Lebanese, Panamanians, Kuwaitis, Somalis, Haitians, Bosnians, and Kosovars all remember their tangles with American power for a long time. What was a passing event for the United States becomes a defining moment in the other countries' histories. Here we discover the first and crucial asymmetry of the twenty-first century. The United States has global interests and involves itself in a large number of global skirmishes. No one involvement is crucial. For the countries that are the object of American interest, however, any intervention is a transformative event. Frequently the object nation is helpless in the face of the American actions, and that sense of helplessness breeds rage even under the best of circumstances. The rage grows all the more when the object of the rage, the United States, is generally both invulnerable and indifferent. The twenty-first century will see both American indifference to the consequences of its actions and the world's resistance and anger toward America.

SUMMING UP

As the U.S.–jihadist war slithers to an end, the first line of defense against Islamic radicals will be the Muslim states themselves. They are the ultimate targets of al Qaeda, and whatever their views of Islam or the West, the Muslim states are not about to turn over political power to al Qaeda. Rather, they will use their national power—their intelligence, security, and military capabilities—to crush al Qaeda.

The United States wins as long as al Qaeda loses. An Islamic world in chaos, incapable of uniting, means the United States has achieved its strategic goal. One thing the United States has indisputably done since 2001 is to create chaos in the Islamic world, generating animosity toward America—and perhaps terrorists who will attack it in the future. But the regional earthquake is not coalescing into a regional superpower. In fact, the region is more fragmented than ever, and that is likely to close the book on this era. U.S. defeat or stalemate in Iraq and Afghanistan is the likely outcome, and both wars will appear to have ended badly for the United States. There is no question that American execution of the war in Iraq has been clumsy, graceless, and in many ways unsophisticated. The United States was, indeed, adolescent in its simplification of issues and in its use of power. But on a broader, more strategic level, that does not matter. So long as the Muslims are fighting each other, the United States has won its war.

This does not mean that it would be impossible for a nation-state to emerge in the Islamic world at some point that could develop into a regional power and a challenge to American interests. Turkey is the historic power in the Muslim world, and as we will see in the chapters that lie ahead, it is emerging again. Its rise will be the result not of the chaos caused by the fall of the Soviet Union, but of new dynamics. Anger does not make history. Power does. And power may be supplemented by anger, but it derives from more fundamental realities: geography, demographics, technology, and culture. All of these will define American power, just as American power will define the twenty-first century.

CHAPTER 3

POPULATION, COMPUTERS, AND CULTURE WARS

n 2002, Osama bin Laden wrote in his "Letter to America": "You are a nation that exploits women like consumer products or advertising tools, calling upon customers to purchase them. You use women to serve passengers, visitors, and strangers to increase your profit margins. You then rant that you support the liberation of women."

As this quote indicates, what al Qaeda is fighting for is a traditional understanding of the family. This is not a minor part of their program: it is at its heart. The traditional family is built around some clearly defined principles. First, the home is the domain of the woman and life outside the house is the purview of the man. Second, sexuality is something confined to the family and the home, and extramarital, extrafamilial sexuality is unacceptable. Women who move outside the home invite extramarital sexuality just by being there. Third, women have as their primary tasks reproduction and nurturing of the next generation. Therefore, intense controls on women are necessary to maintain the integrity of the family and of society. In an interesting way it is all about women, and bin Laden's letter drives this home. What he hates about America is that it promotes a completely different view of women and the family.

Al Qaeda's view is not unique to Osama bin Laden or Islam. The lengths to which that group is prepared to go may be unique, but the issue of women and the family defines most major religions. Traditional Catholicism, fundamentalist Protestantism, Orthodox Judaism, and various branches of Buddhism all take very similar positions. All of these religions are being split internally, as are all societies. In the United States, where we speak of the "culture wars," the battlefield is the family and its definition. All societies are being torn between traditionalists and those who are attempting to redefine the family, women, and sexuality.

This conflict is going to intensify in the twenty-first century, but the traditionalists are fighting a defensive and ultimately losing battle. The reason is that over the past hundred years the very fabric of human life—and particularly the life of women—has been transformed, and with it the structure of the family. What has already happened in Europe, the United States, and Japan is spreading to the rest of the world. These issues will rip many societies apart, but in the end, the transformation of the family can't be stopped.

This is not to say that transformation is inherently a good idea or a bad one. Instead, this trend is unstoppable because the demographic realities of the world are being transformed. The single most important demographic change in the world right now is the dramatic decline everywhere in birthrates. Let me repeat that: the most meaningful statistic in the world is an overall decline in birthrates. Women are having fewer and fewer children every year. That means not only that the population explosion of the last two centuries is coming to an end but also that women are spending much less time bearing and nurturing children, even as their life expectancy has soared.

This seems like a simple fact, and in a way it is, but what I want to show you is the way in which something so mundane can lead to groups like al Qaeda, why there will be more such groups, and why they can't win. It also will illustrate why the European Age, which was built on a perpetually expanding population (whether through conquering other people or having more babies), is being replaced by the American Age—a country in which living with underpopulation has always been the norm. Let's begin with the end of the population explosion.

THE POPULATION BUST

It has been generally accepted in recent decades that the globe was facing a severe population explosion. Uncontrolled population growth would outstrip scarce resources and devastate the environment. More people would require more resources in the form of food, energy, and goods, which in turn would lead to a rise in global warming and other ecological catastrophes. There was no disagreement on the basic premise that population was growing.

This model no longer holds true, however. We already see a change taking place in advanced industrial countries. People are living longer, and because of declining birthrates there are fewer younger workers to support the vast increase in retirees. Europe and Japan are experiencing this problem already. But an aging population is only the tip of the iceberg, the first problem presented by the coming population bust.

People assume that while population growth might be slowing down in Europe, the world's total population will continue to spiral out of control because of high birthrates in less developed countries. In fact, the opposite is true. Birthrates are plunging everywhere. The advanced industrial countries are on the cutting edge of the decline, but the rest of the world is following right behind them. And this demographic shift will help shape the twenty-first century.

Some of the most important, advanced countries in the world, like Germany and Russia, are going to lose large percentages of their population. Europe's population today, taken as a whole, is 728 million people. The United Nations forecasts that by 2050 it will drop to between 557 and 653 million, a remarkable decline. The lower number assumes that women will average 1.6 children each. The second number assumes 2.1 children. In Europe today, the fertility rate per woman is 1.4 children. This is why we will be focusing on the lower projections going forward.

Traditionally, declining population has meant declining power. For Europe, this will indeed be the case. But for other countries, like the United States, maintaining population levels or finding technological ways to augment a declining population will be essential if political power is to be retained in the next hundred years.

An assertion this extreme has to be supported, so we must pause and drill into the numbers a bit before we consider the consequences. This is a pivotal event in human history and we need to understand why it's happening.

Let's start simply. Between about 1750 and 1950, the world's population grew from about one billion people to about three billion. Between 1950 and 2000, it doubled, from three billion to six billion. Not only was the population of the world growing, but the growth was accelerating at an amazing rate. If that trajectory had continued, the result would have been global catastrophe.

But the growth rate has not accelerated. It has actually slowed down dramatically. According to the United Nations, between 2000 and 2050 the population will continue to grow, but only by about 50 percent, halving the growth rate of the previous fifty years. In the second half of the century, it becomes more interesting. Again, the population will continue to grow, but only by 10 percent statistically, according to other forecasters. This is like slamming on the brakes. In fact, some forecasts (not by the UN) have indicated that the total human population will decline by 2100.

The most dramatic effect will be seen in the advanced industrial countries, many of which will experience remarkable declines in population. The middle tier of countries, like Brazil and South Korea, will see their populations stabilize by mid-century and slowly decline by 2100. Only in the least developed part of the world, in countries like Congo and Bangladesh, will populations continue to increase until 2100, but not by nearly as much as over the past hundred years. Any way you look at it, the population explosion is ending.

Let's examine a critical number: 2.1. This is the number of children that each woman must have, on average, in order to maintain a generally stable world population. Anything above that number and the population grows; anything below, the population declines, all other things being equal. According to the United Nations, women had an average of 4.5 children in 1970. In 2000, that number had dropped to 2.7 children. Remember, this is a worldwide average. That is a dramatic drop and explains why the population continued to grow, but more slowly than before.

The United Nations forecasts that in 2050, the global fertility rate will decline to an average of 2.05 births per woman. That is just below the 2.1 needed for a stable world population. The UN has another forecast, based on different assumptions, where the rate is 1.6 babies per woman. So the United Nations, which has the best data available, is predicting that by the year 2050, population growth will be either stable or declining dramatically. I believe the latter is closer to the truth.

The situation is even more interesting if we look at the developed regions of the world, the forty-four most advanced countries. In these countries women are currently having an average of 1.6 babies each, which means that populations are already contracting. Birthrates in the middle tier of countries are down to 2.9 and falling. Even the least developed countries are down from 6.6 children per mother to 5.0 today, and expected to drop to 3.0 by 2050. There is no doubt that birthrates are plunging. The question is why. The answer can be traced to the reasons that the population explosion occurred in the first place; in a certain sense, the population explosion halted itself.

There were two clear causes for the population explosion that were equally significant. First, there was a decline in infant mortality; second there was an increase in life expectancies. Both were the result of modern medicine, the availability of more food, and the introduction of basic public health that began in the late eighteenth century.

There are no really good statistics on fertility rates in 1800, but the best estimates fall between 6.5 and 8.0 children per woman on average. Women in Europe in 1800 were having the same number of babies as women in Bangladesh are having today, yet the population wasn't growing. Most children born in 1800 didn't live long enough to reproduce. Since the 2.1 rule still held, out of eight children born, six died before puberty.

Medicine, food, and hygiene dramatically reduced the number of infant and childhood deaths, until by late in the nineteenth century, most children survived to have their own children. Even though infant mortality declined, family patterns did not shift. People were having the same number of babies as before.

It's not hard to understand why. First, let's face the fact that people like to have sex, and sex without birth control makes babies—and there was no birth control at the time. But people didn't mind having a lot of children because children had become the basis of wealth. In an agricultural society, every pair of hands produces wealth; you don't have to be able to read or program computers to weed, seed, or harvest. Children were also the basis for retirement, if someone lived long enough to have an old age. There was no Social Security, but you counted on your children to take care of you. Part of this was custom, but part of it was rational economic thinking. A father owned land or had the right to farm it. His child needed to have access to the land to live, so the father could dictate policy.

As children brought families prosperity and retirement income, the major responsibility of women was to produce as many children as possible. If women had children, and if they both survived childbirth, the family as a whole was better off. This was a matter of luck, but it was a chance worth taking from the standpoint of both families and the men who dominated them. Between lust and greed, there was little reason not to bring more children into the world.

Habits are hard to change. When families began moving into cities en masse, children were still valuable assets. Parents could send them to work in primitive factories at the age of six and collect their pay. In early industrial society factory workers didn't need many more skills than farm laborers did. But as factories became more complex, they had less use for six-year-olds. Soon they needed somewhat educated workers. Later they needed managers with MBAs.

As the sophistication of industry advanced, the economic value of children declined. In order to continue being economically useful, children had to go to school to learn. Rather than adding to family income, they consumed family income. Children had to be clothed, fed, and sheltered, and over time the amount of education they needed increased dramatically, until today many "children" go to school until their mid-twenties and still have not earned a dime. According to the United Nations, the average number of years of schooling in the leading twenty-five countries in the world ranges from fifteen to seventeen.

The tendency to have as many babies as possible continued into the late nineteenth and early twentieth centuries. Many of our grandparents or great-grandparents come from families that had ten children. A couple of generations before, you'd be lucky if three out of ten children survived. Now they were almost all surviving. However, in the economy of 1900, they could all head out and find work by the time they reached puberty. And that's what most of them did.

Ten children in eighteenth-century France might have been a godsend. Ten children in late-nineteenth-century France might have been a burden. Ten children in late-twentieth-century France would be a catastrophe. It took a while for reality to sink in, but eventually it became clear that most children wouldn't die and that children were extremely expensive to raise. Therefore, people started having a lot fewer children, and had those children more for the pleasure of having them than for economic benefits. Medical advances such as birth control helped achieve this, but the sheer cost of having and raising children drove the decline in birthrates. Children went from being producers of wealth to the most conspicuous form of consumption. Parents began satisfying their need for nurturing with one child, rather than ten.

Now let's consider life expectancy. After all, the longer people live, the more people there will be at any given time. Life expectancy surged at the same time that infant mortality declined. In 1800, estimated life expectancy in Europe and the United States was about forty years. In 2000 it was close to eighty years. Life expectancy has, in effect, doubled over the last two hundred years.

Continued growth in life expectancy is probable, but very few people anticipate another doubling. In the advanced industrial world, the UN projects a growth from seventy-six years in 2000 to eighty-two years in 2050. In the poorest countries it will increase from fifty-one to sixty-six. While this is growth, it is not geometric growth and it, too, is tapering off. This will also help reduce population growth.

The reduction process that took place decades ago in the advanced industrial world is now under way in the least developed countries. Having ten children in São Paolo is the surest path to economic suicide. It may take several generations to break the habit, but it will be broken. And it won't return while the process of educating a child for the modern workforce continues to become longer and costlier. Between declining birthrates and slowing increases in life expectancy, population growth has to end.

THE POPULATION BUST AND THE WAY WE LIVE

What does all this have to do with international power in the twenty-first century? The population bust affects all nations, as we will see in later chapters. But it also affects the life cycles of people within these nations. Lower populations affect everything from the number of troops that can fight in a war to how many people there are in the workforce to internal political conflicts. The process we are talking about will affect more than just the number of people in a country. It will change how those people live, and therefore how those countries behave.

Let's start with three core facts. Life expectancy is moving toward a high of eighty years in the advanced industrial world; the number of children women have is declining; and it takes longer and longer to become educated. A college education is now considered the minimum for social and economic success in advanced countries. Most people graduate from college at twenty-two. Add in law or graduate school, and people are not entering the workforce until their mid-twenties. Not everyone follows this pattern, of course, but a sizable portion of the population does and that portion includes most of those who will be part of the political and economic leadership of these countries.

As a result, marriage patterns have shifted dramatically. People are putting off marriage longer and are having children even later. Let's consider the effect on women. Two hundred years ago, women started having children in their early teens. Women continued having children, nurturing them, and frequently burying them until they themselves died. This was necessary for the family's well-being and that of society. Having and raising children was what women did for most of their lives.

In the twenty-first century this whole pattern changes. Assuming that a woman reaches puberty at age thirteen and enters menopause at age fifty, she will live twice as long as her ancestors and will for over half her life be incapable of reproduction. Let's assume a woman has two children. She will spend eighteen months being pregnant, which is roughly 2 percent of her life. Now assume a fairly common pattern, which is that the woman will have these two children three years apart, that each child enters school at the age of five, and that the woman returns to work outside the home when the oldest starts school.

The total time the woman is engaged in reproduction and full-time nurturing is eight years of her life. Given a life expectancy of eighty years, the amount of time exclusively devoted to having and raising children will be reduced to an astounding 10 percent of her life. Childbearing is reduced from a woman's primary activity to one activity among many. Add to this analysis the fact that many women have only one child, and that many use day care and other mass nurturing facilities for their children well before the age of five, and the entire structure of a woman's life is transformed.

We can see the demographic roots of feminism right here. Since women spend less of their time having and nurturing children, they are much less dependent on men than even fifty years ago. For a woman to reproduce without a husband would have created economic disaster for her in the past. This is no longer the case, particularly for better-educated women. Marriage is no longer imposed by economic necessity.

This brings us to a place where marriages are not held together by need as much as by love. The problem with love is that it can be fickle. It comes and goes. If people stay married only for emotional reasons, there will inevitably be more divorce. The decline of economic necessity removes a powerful stabilizing force in marriage. Love may endure, and frequently does, but by itself it is less powerful than when linked to economic necessity.

Marriages used to be guaranteed "till death do us part." In the past, that parting was early and frequent. There were a great many fifty-year marriages during the transition period when people were having ten surviving children. But prior to that, marriages ended early through death, and the survivor remarried or faced economic ruin. Europe practiced what we might call serial polygamy, in which widowers (usually, since women tended to die in childbirth) remarried numerous times throughout their lives. In the late nineteenth and early twentieth centuries, habit kept marriages together for extraordinarily long periods of time. A new pattern emerged in the later twentieth century, however, in which serial polygamy reasserted itself, but this time the trend was being driven by divorce rather than death.

Let's add another pattern to this. Whereas many marriages used to take place when one or both partners were in their early teens, people are now marrying in their late twenties and early thirties. It was typical for men and women to remain sexually inactive until marriage at age fourteen, but today it is, shall we say, unrealistic to expect someone marrying at age thirty to remain a virgin. People would be living seventeen years after puberty without sexual activity. That's not going to happen.

There is now a period built into life patterns where people are going to be sexually active but not yet able to support themselves financially. There is also a period in which they can support themselves and are sexually active, but choose not to reproduce. The entire pattern of traditional life is collapsing, and no clear alternative patterns are emerging yet. Cohabitation used to be linked to formal, legal marriage, but the two are now completely decoupled. Even reproduction is being uncoupled from marriage, and perhaps even from cohabitation. Longer life, the decline in fertility rates, and the additional years of education have all contributed to the dissolution of previous life and social patterns.

This trend cannot be reversed. Women are having fewer children because supporting a lot of children in industrial, urban society is economic suicide. That won't change. The cost of raising children will not decline, nor will there be ways found to put six-year-olds to work. The rate of infant mortality is also not going to rise. So in the twenty-first century the trend toward having fewer, rather than more, children will continue.

POLITICAL CONSEQUENCES

The more educated segments of the population are the ones where life patterns have diverged the most. The very poorest, on the other hand, have lived in a world of dysfunctional families since the industrial revolution began. For them, chaotic patterns of reproduction have always been the norm. However, between the college-educated professional and business classes on the one side and the underclass on the other, there is a large layer of society that has only partially experienced the demographic shifts.

Among blue- and pink-collar workers there have been other trends, the most important of which is that they have shorter educations. The result is less of a gap between puberty and reproduction. These groups tend to marry earlier and have children earlier. They are far more dependent on each other economically, and it follows that the financial consequences of divorce can be far more damaging. There are nonemotional elements holding their marriages together, and divorce is seen as more consequential, as are extramarital and premarital sex.

This group comprises many social conservatives, a small but powerful social cohort. They are powerful because they speak for traditional values. The chaos of the more highly educated classes can't be called values yet; it will be a century before their lifestyles congeal into a coherent moral system. Therefore social conservatives have an inherent advantage, speaking coherently from the authoritative position of tradition.

However, as we have seen, traditional distinctions between men and women are collapsing. As women live longer and have fewer children, they no longer are forced by circumstance into the traditional roles they had to maintain prior to urbanization and industrialization. Nor is family the critical economic instrument it once was. Divorce is no longer economically catastrophic, and premarital sex is inevitable. Homosexuality—and civil unions without reproduction—also becomes unextraordinary. If sentiment is the basis of marriage, then why indeed is gay marriage not as valid as heterosexual marriage? If marriage is decoupled from reproduction, then gay marriage logically follows. All these changes are derived from the radical shifts in life patterns that are part of the end of the population explosion.

It is no accident, therefore, that traditionalists within all religious groups—Catholics, Jews, Muslims, and others—have focused on returning to traditional patterns of reproduction. They all argue for, and many have, large families. Maintaining traditional roles for women in this context makes sense, as do traditional expectations of early marriage, chastity, and the permanence of marriage. The key is having more children, which is a traditionalist principle. Everything else follows.

The issue is not only cropping up in advanced industrial societies. One of the foundations of anti-Americanism, for example, is the argument that American society breeds immorality, that it celebrates immodesty among women and destroys the family. If you read the speeches of Osama bin Laden, this theme is repeated continually. The world is changing and, he argues, we are moving away from patterns of behavior that have traditionally been regarded as moral. He wants to stop this process.

These issues have become a global battleground as well as an internal political maelstrom in most advanced industrial countries, particularly the United States. On one side there is a structured set of political forces that have their roots in existing religious organizations. On the other side, there is less a political force than an overwhelming pattern of behavior that is indifferent to the political consequences of the actions that are being taken. This pattern of behavior is driven by demographic necessity. Certainly there are movements defending various aspects of this evolution, like gay rights, but the transformation is not being planned. It is simply happening.

THE COMPUTER AND AMERICAN CULTURE

Let's look at this from another perspective, that of technology. As the American Age opens, the United States has a vested interest in the destruction of traditional social patterns, which creates a certain amount of instability and gives the United States maximum room to maneuver. American culture is an uneasy melding of the Bible and the computer, of traditional values and radical innovation. But along with demography, it is the computer that is reshaping American culture and is the real foundation of American cultural hegemony. This will become extraordinarily important in the next hundred years.

The computer represents both a radical departure from previous technology and a new way of looking at reason. The purpose of a computer is the manipulation of quantitative data, that is, numbers. As a machine that manipulates data, it is a unique technology. But since it reduces all information—music, film, and the written word—to a number, it is also a unique way of looking at reason.

The computer is based on binary logic. This simply means that it reads electrical charges, which are either negative or positive and are treated as a 0 or a 1. It uses a string of these binary numbers to represent things we think of as being very simple. So the capital letter A is represented as 01000001.

The small letter *a* is 01100001. These strings of numbers are reorganized into machine language that in turn is managed by computer code written in any of a number of languages, from Basic to C++ to Java.

If that seems complex, then simply remember this: To a computer, everything is a number, from a letter on a screen to a bit of music. Everything is reduced to zeros and ones. In order to manage computers, completely artificial languages have been created. The purpose of those languages is getting the computer to use the data it has been given.

But the computer can only manage things that can be expressed in binary code. It can play music, but it cannot write it (not well at least), or explain its beauty. It can store poetry but cannot explain its meaning. It can allow you to search every book imaginable, yet it cannot distinguish between good and bad grammar, at least not well. It is superb at what it can do, but it excludes a great deal of what the human mind is capable of doing. It is a tool.

It is a powerful and seductive tool. Yet it operates using a logic that lacks other, more complex, elements of reason. The computer focuses ruthlessly on things that can be represented in numbers. By doing so, it also seduces people into thinking that other aspects of knowledge are either unreal or unimportant. The computer treats reason as an instrument for achieving things, not for contemplating things. It narrows dramatically what we mean and intend by reason. But within that narrow realm, the computer can do extraordinary things.

Anyone who has learned a programming language understands its logical rigor, and its artificiality. It doesn't in the least resemble natural language. In fact, it is the antithesis of natural language. The latter is filled with subtlety, nuance, and complex meaning determined by context and inference. The logical tool must exclude all of these things, as the binary logic of computing is incapable of dealing with them.

American culture preceded American computing. The philosophical concept of pragmatism was built around statements such as this by Charles Peirce, a founder of pragmatism: "In order to ascertain the meaning of an intellectual conception one should consider what practical consequences might conceivably result by necessity from the truth of that conception; and the sum of these consequences will constitute the entire meaning of the con-

ception." In other words, the significance of an idea is in its practical consequences. An idea without practical consequences, it follows, lacks meaning.
The entire notion of contemplative reason as an end in itself is excluded.

American pragmatism was an attack on European metaphysics on the
grounds of impracticality. American culture was obsessed with the practical
and contemptuous of the metaphysical. The computer and computer language are the perfect manifestations of the pragmatic notion of reason.
Every line of code must have a practical consequence. Functionality is the
only standard. That a line of code could be appreciated not for its use but
for its intrinsic beauty is inconceivable.

The idea of pragmatism, as it has evolved into languages like C++, is a
radical simplification and contraction of the sphere of reason. Reason now
deals only with some things, all of which are measured by their practical
consequences. Everything that lacks practical consequence is excluded from
the sphere of reason and sent to another, inferior sphere. In other words,
American culture does not deal easily with the true and beautiful. It values
getting things done and not worrying too much about why whatever thing
you are doing is important.

This gives American culture its central truth and its enormous drive.
The charge against American culture is that it has elevated the practical beyond all other forms of truth. The charge is valid, but it also fails to appre-
ciate the power of that reduction. It is in the practical that history is made.

If we look for the essence of American culture, it is not only in pragmatism as a philosophy but also in the computer as the embodiment of pragmatism. Nothing exemplifies American culture more than the computer,
and nothing has transformed the world faster and more thoroughly than its
advent. The computer, far more than the car or Coca-Cola, represents the
unique manifestation of the American concept of reason and reality.

Computing culture is also, by definition, barbaric. The essence of barbarism is the reduction of culture to a simple, driving force that will tolerate
no diversion or competition. The way the computer is designed, the manner
in which it is programmed, and the way it has evolved represent a powerful,
reductionist force. It constitutes not reason contemplating its complexity,
but reason reducing itself to its simplest expression and justifying itself
through practical achievement.

Pragmatism, computers, and Microsoft (or any other American corpora-tion) are ruthlessly focused, utterly instrumental, and highly effective. The fragmentation of American culture is real, but it is slowly resolving itself into the barbarism of the computer and the instrument that ultimately uses and shapes the computer, the corporation. Corporations are an American adaptation of a European concept. In its American form it turns into a way of life. Corporations are as fragmented as the rest of American culture. But in their diversity, they express the same self-certainty as any American ideology.

SUMMING UP

The United States is socially imitated and politically condemned. It sits on the ideological fault line of the international system. As populations decline due to shifts in reproductive patterns, the United States becomes the center for radically redefined modes of social life. You can't have a modern econ-omy without computers and corporations, and if you are going to program computers, you need to know English, the language of computing. On one hand, those who want to resist this trend must actively avoid the American model of life and thought. On the other hand, those who don't adopt Amer-ica's ways can't have a modern economy. This is what gives America its strength and continually frustrates its critics. Falling populations are re-structuring the pattern of families and daily lives. Computers are trans-forming, simplifying, and focusing the way people think. Corporations are constantly reorganizing the way we work. Between these three factors, love, reason, and daily life are being transformed, and through that trans-formation American power is growing.

Old institutions have shattered, but new ones have not yet emerged. The twenty-first century will be a period in which a range of new institutions, moral systems, and practices will begin their first tentative emergence. The first half of the twenty-first century will be marked by intense social conflict globally. All of this frames the international struggles of the twenty-first cen-tury.

CHAPTER 4

THE NEW FAULT LINES

Where will the next earthquake strike and what will it look like? To answer that question we need to examine the geopolitical fault lines of the twenty-first century. As with geology, there are many such fault lines. Without pushing this analogy too far, we have to identify the active fault lines in order to identify areas where friction might build up into conflict. As the focus on the Islamic world subsides, what will be the most unstable point in the world in the next era?

There are five areas of the world right now that are viable candidates. First, there is the all-important Pacific Basin. The United States Navy dominates the Pacific. The Asian rim of the Pacific consists entirely of trading countries dependent on access to the high seas, which are therefore dependent on the United States. Two of them—China and Japan—are major powers that could potentially challenge U.S. hegemony. From 1941 to 1945 the United States and Japan fought over the Pacific Basin, and control of it remains a potential issue today.

Second, we must consider the future of Eurasia after the fall of the Soviet Union. Since 1991, the region has fragmented and decayed. The successor state to the Soviet Union, Russia, is emerging from this period with renewed self-confidence. Yet Russia is also in an untenable geopolitical position. Unless Russia exerts itself to create a sphere of influence, the Russian Federation could itself fragment. On the other hand, creating that sphere of influence could generate conflict with the United States and Europe.

Third, there is continuing doubt about the ultimate framework of Europe. For five centuries Europe has been an arena of constant warfare. For the last sixty years it has been either occupied or trying to craft a federation that would make the return of war impossible. Europe may yet have to deal with the resurgence of Russia, the bullying of the United States, or internal tensions. The door is certainly not closed on conflict.

Fourth, there is the Islamic world. It is not instability that is troubling, but the emergence of a nation-state that, regardless of ideology, might form the basis of a coalition. Historically, Turkey has been the most successful center of power in the Muslim world. Turkey is also a dynamic and rapidly modernizing country. What is its future, and what is the future of other Muslim nation-states?

Fifth, there is the question of Mexican–American relations. Normally, the status of Mexico would not rise to the level of a global fault line, but its location in North America makes it important beyond its obvious power. As the country with the fifteenth highest GDP in the world, it should not be underestimated on its own merits. Mexico has deep and historical issues with the United States, and social forces may arise over the next century that cannot be controlled by either government.

In order to pinpoint events that will occur in the future, we need to examine now which of these events are likely to occur and in what order. A fault line does not necessarily guarantee an earthquake. Fault lines can exist for millennia causing only occasional tremors. But with this many major fault lines, conflict in the twenty-first century is almost certain.

THE PACIFIC BASIN

The western shore of the Pacific has been the fastest-growing region in the world for the past half century. It contains two of the world's largest economies, those of Japan and China. Along with other East Asian economies, they are heavily dependent on maritime trade, shipping goods to the United States and Europe and importing raw material from the Persian Gulf and the rest of the Pacific Basin. Any interruption in the flow of commodities would be damaging. An extended interruption would be catastrophic.

Let's consider Japan, the world's second-largest economy and the only major industrial power to possess no major natural resources of any sort. Japan must import all of its major minerals, from oil to aluminum. Without those imports—particularly oil—Japan stops being an industrial power in a matter of months. To gauge the importance of this flow, bear in mind that Japan attacked Pearl Harbor in 1941 because the United States had interfered with its access to raw materials.

China has also emerged as a major industrial power in the last generation, with growth surpassing that of any other major economy in the world, although its economy is still far smaller than that of Japan or the United States. Nevertheless, China is now a key player in the Pacific Basin. Previously, it was much more self-sufficient than Japan in terms of primary commodities. But as China has grown, it has outstripped its own resources and become a net importer of raw materials.

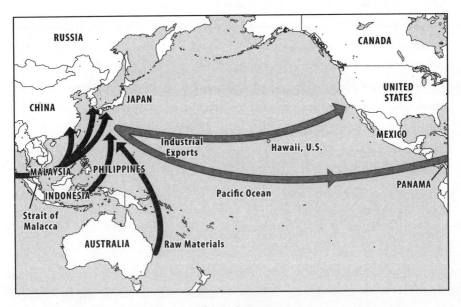

Pacific Trade Routes

The Pacific now has two major Asian powers that are heavily dependent on imports to fuel their economy and on exports to grow their economy. Japan and China, along with South Korea and Taiwan, all depend on access to the Pacific in order to transport their goods and commodities. Since the U.S. Navy controls the Pacific Ocean, they rely on the United States for their economic well-being. That is a huge bet for any nation to make on another.

There is another side to this. The United States consumes massive amounts of Asia's industrial products, which benefits the United States as a whole by providing consumers with cheap goods. At the same time, this trade pattern devastates certain American economic sectors and regions by undermining domestic industry. What benefits consumers can simultaneously increase unemployment and decrease wages, creating complex political crosscurrents within the United States. One of the characteristics of the United States is that it tends to be oversensitive to domestic political concerns because it has a great deal of room to maneuver in foreign policy. Therefore, regardless of the overall benefits of trade with Asia, the United States could wind up in a situation where domestic political considerations force it to change its policy toward Asian imports. That possibility, however remote, represents a serious threat to the interests of East Asia.

China sends almost one-quarter of all its exports to the United States. If the United States barred Chinese products, or imposed tariffs that made Chinese goods uncompetitive, China would face a massive economic crisis. The same would be true for Japan and other Asian countries. Countries facing economic disaster become unpredictable. They can become aggressive in trying to open up other markets, sometimes through political or military pressure.

Militarily, however, the United States could shut down access to the Pacific Ocean whenever it wished. Economically, the United States is dependent on trade with Asia, but not nearly as dependent as Asia is on trade with the United States. The United States is also susceptible to internal political pressures from those groups disproportionately affected by cheaper Asian imports. It is possible that the United States, responding to domestic pressures, might try to reshape economic relations in the Pacific Basin. One of the tools it can use is protectionist legislation, backed up by its military strength. So East Asia has no real effective counter to an American military or economic move.

Subjectively, the last thing any nation in the region wants is conflict. Objectively, however, there is a massive imbalance of power. Any shift in America's policies could wreak havoc on East Asia, and a shift in American policy is far from unimaginable. The threat of American sanctions on China, for example, through which the United States might seek to limit Chinese importation of oil, strikes at the very heart of the Chinese national interest. Therefore, the Chinese must use their growing economic strength to develop military options against the United States. They will simply be acting in accordance with the fundamental principle of strategic planning: hope for the best, plan for the worst.

Over the course of the last fifty years, the western Pacific has dramatically increased its economic power, but not its military power—and that imbalance has left East Asia vulnerable. China and Japan will therefore have no choice but to try to increase their military power in the coming century, which the United States will see as a potential threat to U.S. control of the western Pacific. It will interpret a defensive move as aggressive, which objectively it is, whatever their subjective intent. Add to this the ever-evolving nations of South Korea and Taiwan, and the region is certain to be a powder keg during the twenty-first century.

What's more, any Asian country that believes that huge mega-surges in the price of oil are a realistic possibility cannot discount the threat of an American energy grab. In the near term, the next twenty to fifty years, this is actually a very real scenario. Any rational Asian power must plan for this. The only two that have the resources to challenge the United States at sea are China and Japan, each antagonistic to the other yet sharing a common fear of American behavior during an energy price spike.

Control of the Pacific intersects with a more specific issue—control of the sea lanes used for energy transportation. The higher the price of oil, and the longer non-hydrocarbon energy sources are from being a reality, the greater the likelihood of a confrontation over sea lanes. The imbalance of power in this region is severe. That, coupled with the issues of energy transport and access to the American markets, gives the Pacific Basin its massive geopolitical fault line.

EURASIA

For most of the second half of the twentieth century, the Soviet Union controlled Eurasia—from central Germany to the Pacific, as far south as the Caucasus and the Hindu Kush. When the Soviet Union collapsed, its western frontier moved east nearly a thousand miles, from the West German border to the Russian border with Belarus. From the Hindu Kush its border moved northward a thousand miles to the Russian border with Kazakhstan. Russia was pushed from the border of Turkey northward to the northern Caucasus, where it is still struggling to keep its foothold in the region. Russian power has now retreated farther east than it has been in centuries. During the Cold War it had moved farther west than ever before. In the coming decades, Russian power will settle somewhere between those two lines.

After the Soviet Union dissolved at the end of the twentieth century, foreign powers moved in to take advantage of Russia's economy, creating an era of chaos and poverty. They also moved rapidly to integrate as much as they could of the Russian empire into their own spheres of influence. Eastern Europe was absorbed into NATO and the EU, and the Baltic states were also absorbed into NATO. The United States entered into a close relationship with both Georgia in the Caucasus and with many of the Central Asian "stans," particularly after September 11, when the Russians allowed U.S. forces into the area to wage the war in Afghanistan. Most significantly, Ukraine moved into an alignment with the United States and away from Russia—this was a breaking point in Russian history.

The Orange Revolution in Ukraine, from December 2004 to January 2005, was the moment when the post–Cold War world genuinely ended for Russia. The Russians saw the events in Ukraine as an attempt by the United States to draw Ukraine into NATO and thereby set the stage for Russian disintegration. Quite frankly, there was some truth to the Russian perception.

If the West had succeeded in dominating Ukraine, Russia would have become indefensible. The southern border with Belarus, as well as the southwestern frontier of Russia, would have been wide open. In addition, the distance between Ukraine and western Kazakhstan is only about four hundred miles, and that is the gap through which Russia has been able to project power toward the Caucasus (see map, page 71). We should assume,

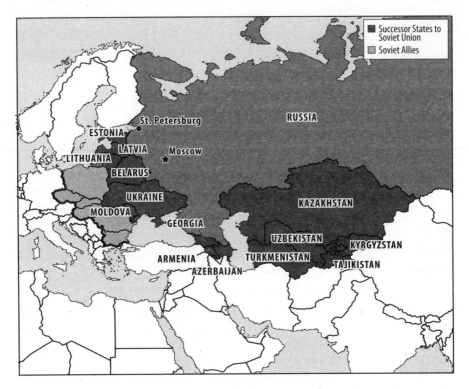

Successor States to the Soviet Union

then, that under these circumstances Russia would have lost its ability to control the Caucasus and would have had to retreat farther north from Chechnya. The Russians would have been abandoning parts of the Russian Federation itself, and Russia's own southern flank would become highly vulnerable. Russia would have continued to fragment until it returned to its medieval frontiers.

Had Russia fragmented to this extent, it would have created chaos in Eurasia—to which the United States would not have objected, since the U.S. grand strategy has always aimed for the fragmentation of Eurasia as the first line of defense for U.S. control of the seas, as we have seen. So the United States had every reason to encourage this process; Russia had every reason to block it.

After what Russia regarded as an American attempt to further damage it, Moscow reverted to a strategy of reasserting its sphere of influence in the areas of the former Soviet Union. The great retreat of Russian power ended in

Ukraine's Strategic Significance

Ukraine. Russian influence is now increasing in three directions: toward Central Asia, toward the Caucasus, and, inevitably, toward the West, the Baltics, and Eastern Europe. For the next generation, until roughly 2020, Russia's primary concern will be reconstructing the Russian state and reasserting Russian power in the region.

Interestingly, the geopolitical shift is aligning with an economic shift. Vladimir Putin sees Russia less as an industrial power than as an exporter of raw materials, the most important of which is energy (particularly natural gas). Moving to bring the energy industry under state supervision, if not direct control, he is forcing out foreign interests and reorienting the industry toward exports, particularly to Europe. High energy prices have helped stabilize Russia's economy internally. But he will not confine his efforts to energy alone. He also is seeking to capitalize on Russian agriculture, timber, gold, diamonds, and other commodities. He is transforming Russia from an impoverished disaster into a poor but more productive country. Putin also is giving Russia the tool with which to intimidate Europe: the valve on a natural gas pipeline.

Russia is pressing back along its frontiers. It is deeply focused on Central Asia and will over time find success there, but Russia will have a more difficult time in the even more crucial Caucasus. The Russians do not intend to allow any part of the Russian Federation to break away. As a result, there will be friction, particularly in the next decade, with the United States and other countries in the region as Russia reasserts itself.

But the real flash point, in all likelihood, will be on Russia's western frontier. Belarus will align itself with Russia. Of all the countries in the former Soviet Union, Belarus has had the fewest economic and political reforms and has been the most interested in re-creating some successor to the Soviet Union. Linked in some way to Russia, Belarus will bring Russian power back to the borders of the former Soviet Union.

From the Baltics south to the Romanian border there is a region where borders have historically been uncertain and conflict frequent. In the north, there is a long, narrow plain, stretching from the Pyrenees to St. Petersburg. This is where Europe's greatest wars were fought. This is the path that Napoleon and Hitler took to invade Russia. There are few natural barriers. Therefore, the Russians must push their border west as far as possible to create a buffer. After World War II, they drove into the center of Germany on this plain. Today, they have retreated to the east. They have to return, and move as far west as possible. That means the Baltic states and Poland are, as before, problems Russia has to solve.

Defining the limits of Russian influence will be controversial. The United States—and the countries within the old Soviet sphere—will not want Russia to go too far. The last thing the Baltic states want is to fall under Russian domination again. Neither do the states south of the northern European plain, in the Carpathians. The former Soviet satellites—particularly Poland, Hungary, and Romania—understand that the return of Russian forces to their frontiers would represent a threat to their security. And since these countries are now part of NATO, their interests necessarily affect the interests of Europe and the United States. The open question is where the line will be drawn in the west. This has been a historical question, and it was a key challenge in Europe over the past hundred years.

Russia will not become a global power in the next decade, but it has no choice but to become a major regional power. And that means it will clash with Europe. The Russian–European frontier remains a fault line.

EUROPE

Europe is still in the process of reorganizing itself after the loss of its empire and two devastating world wars, and it remains to be seen whether that reorganization will be peaceful. Europe is not going to regain its empire, but the complacent certainty that intra-European wars have ended needs to be examined. Central to this is the question of whether Europe is a spent volcano or whether it is merely dormant. The European Union has a total GDP of over $14 trillion, a trillion more than the United States. It is possible that a region of such wealth—and of such diversity in wealth—will remain immune from conflict, but it is not guaranteed.

It is unreasonable to talk of Europe as if it were one entity. It is not, in spite of the existence of the European Union. Europe consists of a series of sovereign and contentious nation-states. There is a general entity called Europe, but it is more reasonable to think of four Europes (we exclude Russia and the nations of the former Soviet Union from this list—although geographically European, these have a very different dynamic from that of Europe):

- Atlantic Europe: the nations that front the Atlantic Ocean and North Sea directly and that were the major imperial powers during the past five hundred years.
- Central Europe: essentially Germany and Italy, which did not come into existence until the late nineteenth century as modern nation-states. It was their assertion of national interest that led to the two world wars of the twentieth century.
- Eastern Europe: the nations running from the Baltic to the Black Sea

that were occupied by Soviet troops in World War II and developed their recent national identities from this experience.

- There is, of course, a fourth less significant Europe, the Scandinavian countries.

In the first half of the twentieth century, Atlantic Europe was the imperial heart of the world. Central Europeans were later comers and challengers. Eastern Europeans were the victims. Torn apart by two world wars, Europe faced a fundamental question: What was the status of Germany in the European system? The Germans, frozen out of the imperial system created by Atlantic Europe, sought to overturn that system and assert their

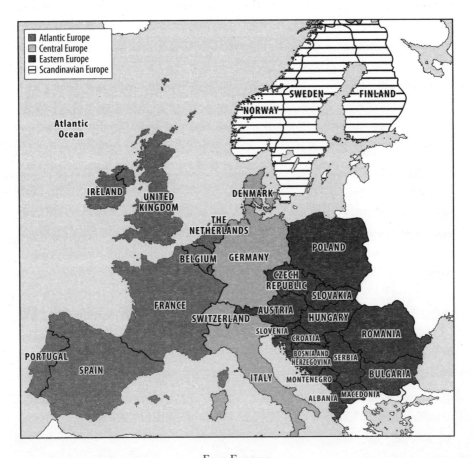

Four Europes

dominance. The conclusion of World War II found Germany shattered, divided and occupied, controlled by Soviets in the east, and England, France, and the United States in the west.

West Germany was indispensable to the United States and its NATO alliance because of the confrontation with the Soviets. Creating a German army, obviously, posed a problem. If the origins of the two world wars were in the growth of German power, and Germany was encouraged to be powerful again, what was to prevent a third European war? The answer rested in the integration of the German army into NATO—essentially putting it under American command in the field. But the broader answer lay in the integration of Germany into Europe as a whole.

During the 1950s, when NATO was created, the European Economic Community was also conceived. The European Union, which emerged from it, is a schizophrenic entity. Its primary purpose is the creation of an integrated European economy, while leaving sovereignty in the hands of individual nations. Simultaneously, it is seen as the preface to a federation of European countries, in which a central European government, with a parliament and professional civil service, would govern a federal Europe where national sovereignty was limited to local matters, and defense and foreign policy rested with the whole.

Europe has not achieved this goal. It has created a free-trade zone and a European currency, which some members of the free-trade zone use and others do not. It has failed to create a political constitution, however, leaving individual nations sovereign—and therefore never has produced a united defense or foreign policy. Defense policy, to the extent it is coordinated, is in the hands of NATO, and not all members of NATO are members of the EU (notably the United States). With the collapse of the Soviet empire, individual countries in Eastern Europe were admitted to the EU and NATO.

In short, post–Cold War Europe is in benign chaos. It is impossible to unravel the extraordinarily complex and ambiguous institutional relationships that have been created. Given the history of Europe, such confusion would normally lead to war. But Europe, excepting the former Yugoslavia, has no energy for war, no appetite for instability, and certainly no desire for conflict. Europe's psychological transformation has been extraordinary.

Where, prior to 1945, slaughter and warfare had been regular pastimes for centuries, after 1945 even the conceptual chaos of European institutions could not generate conflict beyond rhetoric.

Underneath the surface of the EU, the old European nationalisms continue to assert themselves, albeit sluggishly. This can be seen in economic negotiations within the EU. The French, for example, assert the right to protect their farmers from excessive competition, or the right not to honor treaties controlling their deficits. Therefore, in a geopolitical context, Europe has not become a unified transnational entity.

For these reasons, talking of Europe as if it were a single entity like the United States, or China, is illusory. It is a collection of nation-states, still shell-shocked by World War II, the Cold War, and the loss of empire. These nation-states are highly insular and determine their geopolitical actions according to their individual interests. Primary interactions are not between Europe and the rest of the world, but among European nations. In this sense, Europe behaves far more like Latin America than like a great power. In Latin America, Brazil and Argentina spend a great deal of time thinking about each other, knowing that their effect on the globe is limited.

Russia is the immediate strategic threat to Europe. Russia is interested not in conquering Europe, but in reasserting its control over the former Soviet Union. From the Russian point of view, this is both a reasonable attempt to establish some minimal sphere of influence and essentially a defensive measure. However, it is a defensive measure that will immediately affect the three Baltic states, which are now integrated into European institutions.

Obviously the Eastern Europeans want to prevent a Russian resurgence. The real question is what the rest of Europe might do—and especially, what Germany might do. The Germans are now in a comfortable position with a buffer between them and the Russians, free to focus on their internal economic and social problems. In addition, the heritage of World War II weighs heavily on the Germans. They will not want to act alone, but as part of a unified Europe.

Germany's position is unpredictable. It is a nation that has learned, given its geopolitical position, that it is enormously dangerous to assert its national interest. In 1914 and 1939, Germany attempted to act decisively in response to geopolitical threats, and each time its efforts ended catastrophically. The German analysis is that engaging in politico-military maneuvers outside of a broad coalition exposes Germany to tremendous danger. Atlantic Europe sees Germany as a buffer against Russia and will see any threat in the Baltics as being irrelevant to their interests. Therefore, they will not join the coalition Germany needs to face the Russians. So the most likely outcome will be German inaction, limited American involvement, and a gradual return of Russian power into the borderland between Europe and Russia.

But there is another scenario. In this scenario Germany will recognize the imminent danger to Poland in Russian domination of the Baltics. Seeing Poland as a necessary part of German national security, it will thus exercise a forward policy, designed to protect Poland by protecting the Baltics. Germany will move to dominate the Baltic basin. Since the Russians will not simply abandon the field, the Germans will find themselves in an extended confrontation with the Russians, competing for influence in Poland and in the Carpathian region.

Germany will find itself, of necessity, both split off from its aggressive past and from the rest of Europe. While the rest of Europe will try to avoid involvement, the Germans will be engaged in traditional power politics. As they do that, their effective as well as potential power will soar and their psychology will shift. Suddenly, a united Germany will be asserting itself again. What starts defensively will evolve in unexpected ways.

This is not the most likely scenario. However, the situation might galvanize Germany back into its traditional role of looking at Russia as a major threat, and looking at Poland and the rest of Eastern Europe as a part of its sphere of influence and as protection against the Russians. This depends partly on how aggressively the Russians move, how tenaciously the Balts resist, how much risk the Poles are willing to take, and how distant the United States intends to be. Finally, it depends on internal German politics.

Internally, Europe is inert, still in shock over its losses. But external forces such as Islamic immigration or Russian attempts to rebuild its empire could bring the old fault line back to life in various ways.

THE MUSLIM WORLD

We have already discussed the Islamic world in general as a fault line. The current crisis is being contained, but the Islamic world, overall, remains unstable. While this instability will not gel into a general Islamist uprising, it does raise the possibility of a Muslim nation-state taking advantage of the instability, and therefore the weaknesses within other states, to assert itself as a regional power. Indonesia, the largest Muslim state in the world, is in no position to assert itself. Pakistan is the second-largest Muslim state. It is also a nuclear power. But it is so internally divided that it is difficult to see how it could evolve into a major power or, geographically, how it could spread its power, bracketed by Afghanistan to the west, China and Russia to the north, and India to the east. Between instability and geography, Pakistan is not going to emerge as a leading Muslim state.

After Indonesia and Pakistan, there are three other major Muslim nation-states. The largest is Egypt with 80 million people, Turkey is second with 71 million people, and Iran is third with 65 million.

When we look at the three economically, Turkey has the seventeenth-largest economy in the world, with a GDP of about $660 billion. Iran is twenty-ninth, with a GDP of just under $300 billion. Egypt is fifty-second, with a GDP of about $125 billion a year. For the past five years Turkey's economy has been growing at 5 to 8 percent a year, one of the highest sustained growth rates for any major country. With the exception of two years of recession, Iran has also had a sustained GDP growth rate of over 6 percent for the past five years, as has Egypt. These two countries are growing fast, but they are starting with a much smaller base than Turkey. Compared to European countries, Turkey already has the seventh-largest economy and is growing faster than most.

Now, it's true that economic size is not everything. Iran appears to be the most aggressive of the three geopolitically—but that is actually its basic weakness. In trying to protect its regime against the United States, Sunni Muslims, and anti-Iranian Arabs (Iran is not an Arab country), Iran is constantly forced to be prematurely assertive. In the process, it draws the attention of the United States, which then inevitably focuses on Iran as a dangerous power.

Because of its interests in the Persian Gulf and Iraq, Iranian goals run counter to those of the United States. That means Iran must divert resources to protect itself against the possibility of American attack at a time when its economy needs to develop very rapidly in order to carry it into the first rank regionally. The bottom line is that Iran irritates the United States. Sufficiently alarmed, the United States could devastate Iran. Iran is simply not ready for regional power status. It is constantly forced to dissipate its power prematurely. Attempting to become a major regional power while the world's greatest power is focused on your every move is, to say the least, difficult.

There is also the question of geography. Iran is on the margins of the region. Afghanistan is to the east, and there is little to be gained there. In any expansion of influence to the north, Iran would collide with the Russians. Iraq is a possible direction in which to move, but it can also become both a morass and a focal point for Arab and American countermeasures. It is not easy to increase Iranian regional power. Any move will cost more than it is worth.

Egypt is the largest country in the Arab world and has been its traditional leader. Under Gamal Abdel Nasser, it made a major play to become the leader of the Arab world. The Arab world, however, was deeply fragmented, and Egypt managed to antagonize key players like Saudi Arabia. After the Camp David accords with Israel in 1978, Egypt stopped trying to expand its power. It had failed anyway. Given its economy, and its relative isolation and insularity, it is hard to see Egypt becoming a regional power within any meaningful time frame. It is more likely to fall into someone else's sphere of influence, whether Turkish, American, or Russian, which has been its fate for several centuries.

Turkey is a very different case. It is not only a major modern economy, but it is by far the largest economy in the region—much larger than Iran, and perhaps the only modern economy in the entire Muslim world. Most important, it is strategically located between Europe, the Middle East, and Russia.

Turkey is not isolated and tied down; it has multiple directions in which it can move. And, most important, it does not represent a challenge to American interests and is therefore not constantly confronted with an American threat. This means it does not have to devote resources to blocking the

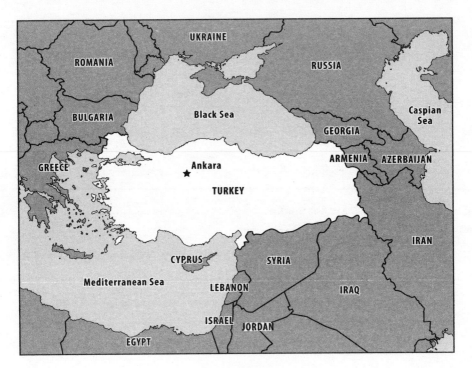

Turkey in 2008

United States. With its economy surging, it will likely soon reemerge in its old role, as the dominant force in the region.

It must be remembered that until World War I, Turkey was the seat of a major empire (see map, page 82). Shorn of its empire, Turkey became a secular state governing a Muslim population. It was, until 1918, the most powerful Muslim country in the world. And, at its height in the fourteenth to sixteenth centuries, the Turkish empire was far reaching and extremely powerful.

By the sixteenth century, Turkey was the dominant Mediterranean power, controlling not only North Africa and the Levant but also southeastern Europe, the Caucasus, and the Arabian Peninsula.

Turkey is an internally complex society, with a secular regime protected by a military charged constitutionally with that role and a growing Islamist movement. It is far from certain what sort of internal government it might end up having. But when we look at the wreckage of the Islamic world after

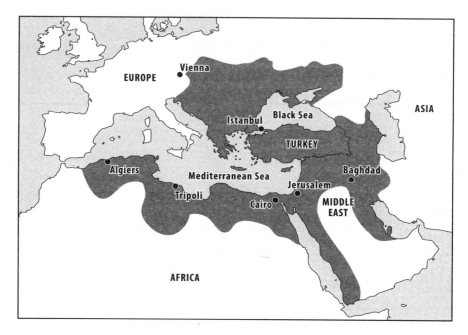

Ottoman Empire

the American invasion of Iraq in 2003 and consider which country must be taken seriously in the region, it seems obvious that it must be Turkey, an ally of the United States and the region's most important economic power.

MEXICO

If anyone had said in 1950 that the world's great economic powerhouses a half century later would be Japan and Germany, ranked second and third, that person would have been ridiculed. If you argued in 1970 that by 2007 China would be the world's fourth-largest economic power, the laughter would have been even more intense. But it would have been no funnier than arguing in 1800 that the United States by 1900 would be a world power. Things change, and the unexpected should be expected.

It is important to note, therefore, that in 2007 Mexico had the world's fifteenth-largest economy, just a bit behind Australia. Mexico ranked much lower in per capita income, of course, placing sixtieth, with a per capita income of roughly $12,000 a year as measured by the International Monetary Fund, ranking with Turkey and way ahead of China, undoubtedly a major power.

Per capita income is important. But the total size of the economy is even more important for international power. Poverty is a problem, but the size of the economy determines what percentage of your resources you can devote to military and related matters. The Soviet Union and China both had low per capita incomes. Yet the sheer sizes of their economies made them great powers. In fact, a substantial economy plus a large population have historically made a nation something to be reckoned with, regardless of poverty.

Mexico's population was about 27 million in 1950. It surged to about 100 million over the next fifty years and to 107 million by 2005. The UN forecast for 2050 is between 114 million and 139 million people, with 114 million being more probable. Having increased about fourfold in the last fifty years, Mexico's population will be basically stable in the next fifty. But Mexico will not lose population (like the advanced industrial countries will in the future), and Mexico has the workforce it needs to expand. This gives it an advantage. So, in terms of population or size, Mexico is not a small country. Certainly it is an unstable country, torn by drugs and cartels, but China was in chaos in 1970. Chaos can be overcome.

There are plenty of other countries like Mexico that we would not label as significant geopolitical fault lines. But Mexico is fundamentally different from any of these, like Brazil or India. Mexico is in North America, which, as we have discovered, is now the center of gravity of the international system. It also fronts both the Atlantic and Pacific oceans and shares a long and tense border with the United States. Mexico has already fought a major war with the United States for domination of North America, and lost. Mexico's society and economy are intricately bound together with those of the United States. Mexico's strategic location and its increasing importance as a nation make it a potential fault line.

To understand the nature of the fault line, let me briefly touch on the concept of borderland. Between two neighboring countries, there is frequently an area that has, over time, passed back and forth between them. It is an area of mixed nationalities and cultures. For example, Alsace-Lorraine lies between France and Germany. It has a unique mixed culture and individuals with different national loyalties. French, German, and a mixed regional argot are spoken there. Right now, France controls the region. But regardless of who controls it at any given time, it is a borderland, with two cultures and an underlying tension. The world is filled with borderlands. Think of Northern Ireland as the borderland between the United Kingdom and Ireland. Kashmir is a borderland between India and Pakistan. Think of the Russian–Polish border, or of Kosovo, the borderland between Serbia and Albania. Think of the French-Canadian–U.S. border. These are all borderlands of varying degrees of tension.

There is a borderland between the United States and Mexico, with Mexicans and Americans sharing a mixed culture. The borderland is on both sides of the official border. The U.S. side is unlike the rest of the United States, and the Mexican side is unlike the rest of Mexico. Like other borderlands, this one is its own unique place, with one exception: Mexicans on both sides of the border have deep ties to Mexico, and Americans have deep ties to the United States. Underneath the economic and cultural mixture, there is always political tension. This is particularly true here because of the constant movement of Mexicans into the borderland, across the border, and throughout the United States. The same cannot be said of Americans migrating south into Mexico.

Most borderlands change hands many times. The U.S.–Mexican borderland has changed hands only once so far.

Northern Mexico was slowly absorbed by the United States beginning with the 1835–1836 revolution in Texas and culminating in the Mexican-American War of 1846–1848. It constituted the southwestern part of today's United States. The border was set at the Rio Grande, and later adjusted in the west to include the south of Arizona. The indigenous Mexican population was not forcibly displaced. Mexicans continued to live in the area, which was later occupied by a much larger number of American settlers from the east. During the second half of the twentieth century, another population movement from Mexico into the borderland and beyond took place, further complicating the demographic picture.

We can draw a distinction between conventional immigration and population movements in a borderland. When other immigrant groups arrive in a country, they are physically separated from their homeland and sur-

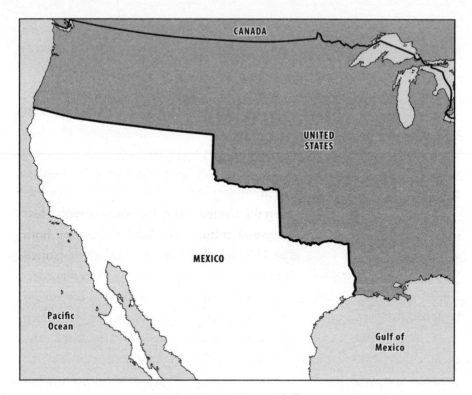

Mexico Prior to Texas Rebellion

rounded by powerful forces that draw their children into the host culture and economy. A movement into a borderland is different. It is an extension of one's homeland, not a separation from it. The border represents a political boundary, not a cultural or economic boundary, and immigrants are not at a great distance from home. They remain physically connected, and their loyalties are complex and variable.

Mexicans who move into the borderland behave differently from Mexicans living in Chicago. Those in Chicago behave more like conventional immigrants. Mexicans in the borderland potentially can regard themselves as living in occupied territory rather than a foreign country. This is no different from the way American settlers in Texas viewed their position prior to the revolution. They were Mexican citizens, but they saw themselves primarily as Americans and created a secessionist movement that tore Texas away from Mexico.

At a certain point, the status of the borderland simply becomes a question of military and political power. The borderland belongs to the stronger side, and the question of strength is determined on the ground. Since 1848, the political border has been fixed by the overwhelming power of the United States. Populations might shift. Smuggling might take place. But the political boundaries are fixed by military reality.

Later in the century, the current border will have been in place for two hundred years. Mexican national power might reemerge, and the demography of the borderland on the American side may have shifted so dramatically that the political boundaries might not be able to hold. At that time, it's quite possible that Mexico may no longer be the fifteenth-biggest country economically, but well into the top ten. Stranger things have happened, and free trade with the United States helps. The countries currently ranked ahead of Mexico include many European countries with severe demographic problems.

Given the impact of a potential Mexican–American confrontation on the border, there is no question but that this fault line must be taken seriously.

SUMMING UP

If we are looking for new challenges after the U.S.–jihadist war is over, there are two obvious places to look. Mexico and Turkey are clearly not yet ready for a significant global role, and Europe will remain insular and divided (it will react to events but will not initiate them). That leaves two fault lines, the Pacific and Eurasia, and, in the context of 2020, that means two countries possibly asserting themselves: China or Russia. A third possibility, more distant in the context of 2020, is Japan, but Japan's behavior will depend heavily on China's. Therefore, we need to examine with some care the geopolitical positions of China and Russia in order to predict which will become active first, and which will therefore pose the greatest challenge to the United States in the next decade.

What we are talking about here, geopolitically, are what we call "systemic" conflicts. The Cold War was a systemic conflict. It pitted the two leading powers against each other in a way that defined the entire international system. There were other conflicts, but most of them got sucked into the vortex of the major conflict. Thus everything from the Arab–Israeli wars to Chilean internal politics to Congolese independence got drawn into the Cold War and shaped by it. The two world wars were also systemic conflicts.

By definition, such a conflict must include the dominant geopolitical power at the time. Therefore, it must include the United States. And, again by definition, the United States will include itself in any major confrontation. If Russia and China were to confront each other, U.S. indifference or neutrality would be highly improbable. The outcome of the confrontation would mean too much to the United States. Moreover, Russia and China could not fight each other without absolute guarantees that the United States would stay out of the war. The United States is so powerful that its alliance with either would mean the defeat of the other.

Which country, China or Russia, is more likely to act in such a way as to bring it into confrontation with the United States? Given what we have seen of American grand strategy, the United States is not inclined to begin a conflict itself, unless it is faced with an aggressive regional power seeking to increase its security to the point of being able to threaten American interests in a fragmented Eurasian landmass. So, looking into future decades, we need to address the inclinations of China and Russia. Let's begin with the power everyone takes most seriously—China.

CHAPTER 5

CHINA 2020

PAPER TIGER

Any discussion of the future has to begin with a discussion of China. One-quarter of the world lives in China, and there has been a great deal of discussion of China as a future global power. Its economy has been surging dramatically in the past thirty years, and it is certainly a significant power. But thirty years of growth does not mean unending growth. It means that the probability of China continuing to grow at this rate is diminishing. And in the case of China, slower growth means substantial social and political problems. I don't share the view that China is going to be a major world power. I don't even believe it will hold together as a unified country. But I do agree that we can't discuss the future without first discussing China.

China's geography makes it unlikely that it will become an active fault line. If it were to become an area of conflict, it would be less China striking out than China becoming the victim of others taking advantage of its weakness. China's economy is not nearly as robust as it might seem, and its political stability, which depends heavily on continuing rapid growth, is even more precarious. China is important, however, because it appears to be the most likely global challenger in the near term—at least in the minds of others.

Again, using geopolitics as our framework, we will begin by considering the basics.

First, China is an island. It is obviously not surrounded by water, but it is surrounded by impassable terrain and wastelands that effectively isolate it from the rest of the world (see map below).

To China's north are Siberia and the Mongolian steppe—inhospitable, lightly settled, and difficult to traverse. To the southwest are the impassable Himalayas. The southern border with Myanmar, Laos, and Vietnam is simultaneously mountains and jungle, and to the east are oceans. Only its western border with Kazakhstan can be traveled by large numbers of people, but there too, movement involves a level of effort not frequently justified in Chinese history.

The vast majority of China's population lives within one thousand miles of the coast, populating the eastern third of the country, with the other two-thirds being quite underpopulated (see map, page 90).

China was completely conquered only once—by the Mongols in the

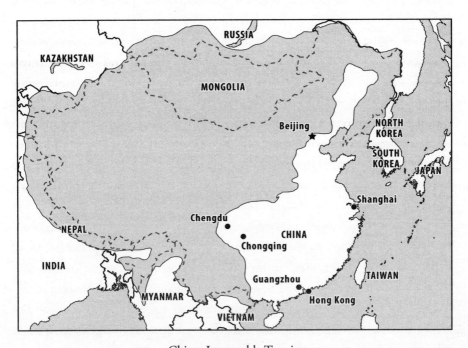

China: Impassable Terrain

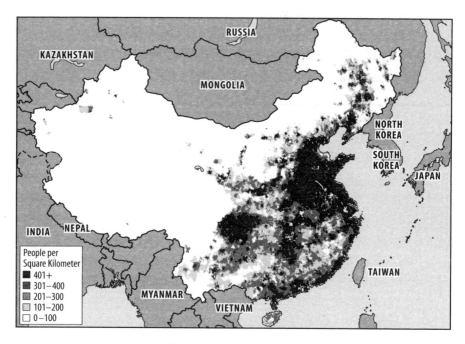

China's Population Density

twelfth century—and it has rarely extended its power beyond its present borders. China is not historically aggressive and has only intermittently involved itself with the rest of the world. It must be remembered that China has not always engaged in international trade, periodically closing itself off and avoiding contact with foreigners. When it does engage in trade, it does so using overland routes like the Silk Road through Central Asia and merchant ships sailing from its eastern ports (see map, page 91). The Europeans encountered a China in the mid-nineteenth century that was going through one of its isolationist periods. It was united but relatively poor. The Europeans forced their way in, engaging coastal China in intense trade. This had two effects. The first was the dramatic increase in wealth in the coastal areas that were engaged in trade. The second was the massive increase in inequality between China's coast and the poor interior regions. This disparity also led to the weakening of the central government's control over the coastal regions, and to increased instability and chaos. The coastal regions preferred close ties to (and even domination by) the Europeans.

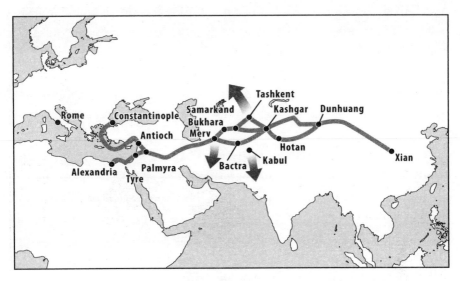

Silk Road

The period of chaos lasted from the mid-nineteenth century until the Communists took power in 1949. Mao had tried to foment a revolution in coastal cities like Shanghai. Having failed, he took the famous long march into the interior, where he raised an army of poor peasants, fought a civil war, and retook the coast. He then returned China to its pre-European enclosure. From 1949 until Mao's death, China was united and dominated by a strong government, but was isolated and poor.

CHINA'S GAMBLE

Mao's death led his successors to try once more for the historic Chinese dream. They wanted a China that was wealthy from international trade but united under a single powerful government. Deng Xiaoping, Mao's successor, knew that China could not remain isolated permanently and still be secure. Someone would take advantage of China's economic weakness. Deng therefore gambled. He bet that this time China could open its borders, engage in international trade, and not be torn apart by internal conflict.

The coastal regions again became prosperous and closely tied to outside powers. Inexpensive products and trade produced wealth for the great coastal cities like Shanghai, but the interior remained impoverished. Tensions between the coast and the interior increased, but the Chinese government maintained its balance and Beijing continued to rule, without losing control of any of the regions and without having to risk generating revolt by being excessively repressive.

This has gone on for about thirty years, which is not very long by any standard (and certainly not by Chinese ones). The open question is whether the internal forces building up in China can be managed. And this is the point at which we begin our analysis of China and its effect on the international system in the twenty-first century. Will China remain part of the global trading system? And if it does, will it disintegrate again?

China is gambling at the beginning of the twenty-first century that it can carry out an indefinite balancing act. The assumption is that it will be able to gradually shift resources away from the wealthier coastal regions toward the interior without meeting resistance from the coast and without encountering restlessness in the interior. Beijing wants to keep the various parts of China happy and is doing everything in its power to achieve that end.

Underlying this is another serious, and more threatening, problem. China appears to be a capitalist country with private property, banks, and all the other accoutrements of capitalism. But it is not truly capitalist in the sense that the markets do not determine capital allocation. Who you know counts for much more than whether you have a good business plan. Between Asian systems of family and social ties and the communist systems of political relationships, loans have been given out for a host of reasons, none of them having much to do with the merits of the business. As a result, not surprisingly, a remarkably large number of these loans have gone bad—"nonperforming," in the jargon of banking. The amount is estimated at somewhere between $600 billion and $900 billion, or between a quarter and a third of China's GDP, a staggering amount.

These bad debts are being managed through very high growth rates driven by low-cost exports. The world has a huge appetite for cheap exports, and the cash coming in from them keeps businesses with huge debts afloat.

But the lower China sets its prices, the less profit there is in them. Profitless exports drive a giant churning of the economic engine without actually getting it anywhere. Think of it as a business that makes money by selling products at or below cost. A huge amount of cash flows into the business, but it flows out just as fast.

This has been an ongoing issue in East Asia, and the example of Japan is instructive. Japan during the 1980s was seen as an economic superpower. It was devastating American businesses—MBAs were being taught to learn from the Japanese and emulate their business practices. Certainly Japan was growing extremely rapidly, but its rapid growth had less to do with management than with Japan's banking system.

Japanese banks, under government regulation, paid extremely low interest rates on money deposited by ordinary Japanese. Under the various laws, the only option for most Japanese was to put money into Japan's post office, which doubled as a bank. The post office paid minimal interest rates. The government turned around and lent this money to Japan's largest banks, again at interest rates well below international levels. These banks lent it again cheaply to businesses with which they were linked, so Sumitomo Bank loaned the money to Sumitomo Chemical. While American companies were borrowing money at double-digit rates in the 1970s, Japanese companies were borrowing money at a fraction of that amount.

It was no surprise that Japanese businesses did better than American ones. The cost of money was much lower. It is also no surprise that the Japanese had extremely high savings rates. Japan had virtually no public retirement plan at the time, and corporate pensions were minimal. Japanese planned for retirement through savings. They weren't more frugal, just more desperate. And this pool of desperate depositors had no alternative but to make deposits at very low interest rates.

While high interest rates imposed discipline on Western economies, culling out the weaker companies, Japanese banks were lending money at artificially low rates to friendly corporations. No real market existed. Money was flowing and relationships were the key. As a result, a lot of bad loans were made.

The primary means of financing in Japan was not raising equity in the stock market. It was borrowing money from banks. Boards of directors consisted of company employees and bankers who were not interested in profits nearly as much as they were in cash flow that would keep their companies afloat and pay off their debts. So Japan had one of the lowest rates of return on capital in the industrialized world. But it had a fabulous growth rate in terms of size because of the way the Japanese structured their economy. They lived by exporting.

The Japanese had to. With an extremely high savings rate driving the system, average Japanese citizens were not spending money, and therefore Japan could not build the economy on domestic demand. And since Japanese companies were controlled not by investors but by insiders and bankers, what they wanted to do was increase the cash coming in. How much, if any, profit was generated mattered less. Therefore, low-cost exports surged. More money was lent, more cash was needed, and more exports were sent out. The economy grew. But underneath it, a crisis was brewing.

The casual ways in which Japanese banks made loans increased the number of nonperforming loans—loans that were not being repaid. A lot of bad ideas were funded. Rather than write these off and let the businesses involved go into bankruptcy, Japanese banks covered up with more loans to keep the companies alive. Loans surged, and since depositors' money was spent maintaining the system, exports to bring in even more money were essential. The system was awash with money, but underneath it a vast array of companies on life support—and companies struggling to increase cash without regard for profit—were undermining the entire financial system. Massive surges in exports were producing very little profit. The entire system was churning just to keep itself afloat.

From the outside, Japan was surging, taking over markets with incredible products at cheap prices. It was not obsessed with profits like American firms were, and the Japanese appeared to have a hammerlock on the future. In fact, the opposite was true. Japan was living off a legacy of cheap, government-controlled money, and low prices were a desperate attempt to keep the cash coming in so the banking system would hold together.

In the end, the debt structure grew too massive and it became impossible to stay in front of it with exports. Japanese banks began to collapse and were bailed out by the government. Instead of permitting a massive recession to impose discipline, Japan used various salvaging means to put off extreme pain in return for a long-term malaise that is still lingering. Growth plunged, markets plunged. Interestingly, while the crisis hit in the early 1990s, many Westerners did not notice that the Japanese economy had failed until years later. They were still talking about the Japanese economic miracle in the mid-1990s.

How is this relevant to China? China is Japan on steroids. It is not only an Asian state that values social relations above economic discipline but a communist state that allocates money politically and manipulates economic data. It is also a state in which equity holders—demanding profits—are less important than bankers and government officials, who demand cash. Both economies rely heavily on exports, both have staggeringly high growth rates, and both face collapse when the growth rate begins even to barely slow. Japan's bad debt rate around 1990 was, by my estimate, about 20 percent of GDP. China's, under the most conservative estimate, is about 25 percent— and I would argue the number is closer to 40 percent. But even 25 percent is staggeringly high.

China's economy appears healthy and vibrant, and if you look only at how fast the economy is growing, it is breathtaking. Growth is only one factor to examine, however. The more important question is whether such growth is profitable. Much of China's growth is very real, and it generates the money necessary to keep the banks satisfied. But this growth really does not strengthen the economy. And if and when it slacks off, for example because of a recession in the United States, the entire structure could crumble very fast.

This is not a new story in Asia. Japan was a growth engine in the 1980s. Conventional wisdom said it was going to bury the United States. But in reality, while Japan's economy was growing fast, its growth rates were unsustainable. When growth slumped, Japan had a massive banking crisis from which it has not really fully recovered almost twenty years later. Similarly, when East Asia's economy imploded in 1997, it came as a surprise to many, since the economies had been growing so fast.

China has expanded extraordinarily for the last thirty years. The idea that such growth rates can be sustained indefinitely or permanently violates basic principles of economics. At some point the business cycle, culling weak business, must rear its ugly head—and it will. At some point a simple lack of skilled labor will halt continued growth. There are structural limits to growth, and China is reaching them.

CHINA'S POLITICAL CRISIS

Japan solved its problem with a generation of low growth. It had the political and social discipline to do this without unrest. East Asia solved it in two ways. Some countries, like South Korea and Taiwan, imposed painful measures and came out stronger than ever, but this was possible only because they had strong states able to impose pain. Some countries, like Indonesia, never really recovered.

The problem for China is political. China is held together by money, not ideology. When there is an economic downturn and the money stops rolling in, not only will the banking system spasm, but the entire fabric of Chinese society will shudder. Loyalty in China is either bought or coerced. Without available money, only coercion remains. Business slowdowns can generally lead to instability because they lead to business failure and unemployment. In a country where poverty is endemic and unemployment widespread, the added pressure of an economic downturn will result in political instability.

Recall how China split into coastal and interior regions between the British intrusion and Mao's triumph. Businesses on the coast, prosperous from foreign trade and investment, gravitated to their foreign interests, trying to break free from the central government. They drew in European imperialists—and Americans—who had financial interests in China. Today's situation is potentially the same. A businessman in Shanghai has interests in common with Los Angeles, New York, and London. In fact, he makes far more money from these relationships than he does from Beijing. As Beijing tries to clamp down on him, not only will he want to break free of its control, but he will try to draw in foreign powers to protect his and their interests. In the meantime, the much poorer people in the interior of the country will be either trying to move to the coastal cities or pressuring Beijing to tax the coast and give them money. Beijing, caught in the middle, either weakens and loses control or clamps down so hard that it moves back to a Maoist enclosure of the country. The critical question is which outcome is more likely.

The Chinese regime rests on two pillars. One is the vast bureaucracy that operates China. The second is the military-security complex that enforces the will of the state and the Communist Party. A third pillar, the ideological principles of the Communist Party, has now disappeared. Egalitarianism, selflessness, and service to the people are now archaic values, preached but not believed by or practiced by the Chinese people.

State, party, and security apparati are as affected by the decline in ideology as the rest of society. Communist Party officials have been the personal beneficiaries of the new order. If the regime were to try to bring the coastal regions under control, it is hard to imagine the apparatus being particularly aggressive, as it is part of the same system that enriched those regions. In the nineteenth century the same problem emerged when government officials along the coast didn't want to enforce Beijing's edicts. They were on the side of doing business with foreigners.

If there is indeed a serious economic crisis, the central government will have to find a substitute ideology for communism. If people are to sacrifice, it must be for something they believe in—and if the Chinese cannot believe in communism, they can still believe in China. The Chinese government will attempt to limit disintegration by increasing nationalism and the natural companion of nationalism, xenophobia. Historically, China has a deep distrust of foreigners, and the party will need to blame someone for economic devastation. As Mao blamed foreigners for China's weakness and poverty, the party will again blame foreigners for China's economic problems.

Since there will be substantial confrontations with foreign states on economic issues—they will be defending their economic investments in China—playing the nationalist card will come easily. The idea of China as a great power will substitute for the lost ideology of communism. Disputes will help bolster the position of the Chinese government. By blaming foreigners for problems and confronting foreign governments diplomatically and with growing military power, the Chinese will generate public support for the regime. This is most likely to take place in the 2010s.

The most natural confrontation would be with Japan and/or the United States, both historical enemies with whom smoldering disputes already exist. Russia is unlikely to be treated as an enemy. However, the probability of a military confrontation with the Japanese or the Americans is limited. It would be difficult for the Chinese to engage either country aggressively. The Chinese have a weak navy that could not survive a confrontation with the United States. Therefore, invading Taiwan might be tempting in theory but is not likely to happen. China does not have the naval power to force its way across the Taiwan Strait, and certainly not the ability to protect convoys shuttling supplies to Taiwanese battlefields. China is not going to develop a naval capacity that can challenge the United States within a decade. It takes a long time to build a navy.

China, then, has three possible future paths. In the first, it continues to grow at astronomical rates indefinitely. No country has ever done that, and China is not likely to be an exception. The extraordinary growth of the past thirty years has created huge imbalances and inefficiencies in China's economy that will have to be corrected. At some point China will have to go through the kind of wrenching readjustment that the rest of Asia already has undergone.

A second possible path is the recentralization of China, where the conflicting interests that will emerge and compete following an economic slowdown are controlled by a strong central government that imposes order and restricts the regions' room to maneuver. That scenario is more probable than the first, but the fact that the apparatus of the central government is filled with people whose own interests oppose centralization would make this difficult to pull off. The government can't necessarily rely on its own people to enforce the rules. Nationalism is the only tool they have to hold things together.

A third possibility is that under the stress of an economic downturn, China fragments along traditional regional lines, while the central government weakens and becomes less powerful. Traditionally, this is a more plausible scenario in China—and one that will benefit the wealthier classes as well as foreign investors. It will leave China in the position it was in prior to Mao, with regional competition and perhaps even conflict and a central government struggling to maintain control. If we accept the fact that China's economy will have to undergo a readjustment at some point, and that this will generate serious tension, as it would in any country, then this third outcome fits most closely with reality and with Chinese history.

A JAPANESE VARIANT

The advanced industrial world will be experiencing a contraction of population in the 2010s, and labor will be at a premium. For some countries, due to entrenched cultural values, immigration either is not an option or is at least a very difficult one. Japan, for example, is extremely averse to immigration, yet it must find a source of labor that is under its control and that can be taxed to support older workers. Most workers with a choice of where to go will not choose Japan, as it is fairly inhospitable to foreigners who want to become citizens. Koreans in Japan are not citizens of Japan. Even if they have lived all their lives and worked in Japan, they are issued papers by the Japanese police calling them "Korean" (neither north nor south) and are unable to become Japanese citizens.

Consider, however, that China is a vast pool of relatively low-cost labor. If the Chinese won't come to Japan, Japan may come to China, as it has before. Using Chinese labor in enterprises created by the Japanese but located in China will be an alternative to immigration—and it will not only be Japan doing this.

Remember that Beijing will be trying simultaneously to tighten its grip on the country. Traditionally, when the central government is clamping down on China, it is prepared to accept lower economic growth. While a large-scale, concentrated Japanese presence sucking up Chinese labor might make a great deal of economic sense for local entrepreneurs and governments and even for Beijing, it makes little political sense. It would cut directly against Beijing's political interests. But Japan will not want the Chinese government diverting money to its own ends. That would defeat the entire purpose of the exercise.

By approximately 2020, Japan will have Chinese allies in the fight to bring in Japanese investment on terms favorable to Japan. Coastal regions will be competing to attract Japanese investment and resisting Beijing's pressure and its nationalist ideology. Interior China might not benefit from Japan's presence, but businesses and governments along the coast would. The Japanese, with large amounts of money, will have recruited allies in the coastal cities who do not want to pay the price that will be needed to satisfy the demands of the interior. An alliance between one or more coastal regions and Japan will emerge, confronting the power of Beijing. The amount of money that Japan will bring to bear will rapidly divide the central party itself and weaken the central government's ability to assert its control on the coastal cities.

China will be seen as part of the solution for countries like Japan that are feeling heavy pressure from demographic problems but cannot manage large-scale immigration. Unfortunately the timing will not be good. An inevitable downturn in the Chinese economy will make the central government more assertive and more nationalist. But the central government will itself be weakened by the corrosive effect of money. China will remain formally united, but power will tend to devolve to the regions.

A very real future for China in 2020 is its old nightmare—a country divided among competing regional leaders, foreign powers taking advantage of the situation to create regions where they can define economic rules to their advantage, and a central government trying to hold it all together but failing. A second possibility is a neo-Maoist China, centralized at the cost of economic progress. As always, the least likely scenario is the continuation of the current situation indefinitely.

It all boils down to this: China does not represent a geopolitical fault line in the next twenty years. Its geography makes that unlikely under any circumstances, and China's level of military development needs more than a decade to overcome this geographical limit. Internal stresses on the Chinese economy and society will give China far greater internal problems than it can reasonably handle, and therefore it will have little time for foreign policy adventures. To the extent that China will be involved with foreign powers, it will be defending itself against encroachment rather than projecting its own power.

CHAPTER 6

RUSSIA 2020

REMATCH

In geopolitics, major conflicts repeat themselves. France and Germany, for example, fought multiple wars, as did Poland and Russia. When a single war does not resolve an underlying geopolitical issue, it is refought until the issue is finally settled. At the very least, even without another war, tension and confrontation are ongoing. Significant conflicts are rooted in underlying realities—and they do not go away easily. Keep in mind how quickly Balkan geopolitics led to a recurrence of wars that had been fought a century earlier.

Russia is the eastern portion of Europe and has clashed with the rest of Europe on multiple occasions. The Napoleonic wars, the two world wars, and the Cold War all dealt, at least in part, with the status of Russia and its relationship to the rest of Europe. None of these wars ultimately settled this question, because in the end a united and independent Russia survived or triumphed. The problem is that the very existence of a united Russia poses a significant potential challenge to Europe.

Russia is a vast region with a huge population. It is much poorer than the rest of Europe, but it has two assets—land and natural resources. As such it is a constant temptation for European powers, which see an opportunity to increase their size and wealth to the east. Historically, though, Europeans who have invaded Russia have come to a disastrous end. If they are not beaten by the Russians, they are so exhausted from fighting them that someone else defeats them. Russia occasionally pushes its power westward, threatening Europe with the Russian masses. At other times passive and ignored, Russia is often taken advantage of. But, in due course, others pay for underestimating it.

The Cold War only appeared to have settled the Russian question. Had the Russian Federation collapsed in the 1990s and the region fragmented into multiple, smaller states, Russian power would have disappeared, and with it the challenge Russian power poses to Europe. Had the Americans, Europeans, and Chinese moved in for the kill, the Russian question would have been finally settled. But the Europeans were too weak and divided at the end of the twentieth century, the Chinese too isolated and preoccupied with internal issues, and after September 11, 2001, the Americans were too distracted by the Islamist war to act decisively. What actions were taken by the United States were insufficient and unfocused. In fact, these actions only served to alert the Russians to the great potential danger from the United States and ensured they would respond to it.

Given the simple fact that Russia did not disintegrate, the Russian geopolitical question will reemerge. Given the fact that Russia is now reenergizing itself, that question will come sooner rather than later. The conflict will not be a repeat of the Cold War, any more than World War I was a repeat of the Napoleonic wars. But it will be a restatement of the fundamental Russian question: If Russia is a united nation-state, where will its frontiers lie and what will be the relationship between Russia and its neighbors? That question will represent the next major phase in world history—in 2020, and in the years leading up to it.

RUSSIAN DYNAMICS

If we are going to understand Russia's behavior and intentions, we have to begin with Russia's fundamental weakness—its borders, particularly in the northwest. Even when Ukraine is controlled by Russia, as it has been for centuries, and Belarus and Moldavia are part of the Russian empire as well, there are still no natural borders in the north. The center and south are anchored on the Carpathian Mountains, as far north as the Slovakian-Polish border, and to the east of them are the Pripet marshes, boggy and impassable. But in the north and south (east of the Carpathians), there are no strong barriers to protect Russia—or to protect Russia's neighbors.

On the northern European plain, no matter where Russia's borders are drawn, it is open to attack. There are few significant natural barriers anywhere on this plain. Pushing its western border all the way into Germany, as it did in 1945, still leaves Russia's frontiers without a physical anchor. The only physical advantage Russia can have is depth. The farther west into Europe its borders extend, the farther conquerors have to travel to reach Moscow. Therefore, Russia is always pressing westward on the northern European plain and Europe is always pressing eastward.

That is not the case with other borders of Russia—by which we mean to include the former Soviet Union, which has been the rough shape of Russia since the end of the nineteenth century. In the south, there was a natural secure boundary. The Black Sea leads to the Caucasus, separating Russia from Turkey and Iran. Iran is further buffered by the Caspian Sea, and by the Kara Kum Desert in southern Turkmenistan, which runs along the Afghan border, terminating in the Himalayas. The Russians are concerned with the Iranian–Afghan segment, and might push south as they have done several times. But they are not going to be invaded on that border. Their frontier with China is long and vulnerable, but only on a map. Invading Siberia is not a practical possibility. It is a vast wilderness. There is a potential weakness along China's western border, but not a significant one. Therefore, the Russian empire, in any of its incarnations, is fairly secure except in northern Europe, where it faces its worst dangers—geography and powerful European nations.

Russia had its guts carved out after the collapse of communism. St. Petersburg, its jewel, was about a thousand miles away from NATO troops in 1989. Now it is less than one hundred miles away. In 1989, Moscow was twelve hundred miles from the limits of Russian power. Now it is about two hundred miles. In the south, with Ukraine independent, the Russian hold on the Black Sea is tenuous, and it has been forced to the northern extreme of the Caucasus. Afghanistan is occupied, however tentatively, by the Americans, and Russia's anchor on the Himalayas is gone. If there were an army interested in invading, the Russian Federation is virtually indefensible.

Russia's strategic problem is that it is a vast country with relatively poor transportation. If Russia were simultaneously attacked along its entire periphery, in spite of the size of its forces, it would be unable to easily protect itself. It would have difficulty mobilizing forces and deploying them to multiple fronts, so it would have to maintain an extremely large standing army that could be predeployed. This pressure imposes a huge economic burden on Russia, undermines the economy, and causes it to buckle from within. That is what happened to the Soviet state. Of course, this is not the first time Russia has been in peril.

Protecting its frontiers is not Russia's only problem today. The Russians are extremely well aware that they are facing a massive demographic crisis. Russia's current population is about 145 million people, and projections for 2050 are for between 90 million and 125 million. Time is working against it. Russia's problem will soon be its ability to field an army sufficient for its strategic needs. Internally, the number of Russians compared to other ethnic groups is declining, placing intense pressure on Russia to make a move sooner rather than later. In its current geographical position, it is an accident waiting to happen. Given Russia's demographic trajectory, in twenty years it may be too late to act, and its leaders know this. It does not have to conquer the world, but Russia must regain and hold its buffers—essentially the boundaries of the old Soviet Union.

Between their geopolitical, economic, and demographic problems, the Russians have to make a fundamental shift. For a hundred years the Russians sought to modernize their country through industrialization, trying to catch up to the rest of Europe. They never managed to pull it off. Around 2000 Russia shifted its strategy. Instead of focusing on industrial development as they had in the past century, the Russians reinvented themselves as exporters of natural resources, particularly energy, but also minerals, agricultural products, lumber, and precious metals.

By de-emphasizing industrial development, and emphasizing raw materials, the Russians took a very different path, one more common to countries in the developing world. But given the unexpected rise of energy and commodity prices, this move not only saved the Russian economy but also strengthened it to the point where Russia could afford to drive its own selective reindustrialization. Most important, since natural resource production is less manpower-intensive than industrial production, it gave Russia an economic base that could be sustained with a declining population.

It also gave Russia leverage in the international system. Europe is hungry for energy. Russia, constructing pipelines to feed natural gas to Europe, takes care of Europe's energy needs and its own economic problems, and puts Europe in a position of dependency on Russia. In an energy-hungry world, Russia's energy exports are like heroin. It addicts countries once they start using it. Russia has already used its natural gas resources to force neighboring countries to bend to its will. That power reaches into the heart of Europe, where the Germans and the former Soviet satellites of Eastern Europe all depend on Russian natural gas. Add to this its other resources, and Russia can apply significant pressure on Europe.

Dependency can be a double-edged sword. A militarily weak Russia cannot pressure its neighbors, because its neighbors might decide to make a grab for its wealth. So Russia must recover its military strength. Rich and weak is a bad position for nations to be in. If Russia is to be rich in natural resources and export them to Europe, it must be in a position to protect what it has and to shape the international environment in which it lives.

In the next decade Russia will become increasingly wealthy (relative to its past, at least) but geographically insecure. It will therefore use some of its wealth to create a military force appropriate to protect its interests, buffer zones to protect it from the rest of the world—and then buffer zones for the buffer zones. Russia's grand strategy involves the creation of deep buffers along the northern European plain, while it divides and manipulates its neighbors, creating a new regional balance of power in Europe. What Russia cannot tolerate are tight borders without buffer zones, and its neighbors united against it. This is why Russia's future actions will appear to be aggressive but will actually be defensive.

Russia's actions will unfold in three phases. In the first phase, Russia will be concerned with recovering influence and effective control in the former Soviet Union, re-creating the system of buffers that the Soviet Union provided it. In the second phase, Russia will seek to create a second tier of buffers beyond the boundaries of the former Soviet Union. It will try to do this without creating a solid wall of opposition, of the kind that choked it during the Cold War. In the third phase—really something that will have been going on from the beginning—Russia will try to prevent anti-Russian coalitions from forming.

It is important to step back here and look at the reasons why the former Soviet Union stayed intact in the latter half of the twentieth century. The Soviet Union was held together not simply by force but by a system of economic relationships that sustained it in the same way that the Russian empire before it was sustained. The former Soviet Union shares a common geography—that is, vast and mostly landlocked, in the heart of Eurasia. It has extremely poor internal transport systems, as is common in landlocked areas where the river systems don't match with agricultural systems. It is therefore difficult to transport food—and after industrialization, difficult to move manufactured goods.

Think of the old Soviet Union as that part of the Eurasian landmass that stretched westward from the Pacific Ocean along the wastelands north of populated China, northwest of the Himalayas, and continued along the border with South Central Asia to the Caspian, and then on to the Caucasus. It was buffered by the Black Sea and then by the Carpathian Mountains. Along the north, there was only the Arctic. Within this space, there was a vast landmass, marked by republics with weak economies.

If we think of the Soviet Union as a natural grouping of geographically isolated and economically handicapped countries, we can see what held it together. The countries that made up the Soviet Union were bound together of necessity. They could not compete with the rest of the world economically—but isolated from global competition, they could complement and support each other. This was a natural grouping readily dominated by the Russians. The countries beyond the Carpathians (the ones Russia occupied after World War II and turned into satellites) were not included in this natural grouping. If it weren't for Soviet military force, they would have been oriented toward the rest of Europe, not Russia.

The former Soviet Union consisted of members who really had nowhere else to go. These old economic ties still dominate the region, except that Russia's new model, exporting energy, has made these countries even more dependent than they were previously. Attracted as Ukraine was to the rest of Europe, it could not compete or participate with Europe. Its natural economic relationship is with Russia; it relies on Russia for energy, and ultimately it tends to be militarily dominated by Russia as well.

These are the dynamics that Russia will take advantage of in order to re-assert its sphere of influence. It will not necessarily re-create a formal political structure run from Moscow—although that is not inconceivable. Far more important will be Russian influence in the region over the next five to ten years, which will surge. In order to think about this, let's break it down into three theaters of operation: the Caucasus, Central Asia, and the European theater, which includes the Baltics.

THE CAUCASUS

The Caucasus is the boundary between Russian and Turkish power, and has historically been a flash point between the two empires. It was also a flash point during the Cold War. The Turkish–Soviet border ran through the Caucasus, with the Soviet side consisting of three separate republics: Armenia, Georgia, and Azerbaijan, all now independent. The Caucasus also ran north into the Russian Federation itself, including into the Muslim areas of Dagestan and, most important, Chechnya, where a guerrilla war against Russian domination raged after the fall of communism.

From a purely defensive point of view, the precise boundaries of Russian and Turkish influence don't matter so long as both are based somewhere in the Caucasus. The rugged terrain makes defense relatively easy. However, should the Russians lose their position in the Caucasus altogether and be pushed north into the lowlands, Russia's position would become difficult. With the gap between Ukraine and Kazakhstan only a few hundred miles wide, Russia would be in strategic trouble.

This is the reason the Russians are so unwilling to compromise on Chechnya. The southern part of Chechnya is deep in the northern Caucasus. If that were lost, the entire Russian position would unravel. Given a choice, the Rus-

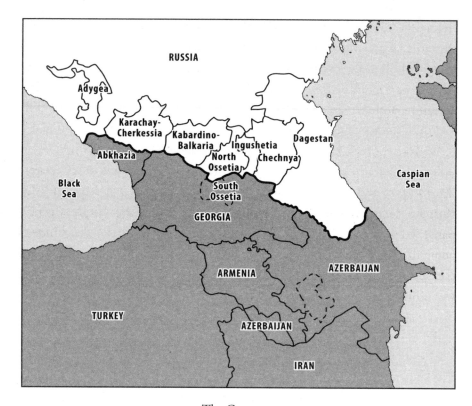

The Caucasus

sians would prefer to be anchored farther south, in Georgia. Armenia is an ally of Russia. If Georgia were Russian, its entire position would be much more stable. Controlling Chechnya is indispensable. Reabsorbing Georgia is desirable. Holding Azerbaijan does not provide a strategic advantage—but the Russians would not mind having it as a buffer with the Iranians. Russia's position here is not intolerable, but Georgia, not incidentally closely allied with the United States, is a tempting target, as was seen in the August 2008 conflict.

Bitter rivalries continue to rage in the region, as always happens in mountainous regions where small nationalities persist. The Armenians, for example, hate the Turks, whom they accuse of conducting genocide against them early in the twentieth century. Armenia looks to the Russians for protection. Armenian–Georgian rivalry is intense and, in spite of the fact that Stalin was a Georgian, the Georgians are hostile to the Armenians and extremely wary of the Russians. The Russians believe the Georgians looked the other way while weapons were shipped through their country to the Chechens, and the fact that the Georgians are very close to the Americans makes the situation even worse. Azerbaijan is hostile to Armenia—and therefore close to Iran and Turkey.

The situation in the Caucasus is not only difficult to understand but also difficult to deal with. The Soviet Union actually managed to solve the complexity by incorporating all these countries into the Soviet Union after World War I and ruthlessly suppressing their autonomy. It is impossible for Russia to be indifferent to the region now or in the future—unless it is prepared to lose its position in the Caucasus. Therefore, the Russians are indeed going to reassert their position, starting with Georgia. Since the United States sees Georgia as a strategic asset, Russia's reassertion there will lead to confrontation with the United States. Unless the Chechen rebellion completely disappears, the Russians will have to move south, then isolate the rebellion and nail down their position in the mountains.

There are two powers that will not want this to happen. The United States is one, and the other is Turkey. Americans will see Russian domination of Georgia as undermining their position in the region. The Turks will see this as energizing the Armenians and returning the Russian army in force to their borders. The Russians will become more convinced of the need to act because of this resistance. A duel in the Caucasus will result.

CENTRAL ASIA

Central Asia is a vast region running between the Caspian Sea and the Chinese border. It is primarily Muslim and therefore, as we have seen, was part of the massive destabilization that took place in the Muslim world after the fall of the Soviet Union. By itself it has some economic value, as a region with energy reserves. But it has little strategic importance to the Russians—unless another great power was to dominate it and use it as a base against them. If that were to happen, it would become enormously important. Whoever controls Kazakhstan would be a hundred miles from the Volga, a river highway for Russian agriculture.

Central Asia

During the 1990s, Western energy companies flocked to the region. Russia had no problem with that. It wasn't in a position to compete, and it wasn't in a position to control the region militarily. Central Asia was a neutral zone of relative indifference to the Russians. All of that changed on September 11, 2001, which redefined the geopolitics of the region. September 11 made it urgent for the United States to invade Afghanistan. Unable to mount an invasion by itself quickly, the United States asked the Russians for help.

One thing they asked for was Russian help in getting the Northern Alliance, an anti-Taliban group in Afghanistan, to play the major role on the ground. The Russians had sponsored the Northern Alliance and effectively controlled it. Another thing the Americans asked for was Russian support in securing bases for the United States in several Central Asian countries. Technically these were independent countries, but the United States was asking for help with the Northern Alliance and couldn't afford to anger the Russians. The Central Asian countries did not want to anger the Russians either—and U.S. planes had to fly over the former Soviet Union to get to them.

The Russians agreed to an American military presence in the region, thinking they had an understanding with the United States that this was a temporary situation. But as the war in Afghanistan dragged on, the United States stayed on; and as it stayed on, it became more and more influential with the various republics in the region. Russia realized that what had been a benign buffer zone was becoming dominated by the main global power—a power that was pressing Russia in Ukraine, the Caucasus, and the Baltics. In addition, as the price of energy rose and Russia adopted its new economic strategy, Central Asia's energy became even more significant.

Russia did not want American forces a hundred miles from the Volga. Russia simply had to react. It didn't act directly, but it began manipulating the political situation in the region, reducing American power. It was a move designed to return Central Asia to the Russian sphere of influence. And the Americans, on the other side of the world, isolated by chaotic Afghanistan, Iran, and Pakistan, were in no position to resist. The Russians reasserted their natural position. And tellingly, it was one of the few places U.S. naval power couldn't reach.

Central Asia is an area where the United States can't remain under Russian pressure. It is a place where the Chinese could potentially cause problems, but as we've seen, that is unlikely to happen. China has economic influence there, but the Russians, in the end, have both military and financial capabilities that can outduel them. The Russians might offer China access to Central Asia, but the arrangements created in the nineteenth century and maintained by the Soviet Union will reassert themselves. Therefore, it is my view that Central Asia will be back in the Russian sphere of influence by the early 2010s, long before the major confrontation begins in the west, in Europe.

THE EUROPEAN THEATER

The European theater is, of course, the area directly west of Russia. In this region, Russia's western border faces the three Baltic states of Estonia, Latvia, and Lithuania, and the two independent republics of Belarus and Ukraine. All of these were part of the former Soviet Union and of the Russian empire. Beyond these countries lies the belt of former Soviet satellites: Poland, Slovakia, Hungary, Romania, and Bulgaria. The Russians must dominate Belarus and Ukraine for their basic national security. The Baltics are secondary but still important. Eastern Europe is not critical, so long as the Russians are anchored in the Carpathian Mountains in the south and have strong forces on the northern European plain. But of course, all of this can get complicated.

Ukraine and Belarus are everything to the Russians. If they were to fall into an enemy's hands—for example, join NATO—Russia would be in mortal danger. Moscow is only a bit over two hundred miles from the Russian border with Belarus, Ukraine less than two hundred miles from Volgograd, formerly Stalingrad. Russia defended against Napoleon and Hitler with depth. Without Belarus and Ukraine, there is no depth, no land to trade for an enemy's blood. It is, of course, absurd to imagine NATO posing a threat to Russia. But the Russians think in terms of twenty-year cycles, and they know how quickly the absurd becomes possible.

They also know that the United States and NATO have systematically expanded their reach by extending membership in NATO to Eastern Europe and the Baltic states. As soon as the United States began trying to recruit Ukraine into NATO, the Russians changed their view both of American intentions and of Ukraine. From the Russian point of view, NATO expanding into Ukraine threatens Russian interests in the same way as if the Warsaw Pact had moved into Mexico. When a pro-Western uprising in 2004—the Orange Revolution—seemed about to sweep Ukraine into NATO, the Russians accused the United States of trying to surround and destroy Russia. What the Americans were thinking is open to debate. That Ukraine in NATO would be potentially devastating to Russian national security is not.

The Russians did not mobilize their army. Rather, they mobilized their intelligence service, whose covert connections in Ukraine were superb. The

Russians undermined the Orange Revolution, playing on a split between pro-Russian eastern Ukraine and pro-European western Ukraine. It proved not to be difficult at all, and fairly quickly Ukrainian politics became gridlocked. It is only a matter of time before Russian influence will overwhelm Kiev.

Belarus is an easier issue. As noted earlier, Belarus is the least reformed member of the former Soviet republics. It remains a centralized, authoritarian state. More important, its leadership has repeatedly mourned the passing of the Soviet Union and has proposed union of some sort with Russia. Such a union will, of course, have to be on Russian terms, which has led to tension, but there is no possibility of Belarus joining NATO.

The reabsorption of Belarus and Ukraine into the Russian sphere of influence is a given in the next five years. When that happens, Russia will have roughly returned to its borders with Europe between the two world wars. It will be anchored in the Caucasus in the south, with Ukraine protected, and in the north its borders on the northern European plain will abut Poland and the Baltic countries. That will pose the questions of who the most powerful country in the north is and where the precise frontiers will be. The real flash point will be the Baltics.

The traditional path to invade Russia is a three-hundred-mile gap between the northern Carpathians and the Baltic Sea. This is flat, easily traversed country with few river barriers. This northern European plain is a smooth ride for invaders. A European invader can move due east to Moscow or to St. Petersburg in the northwest. During the Cold War, the distance from St. Petersburg to NATO's front line was also more than a thousand miles. Today the distance is about seventy miles. This explains the strategic nightmare Russia faces in the Baltics—and what it will need to do to fix the problem.

The three Baltic countries were once part of the Soviet Union. Each became independent after it collapsed. And then, in that narrow window, each became part of NATO. As we have seen, the Europeans are most likely too far into their decadent cycle to have the energy to take advantage of the situation. However, the Russians are not going to risk their national security on that assumption. They saw Germany go from being a cripple in 1932 to being at the gates of Moscow in 1941. The inclusion of the Baltic countries along with Poland in NATO has moved NATO's frontier extraordinarily close to the Russian heartland. For a country that was invaded three times in the last two hundred years, the comfortable assumption that NATO and its members are no threat is not something it can risk.

From the Russian point of view, the major invasion route into their country is not only wide open but also in the hands of countries with a pronounced hostility to Russia. The Baltic countries have never forgiven the Russians for their occupation. The Poles are equally bitter and deeply distrustful of Russian intentions. Now that they are part of NATO, these countries form the front line. Behind them is Germany, a country as distrusted by Russia as Russia is by the Poles and Balts. The Russians are certainly paranoid—but that doesn't mean they don't have enemies or that they are crazy.

This would be the point of any confrontation. The Russians can live with a neutral Baltic region. Living with a Baltic region that is part of NATO and close to the Americans, however, is a much more difficult risk to take. On the other hand, the Americans, having backed down in Central Asia, and being cautious in the Caucasus, can't retreat from the Baltics. Any compromise over the three NATO members would send Eastern Europe into a panic. Eastern Europe's behavior would become unpredictable, and the possibility of Russian influence spreading westward would increase. Russia has the greater interest, but the Americans could bring substantial power to bear if they chose.

Russia's next move likely will be an agreement with Belarus for an integrated defense system. Belarus and Russia have been linked for a very long time, so this will be a natural reversion. And that will bring the Russian army to the Baltic frontier. It will also bring the army to the Polish frontier—and that will start the confrontation in its full intensity.

The Poles fear the Russians and the Germans. Trapped between the two, without natural defenses, they fear whichever is stronger at any time. Unlike the rest of Eastern Europe, which at least has the barrier of the Carpathians between them and the Russians—and shares a border with Ukraine, not Russia—the Poles are on the dangerous northern European plain. When the Russians return to their border in force in the process of confronting the Baltic states, the Poles will react. Poland has almost forty million people. It is not a small country, and since it will be backed by the United States, not a trivial one.

Polish support will be thrown behind the Balts. The Russians will pull the Ukrainians into their alliance with Belarus and will have Russian forces all along the Polish border, and as far south as the Black Sea. At this point the Russians will begin the process of trying to neutralize the Balts. This, I believe, will all take place by the mid-2010s.

The Russians will have three tools at their disposal to exert their influence over the Baltic states. First, covert operations. In the same way the United States has financed and energized non-governmental organizations around the world, the Russians will finance and energize Russian minorities in these countries, as well as whatever pro-Russian elements exist, or can be bought. When the Balts suppress these movements, it will give the Russians a pretext for using their second tool, economic sanctions, particularly by cutting the flow of natural gas. Finally, the Russians will bring military pressure to bear through the presence of substantial forces near these borders. Not surprisingly, the Poles and Balts both remember the unpredictability of the Russians. The psychological pressure will be enormous.

There has been a great deal of talk in recent years about the weakness of the Russian army, talk that in the decade after the collapse of the Soviet Union was accurate. But here is the new reality—that weakness started to reverse itself in 2000, and by 2015 it will be a thing of the past. The coming confrontation in northeastern Europe will not take place suddenly, but will be an extended confrontation. Russian military strength will have time to develop. The one area in which Russia continued research and development in the 1990s was in advanced military technologies. By 2010, it will certainly have the most effective army in the region. By 2015–2020, it will have a military that will pose a challenge to any power trying to project force into the region, even the United States.

Russia will be facing a group of countries that cannot defend themselves and a NATO alliance that is effective only if the United States is prepared to use force. As we have seen, the United States has a single core policy in Eurasia—preventing any power from dominating Eurasia or part of it. If China weakens or fragments and the Europeans are weak and divided, the United States will have a fundamental interest: avoiding general war, by keeping the Russians focused on the Balts and Poles, unable to think globally.

The United States will use its traditional method for supporting these countries: technology transfer. As we approach 2020, this method will be much more effective. The new technology for warfare will require smaller, more efficient military forces, meaning that lesser countries can wield military power disproportionately if they have access to advanced technologies. The United States will be eager to increase the power of Poland and the Baltic countries and have them tie down the Russians. If Russia has to be contained, this is the best way to contain it. Georgia in the Caucasus represents a secondary flash point, irritating to the Russians, something that diverts forces from Europe, and therefore will be an area where the United States will intrude. But it will be Europe, not the Caucasus, that will matter.

Given American power, there will be no direct attack by the Russians, nor will the Americans allow any adventures by their allies. Rather, the Russians will seek to bring pressure on the United States elsewhere in Europe and in other parts of the world. For example, they will seek to destabilize countries on their border, like Slovakia and Bulgaria. The confrontation will spread along the entire frontier between Russia and the rest of Europe.

Russia's basic strategy will be to try to break up NATO and isolate Eastern Europe. The key to this will be the Germans, followed by the French. Neither of them wants another confrontation with Russia. They are insular nations, and Germany is dependent on Russian natural gas. The Germans are trying to reduce this dependency and probably will to some extent, but they will continue to depend on the delivery of a substantial quantity of natural gas, which they will not be able to do without. The Russians will therefore argue to the Germans that the Americans are again using them to contain Russia, but that the Russians, far from threatening Germany, have a shared interest—a stable, neutral buffer between them, consisting of an independent Poland. The question of the Baltic states should not, they will argue, enter into it. The only reason Americans would care about the Baltics is if they were planning aggression against Russia. Russia will be prepared to guarantee Baltic autonomy in the context of a broad confederation, as well as Polish security, in return for reduction of arms and neutrality. The alternative—war—would not be in the interests of the Germans or the French.

The argument will probably work, but I believe this will play out in an unexpected way. The United States, always excessively aggressive from the European point of view, will be stirring up unnecessary trouble in Eastern Europe as a threat to the Russians. If the Germans allow NATO to do this, they will be drawn into a conflict they don't want. Therefore, I believe they will block NATO support for Poland, the Baltics, and the rest of Eastern Europe—NATO requires unanimity to function, and Germany is a major power. The Russian expectation will be that the shock of the withdrawal of NATO support would cause the Poles and others to buckle.

The opposite happens. Poland, caught in its historic nightmare between Russia and Germany, will become even more dependent on the United States. The United States, seeing a low-cost opportunity to tie down the Russians and split Europe down the middle, weakening the European Union in the process, will increase its support for Eastern Europe. Around 2015 a new bloc of nations, primarily the old Soviet satellites coupled with the Baltic states, will emerge. Far more energetic than the Western Europeans, with far more to lose, and backed by the United States, this bloc will develop a surprising dynamism.

The Russians will respond to this subtle American power grab by trying to increase pressure on the United States elsewhere in the world. In the Middle East, for example, where the interminable confrontation between Israel and the Palestinians will continue, the Russians will increase military aid to the Arabs. In general, wherever anti-American regimes exist, Russian military aid will be forthcoming. A low-grade global confrontation will be under way by 2015 and will intensify by 2020. Neither side will risk war, but both sides will be maneuvering.

By 2020 this confrontation will be the dominant global issue—and everyone will think of it as a permanent problem. The confrontation will not be as comprehensive as the first cold war. The Russians will lack the power to seize all of Eurasia, and they will not be a true global threat. They will, however, be a regional threat, and that is the context in which the United States will respond. There will be tension all along the Russian frontier, but the United States will not be able to (or need to) impose a complete cordon around Russia as it did around the Soviet Union.

Given the confrontation, the European dependence on hydrocarbons, much of it derived from Russia, will become a strategic issue. The American strategy will be to de-emphasize the focus on hydrocarbon energy sources. This will kick into high gear the American interest in developing alternative sources of energy. Russia, as before, will focus on its existing industries rather than on the development of new ones. That will mean increased oil and natural gas production rather than new energy sources. As a result, Russia is not going to be in the forefront of the technological developments that will dominate the later portions of the century.

Instead, Russia will need to develop its military capabilities. Thus, as it has over the past two centuries, Russia will devote the bulk of its research and development money to applying new technologies toward military ends and expanding existing industries, causing it to fall behind the United States and the rest of the world in nonmilitary but valuable technology. It will be particularly hurt, paradoxically, by its hydrocarbon riches—because it will not be motivated to develop new technologies and will be burdened by military spending.

During the first phase of Russia's reassertion of power, until about 2010 or so, Russia will be grossly underestimated. It will be perceived as a fractured country with a stagnant economy and a weak military. In the 2010s, when the confrontation intensifies on its borders and its immediate neighbors become alarmed, the greater powers will continue to be dismissive.

The United States in particular tends to first underestimate and then overestimate enemies. By the middle of the 2010s, the United States will again be obsessed with Russia. There is an interesting process to observe here. The United States swings between moods but actually, as we have seen, executes a very consistent and rational foreign policy. In this case, the United States will move to its manic state but will focus on keeping Russia tied in knots without going to war.

It will matter a great deal where the fault line lies. If Russia's resurgence is to be a minimal crisis, the Russians will dominate Central Asia and the Caucasus and possibly absorb Moldova, but they will not be able to absorb the Baltic states, or dominate any nations west of the Carpathians. If the Russians do manage to absorb the Baltics and gain significant allies in the Balkans, like Serbia, Bulgaria, and Greece—or Central European countries such as Slovakia—the competition between the United States and Russia will be more intense and frightening.

In the end though, it won't truly matter. Russian military power will be severely strained confronting the fraction of American military power that the United States decides to wield in responding to Russia's moves. Regardless of what the rest of Europe does, Poland, the Czech Republic, Hungary, and Romania will be committed to resisting Russian advances and will make any deal the United States wants in order to gain its support. The line therefore will be drawn in the Carpathian Mountains this time, rather than in Germany as it was during the Cold War. The Polish northern plains will be the main line of confrontation, but the Russians will not move militarily.

The causes that ignited this confrontation—and the Cold War before it—will impose the same outcome as the Cold War, this time with less effort for the United States. The last confrontation occurred in Central Europe. This one will take place much farther to the east. In the last confrontation China was an ally of Russia, at least in the beginning. In this case China will be out of the game. Last time, Russia was in complete control of the Caucasus, but now it will not be, and it will be facing American and Turkish pressure northward. In the last confrontation Russia had a large population, but this time around it has a smaller and declining population. Internal pressure, particularly in the south, will divert Russian attention from the west and eventually, without war, it will break. Russia broke in 1917, and again in 1991. And the country's military will collapse once more shortly after 2020.

CHAPTER 7

AMERICAN POWER AND
THE CRISIS OF 2030

A wall is being built along the southern border of the United States. The goal is to keep illegal immigrants out. The United States built its economic might on the backs of immigrants, but since the 1920s there has been a national consensus that the flow of immigrants should be limited so that the economy can absorb them, and to ensure that jobs will not be taken away from citizens. The wall along the Mexican border is the logical conclusion to this policy.

In the 1920s, the world was in the midst of an accelerating population explosion. The problem facing the United States, and the world, was what to do with an ever-increasing pool of labor. Labor was cheap, and it tended to move to countries that were wealthy. The United States, facing an onslaught of potential immigrants, decided to limit their entry in order to keep the price of labor—wages—from plunging.

The assumption on which U.S. immigration policy was built will not be true in the twenty-first century. The population surge is abating, and people are living longer. This leads to an older population, with fewer younger workers. It means that the United States will be short of workers no later than 2020 and accelerating throughout the decade, and will need immigrants to fill the gap. But it will need new workers at the same time that the rest of the industrial world needs them. In the twentieth century, the problem was limiting immigration. In the twenty-first century, the problem will be attracting enough immigrants.

The second collapse of Russia will appear to open the door to a golden age for the United States. But a massive internal economic crisis caused by a shortage of labor will emerge just as the confrontation with Russia is ending.

We can already see the leading edge of this crisis today in the graying of the population of advanced industrialized countries. Part of the crisis will be social—the family structures that have been in place for centuries will continue to break down, leaving larger numbers of elderly people with no one to care for them. And as I stated earlier, there will be more and more elderly people to care for. This will create intense political struggle between social conservatism and ever-changing social reality. We are already seeing this in popular culture—from talk shows to politicians—but it will intensify dramatically until a crisis point is reached in the mid-2020s.

The crisis will come to a head, if history is any guide, in the presidential election of either 2028 or 2032. I say that because there is an odd—and not entirely explicable—pattern built into American history. Every fifty years, roughly, the United States has been confronted with a defining economic and social crisis. The problem emerges in the decade before the crisis becomes apparent. A pivotal presidential election is held that changes the country's political landscape over the following decade or so. The crisis is resolved, and the United States flourishes. Over the next generation, the solution to the old problem generates a new one, which intensifies until there is another crisis and the process repeats itself. Sometimes the defining moment is not readily apparent until later, and sometimes it can't be missed. But it is always there.

To understand the reasons why I believe we will see a crisis in the 2020s, it's important to understand this pattern in some detail. Just as you can't invest in stocks without understanding historical patterns, you can't make sense out of my forecasting here without understanding American political and economic cycles.

In its history so far, the United States has had four such complete cycles and is currently about halfway through its fifth. The cycles usually begin with a defining presidency and end in a failed one. So the Washington cycle ends with John Quincy Adams, Jackson ends with Ulysses S. Grant, Hayes with Herbert Hoover, and FDR with Jimmy Carter. Underneath the politics, the crises are defined by the struggle between a declining dominant class linked to an established economic model and the emergence of a new class and a new economic model. Each faction represents a radically different way of viewing the world and a different definition of what it means to be a good citizen, and reflects the changing ways of making a living.

THE FIRST CYCLE: FROM FOUNDERS TO PIONEERS

America was founded in 1776, with the Declaration of Independence. From that moment on, it had a national identity, a national army, and a national congress. The founders consisted primarily of a single ethnic group—Englishmen with a smattering of Scots. These prosperous men saw themselves as the guardians of the new governing regime, different in character from the unlanded and unmonied masses—and certainly from African slaves.

But they couldn't build the country by themselves. Pioneers were needed to move the country outward and settle the land west of the Alleghenies. These pioneers were men completely unlike Jefferson or Washington. Typically they were poor, uneducated immigrants, mostly Scots-Irish, who were searching for small parcels of land to clear and farm. They were men like Daniel Boone.

By the 1820s, a political battle was raging between these two groups, as the ideals of the founders collided with the interests of the settlers. The social tension turned into economic crisis and culminated in the election of the champion of the new generation, Andrew Jackson, in 1828. This followed the failed presidency of John Quincy Adams, the last of the founding generation.

SECOND CYCLE: FROM PIONEERS
TO SMALL-TOWN AMERICA

Under Jackson, the most dynamic class in America was that of the pioneer-farmers who settled the center of the continent. The old founding class didn't vanish, but the balance of political power shifted from them to the poorer (but much more numerous) settlers heading west. Jackson's predecessors had favored a stable currency to protect investors. Jackson championed cheap money to protect debtors, the people who voted for him. Where Washington, the gentleman farmer, soldier, and statesman, was the emblematic hero of the first cycle, Abraham Lincoln, born in a log cabin in Kentucky, was the emblematic hero of the second.

By the end of this cycle, after the Civil War, the West was no longer characterized by the hardscrabble subsistence farming of first-generation pioneers. By 1876, farmers not only owned their land but also were making money at farming. The landscape changed as well, homesteads giving rise to small towns that had developed to serve the increasingly prosperous farmers. Small-town banks took the farmers' deposits and invested the money on Wall Street, which in turn invested the money in railroads and industry.

But there was a problem. The cheap-money policies that had been followed for fifty years might have helped the pioneers, but those same policies were hurting their children, who had turned the farms of the West into businesses. By the 1870s the crisis of cheap money had become unbearable. Low interest rates were making it impossible to invest the profits from the farms—and especially from the businesses that were serving the farmers.

A strong, stable currency was essential if America was to grow. In 1876, Rutherford B. Hayes was elected president after the failed presidency of Ulysses S. Grant. Hayes—or more precisely his secretary of the treasury, John Sherman—championed money backed by gold, which limited inflation, raised interest rates, and made investment more attractive. Poorer farmers were hurt, but wealthier farmers and ranchers and their small-town bankers were helped. This financial policy fueled the rapid industrialization of the United States. For fifty years it drove the American economy in an extraordinary expansion, until it choked on its own success, just as in the two earlier cycles.

THIRD CYCLE: FROM SMALL TOWNS
TO INDUSTRIAL CITIES

Just as Daniel Boone was celebrated long after his day was done, so were the virtues of small-town American life. Millions of immigrant workers had been imported to work in mines and factories, settling mainly in the big cities. They were mostly Irish, Italian, and Eastern European. These immigrants were completely different from anyone seen in the United States before. Think about it: a nation that was essentially white and Protestant with a black underclass was suddenly teeming with immigrants who looked, spoke, and acted very differently. Hence, they were regarded with suspicion and hostility by small-town America. Big cities, where these new immigrants settled to work in factories, came to be viewed as the center of an alien and corrupt culture.

However, small-town values now started to work against America. The financial system had run on tight money since the late 1870s. This encouraged savings and investment but limited consumption and credit. As the population living in cities exploded—both from high birthrates and immigration—low wages made life difficult for new immigrants. As investment grew, the ability of the workers to buy the products they produced became severely constrained. The result was the Great Depression, in which consumers had no money to buy the products they needed, so factories making these products laid workers off, in a seemingly endless cycle. Hard work and frugality, the ethics of small-town America, were hardly sufficient against such powerful macroeconomic forces.

In 1932, Franklin Roosevelt succeeded the failed presidency of Herbert Hoover. Roosevelt proceeded to reverse the policies of the preceding political generation by looking for ways to increase consumption through transfers of wealth from investors to consumers. He championed the industrial, urban workers at the expense of the declining small towns and their values.

Ultimately, though, the New Deal didn't end the Depression—World War II did it, by allowing the government to spend vast amounts of money to build factories and hire workers. The aftermath of World War II was even more decisive in ending the Depression. After the war ended, a series of laws was created that allowed returning soldiers to buy homes on credit, easily finance a college education, and become white-collar professionals. The federal government built an interstate highway system, opening up the areas around cities for residential construction. These measures constituted a vast transfer of wealth, spurring growth in factory and office work and maintaining wartime economic gains. The American middle class was born. Roosevelt's reforms—dictated by World War II—were aimed at supporting the urban working class. They turned the ethnic working classes' children into middle-class suburbanites.

FOURTH CYCLE: FROM INDUSTRIAL CITIES
TO SERVICE SUBURBS

As always, one solution creates the next problem. The Depression was overcome by increasing demand, by creating jobs and social supports and then transferring money to consumers. High tax rates were imposed on the wealthy, relatively low interest rates were offered to facilitate home ownership, and consumer credit was introduced for a range of purchases. The policies kept the economy humming.

But by the 1970s, the formula was no longer working. High tax rates made the risk of starting businesses prohibitive and favored large, increasingly inefficient corporations. Marginal tax rates—the highest rates paid—were in excess of 70 percent for the wealthy and for corporations. By penalizing success, this tax policy discouraged investment. Factories aged and became obsolete, even as consumption remained high due to ready consumer credit. Without investment, the industrial plant, and the economy as a whole, became increasingly less efficient and less competitive globally.

In the late 1970s the baby boomers entered the period of family formation, when demand for credit was the highest. All of these factors, coupled with an energy crisis, brought the situation to a head. Under President Jimmy Carter, the entire economy was teetering. Long-term interest rates were in the mid-teens. Inflation was over 10 percent, as was unemployment.

Carter's solution was tax cuts for the middle and lower classes, which only increased consumption and put further pressure on the system. All of the economic stimuli that had worked in the previous fifty years had not only stopped working but were making the situation even worse.

In 1980, Ronald Reagan was elected president. Reagan faced a crisis of underinvestment and overconsumption. Reagan's solution was maintaining consumption while simultaneously increasing the amount of investment capital. He did so through "supply-side economics": reducing taxes in order to stimulate investment. Reagan did not want to stifle demand, making consumers unable to purchase products. His aim was for the upper classes and corporations to be able to modernize the economy through investment. This represented a radical restructuring of the American economy during the 1980s, setting the stage for the boom of the 1990s.

Reagan's policies transferred political and economic power away from the cities and into the suburbs. Because of the innovations of the FDR–Carter era, a massive population shift to the suburbs had transformed the country. The interstate highway system and other well-maintained roads allowed people access to less developed, less expensive land while permitting them to easily commute into the city. These suburbanites grew more and more wealthy over the course of the second half of the century, and by the 1980s they were primed to benefit from Reagan's economic policies.

Reagan thus completed the reorientation of the American economy away from the principles of the New Deal, which favored urban working class consumption over all other considerations, toward the suburban professional and entrepreneurial classes. In this, he was seen by some as betraying the heart of American society, the cities, and the soul of American labor, unionized workers. Just as FDR, Hayes, and Jackson were vilified, so was Reagan vilified as a betrayer of America's common man. But Reagan had no more choice in the end than did Roosevelt or Hayes or Jackson. Reality dictated this evolution.

FIFTH CYCLE: FROM SERVICE SUBURBS
TO A PERMANENT MIGRANT CLASS

Now we turn to the future.

If the fifty-year pattern holds—and a series of cycles that has lasted 220 years has a fairly reliable track record—we are now exactly in the middle of the fifth cycle, the one ushered in by Ronald Reagan's election in 1980. This pattern indicates that the current structure of American society is in place until approximately 2030, and that no president, regardless of ideology, can alter the basic economic and social trends.

Dwight Eisenhower was elected in 1952, twenty years after Roosevelt, but he was unable to change the basic patterns that had been established by the New Deal. Teddy Roosevelt, the great progressive, couldn't significantly shift the course set by Rutherford Hayes. Lincoln affirmed the principles of Jackson. Jefferson, far from breaking Washington's system, acted to affirm it. In every cycle, the opposition party wins elections, sometimes electing great presidents. But the basic principles remain in place. Bill Clinton could not change the basic realities that had been in place since 1980, nor will any president from either party change them now. The patterns are too powerful, too deeply rooted in fundamental forces.

But we are dealing with cycles, and every cycle ends. If the pattern holds, we will see increasing economic and social tensions in the 2020s, followed by a decisive shift in an election at some point around then, likely 2028 or 2032. The question now is this: What will the crisis of the 2020s be about and what will the solution be? One thing we know: the solution to the last cycle's crisis will engender the problem of the next, and the next solution will dramatically change the United States.

The U.S. economy is currently built on a system of readily available credit for both consumer spending and business development—interest rates are historically low. Much of the wealth comes from equities growth— homes, 401(k)s, land—rather than traditional savings. The savings rate is low, but the growth in wealth is high.

There is nothing artificial about this growth. The restructuring of the 1980s kicked off a massive productivity boom driven by entrepreneurial activity. The introduction not only of new technologies but of new patterns of doing business increased worker productivity dramatically and also increased the real value of businesses. Think of Microsoft and Apple as examples of 1980s-style new industry. Where during the previous cycle corporations like General Motors and U.S. Steel had dominated the economic landscape, in this cycle growth in jobs was centered on more entrepreneurial, less capital-intensive companies.

Consumer demand and equity prices live in a delicate balance. If consumer demand falls for any reason, the value of things, from homes to businesses, will decline. These values help drive the economy, from lines of consumer credit to business loans. They define the net worth of an individual or business. If equity declines, demand decreases, so a downward spiral is created. Until now, the problem has been growing the economy as fast as the population. Now the challenge is making sure the economy doesn't decline faster than the population. Ideally, it should continue to grow in spite of population decline.

A little over a decade away from the likely commencement of the first crisis of the twenty-first century, we should already be able to glimpse its beginnings. There are three storms on the horizon. The first is demographic. In the late 2010s, the major wave of baby boomers will be entering their seventies, cashing in equities and selling homes to live off the income. The second storm is energy. Recent surges in the cost of oil may only be a cyclical upturn following twenty-five years of low energy prices. These surges could also be the first harbingers, though, of the end of the hydrocarbon economy.

Finally, productivity growth from the last generation of innovations is peaking. Great entrepreneurial companies of the 1980s and 1990s like Microsoft and Dell have become major corporations, with declining profit margins reflecting declining productivity growth. In general, the innovations of the last quarter century are already factored into the price of equity. Maintaining the thunderous pace of the past twenty years will be difficult.

All of this will put pressure on equity prices—real estate and stocks. The economic tools for managing equity prices aren't there. During the past hundred years, tools for managing interest rates and money supply—controls of credit—have been created. But tools for managing equity prices are only now beginning to emerge, as the mortgage meltdown of 2008 showed. There has been talk of a speculative bubble in housing and stocks already; it is only beginning, and I suspect that we will not see it at its most intense for another fifteen to twenty years or so. But when this cycle climaxes, the United States will be smashed by demography, energy, and innovation crises.

It is worth pausing to consider the financial crisis in 2008. For the most part, it was a routine culmination of a business cycle. During an aggressive upsurge in an economy, interest rates are necessarily low. Conservative investors seek to increase yield without increasing risk. Financial institutions are first and foremost marketing organizations, designed to devise products satisfying demand. As the business cycle moves to climax, financial institutions must become more aggressive in crafting these products, frequently increasing the hidden risk in the product. At the end of the cycle, the weakness is revealed and the house comes crashing down. Consider the dot-com meltdown at the turn of the century.

When the devastation affects a financial sector, rather than a non-financial economic sector like dot-coms, the consequences are doubled. First, there are financial losses. Second, the ability of the financial sector to function, to provide liquidity to the economy, contracts. In the United States, the normal solution has been federal intervention. In the 1970s, the federal government intervened in a possible meltdown in municipal bonds by bailing out New York City—guaranteeing its bonds. In the 1980s, when third world countries began defaulting on debt because of declining commodity prices, the United States led an international bailout that essentially guaranteed the third world debt via the Brady Bond. In 1989, when a collapse in the commercial real estate market devastated the savings and loan industry, the federal government intervened through the Resolution Trust Corporation. The crisis of 2008 was triggered by the decline of housing prices, forcing the government to intervene to guarantee those loans and other functions of the financial system.

Debt is measured against net worth. If you owe a thousand dollars and have a net worth that's negative, you have problems if you lose your job. If you owe a million dollars but have a net worth of a billion dollars, you don't have a problem. The U.S. economy has a net worth measured in hundreds of trillions of dollars. Therefore, a debt crisis measuring a few trillion cannot destroy it. The problem is, how can this country's net worth be used to cover the bad loans, since that net worth is in hundreds of millions of private hands? Only the government can do that, and it does it by guaranteeing the debts, using the state's sovereign taxing power, and utilizing the Federal Reserve's ability to print money to bail out the system.

In that sense, the 2008 crisis was not materially different from previous crises. While the underlying economy will go through a recession, recessions are normal and common parts of the business cycle. But at the same time, we are seeing an important harbinger of the more distant future. The decline in housing prices has many reasons, but lurking in back of it is a demographic reality. As global population growth declines, the historic assumption that land and other real estate will always rise in price due to greater demand becomes suspect. The crisis of 2008 was not yet really a demographically driven crisis. But it showed a process that will reveal itself more fully over the next twenty years: an equity crisis driven by demographics. Declines in residential real estate prices are startling. They have not been drivers in the past. This one is hardly a defining moment. Think of it as a straw in the wind, a sign of things to come—from pressure on real estate to greater government control of the economy.

When we talk of economic crisis, all fears turn immediately to the Great Depression. In fact, historically, the terminal crisis of a cycle has usually resembled deep discomfort more than the profound agony of the Depression. The stagflation of the 1970s or the short, sharp crises of the 1870s are far more likely than the prolonged, systemic failure of the 1930s. As will be true for the crisis of the 2020s, we don't have to be facing a Great Depression in order to be confronting a historical turning point.

For the first century of the United States, the driving problem was the structure of land ownership. For the next 150 years, the primary issue was how to manage the relationship between capital formation and consumption. The solution swung between favoring capital formation and favoring consumption, sometimes settling on balancing the two. But for 250 years of American history, labor was never an issue. The population always grew and the younger, working-age cohorts were more numerous than the older.

Underlying the crisis of 2030 is the fact that labor will no longer be the reliable component it has been up to that point. The surge in birthrate following World War II and the increase in life expectancy will create a large aging population, increasingly out of the workforce but continuing to consume. And here's a fact that should get you thinking: when Social Security set the retirement age at sixty-five, the average life expectancy for a male was sixty-one. It makes us realize how little Social Security was designed to pay out. The subsequent surge in life expectancy has changed the math of retirement entirely.

The decline in birthrates since the 1970s, coupled with later and later entry into the workforce, reduces the number of workers to each retiree. During the 2020s this trend will intensify. It is not so much that workers will be supporting retirees, although that will be a factor. The problem will be that retirees, drawing on equity in homes and retirement funds, will still be consuming at high rates. Therefore, workers will be needed to fill their demand. With a declining workforce, and steady demand for goods and services, inflation will soar because the cost of labor will go through the roof. It will also accelerate the rate at which retirees exhaust their wealth.

Retirees will divide into two groups. Those lucky or smart enough to have equity reserves in houses and 401(k)s will be forced to sell those assets. A second group of retirees will have few or no assets. Social Security, under the best of circumstances, leaves people in abject poverty. The pressure to maintain reasonable standards of living and health care for the baby boomers will be intense, and it will come from a group that will continue to retain disproportionate political power because of their numbers. Retirees vote disproportionately to other groups, and the baby boomer vote will be particularly huge. They will vote themselves benefits.

Governments around the world—this won't only be happening in the United States—will be forced to either increase taxes or borrow heavily. If the former, they will be taxing the very group that would be benefiting from the increased wages necessitated by the labor shortage. If there is increased borrowing, the government will be entering a shrinking capital market at the same time that boomers are withdrawing capital from that market, further driving up interest rates and, in a replay of the 1970s, increasing inflation due to a surging supply of money. Unemployment is the only thing that won't echo the 1970s. Whoever can work will have a job—at high wages—but those wages will be badly squeezed by taxes or inflation.

Boomers will start retiring in about 2013. If we assume an average retirement age of seventy (and health and financial need will push it there), the years after will see the start of a surging retired population. A significant drop-off won't occur until well after 2025, and the economic repercussions will continue to echo well after that. Those born in 1980 will be coping with this problem from their mid-thirties to their mid-forties. For an important part of their working life, they will be living in an increasingly dysfunctional economy. From a broad historical point of view this is just a passing problem. For those born between 1970 and 1990 this not only will be painful but will define their generation. It may not be on the order of another Great Depression, but those who remember the stagflation of the 1970s will have a point of reference.

Baby boomers came in with a generation gap. They will go out with a generation gap.

Whoever is elected president in 2024 or 2028 will face a remarkable problem. Like Adams, Grant, Hoover, and Carter, this president will be using the last period's solutions to solve the new problem. Just as Carter tried to use Roosevelt's principles to solve stagflation, making the situation worse, the final president in this period will use Reagan's solution, fielding a tax cut for the wealthy to generate investment. Tax cuts will increase investment at a time when labor shortages are most intense, further increasing the price of labor and exacerbating the cycle.

Just as the problems leading to previous crises were unprecedented, so the problem emerging in the 2020s will be unprecedented. How can we increase the amount of available labor? The labor shortage will have two solutions. One is to increase productivity per worker, and the other is to introduce more workers. Given the magnitude and time frame of this problem, the only immediate solution will be to increase the number of workers—and to do that through increased immigration. From 2015 onward, immigration will be rising, but not quickly enough to alleviate the problem.

American political culture, ever since 1932, has been terrified of a labor surplus—of unemployment. The issue of immigration will have been regarded for a century in terms of lowering wages. Immigration has been viewed through the prism of population explosion. The idea that it could resolve a problem—a shortage of labor—would have been as alien a concept as the idea in 1930 that unemployment was not the result of laziness.

In the 2020s this concept will shift again, and by the election of either 2028 or 2032 a sea change in American political thinking will have taken place. Some will argue that there are plenty of workers available, but that they don't have the incentive to work because taxes are too high. The failing president will try to solve the problem with tax cuts to motivate nonexistent workers to join the workforce by stimulating investment.

Rapid and dramatic increases in the workforce through immigration will be the real solution. The breakthrough will be the realization that the historical view of labor scarcity does not work any longer. For the foreseeable future, the problem will be that there is simply not enough labor to be employed. And this will not be a uniquely American problem. Every advanced industrial country will be facing the same problem—and most of them will be in much greater trouble. Quite simply, they will be hungry for new workers and taxpayers. In the meantime, the middle-tier countries that have been the source of immigration will have improved their economies substantially as their own populations stabilized. Any urgency to immigrate to other countries will be subsiding.

It is hard to imagine now, in 2009, but by 2030 advanced countries will be competing for immigrants. Crafting immigrant policy will involve not finding ways to keep them out, but finding ways to induce them to come to the United States rather than Europe. The United States will still have advantages. It is easier now to be an immigrant in the United States than it is in France, and that will continue to be the case. Moreover, the United States has more long-term opportunities than European countries do, if for no other reason than that it has lower population density. But the fact is that the United States will have to do something it hasn't done in a long time—create incentives to attract immigrants to come here.

Retirees will favor the immigration solution for obvious reasons. But the workforce will be divided. Those who fear that their income will be reduced by competition will oppose it vehemently. Other workers, in less precarious positions, will support immigration, particularly in areas that will reduce the cost of services they require. In the end, the politics will turn not so much on the principle of immigration as on identifying the areas in which immigration will be economically useful and the skills immigrants will need, and managing the settlement of immigrants so that they do not overwhelm particular regions.

Back to the incentives. The United States will have to offer immigrants a range of competitive benefits, from highly streamlined green-card processes to specialized visas catering to the needs and wishes of the immigrant workforce and quite possibly to bonuses—paid directly through the government or through firms that are hiring them—along with guarantees of employment. And immigrants will certainly comparison shop.

This process will result in a substantial increase in the power of the federal government. Since 1980 we have seen a steady erosion of government power. The immigration reform that will be needed around 2030 will require direct government management, however. If private businesses manage the process, the federal government at least will be enforcing guarantees to make certain immigrants are not defrauded and that the companies can deliver on their promises. Otherwise, unemployed immigrants will become a burden. Simply opening the borders will not be an option. The management of the new labor force—the counterpart to the management of capital and credit markets—will dramatically enhance federal power, reversing the pattern of the Reagan period.

Imported labor will be of two classes. One will consist of those able to support the aging population, such as physicians and housekeepers. The other will be those who can develop technologies that increase productivity in order to address the labor shortage over the longer term. Therefore, professionals in the physical sciences, engineering, and health care, along with manual laborers of various sorts, will be the primary kinds of workers that are recruited.

This influx of immigrants will not be on the order of the 1880–1920 immigration but will certainly be more substantial than any immigration wave since. It will also change the cultural character of the United States. The very plasticity of American culture is its advantage, and this will be crucial in helping it to attract immigrants. We should expect international friction from the process of recruiting immigrants as well. The United States pursues its ends ruthlessly, and will outbid and outmaneuver other countries for scarce labor as well as drain educated workers from developing countries. This will, as we will see, affect the foreign policy of these countries.

For the United States, on the other hand, it will be merely another fifty-year cycle in its history successfully navigated and another wave of immigrants attracted and seduced by the land of opportunity. Whether they come from India or Brazil, their children will be as American in a generation as previous immigration cohorts were throughout America's history.

This applies to everyone except for one group—the Mexicans. The United States occupies land once claimed by Mexico, and its border with that nation is notoriously porous. Population movements between Mexico and the United States differ from the norm, particularly in the borderlands. This region will be the major pool from which manual labor is drawn in the 2030s, and it will cause serious strategic problems for the United States later in the century.

But around 2030 an inevitable step will be taken. A labor shortage that destabilizes the American economy will force the United States to formalize a process that will have been in place since around 2015 of intensifying immigration into the United States. Once this is done, the United States will resume the course of its economic development, accelerating in the 2040s as the boomers die and the population structure begins to resemble the normal pyramid once again, rather than a mushroom. The 2040s should see a surge in economic development similar to those of the 1950s or 1990s. And this period will set the stage for the crisis of 2080. But there is a lot of history to come between now and then.

CHAPTER 8

A NEW WORLD EMERGES

The collapse of Russia in the early 2020s will leave Eurasia as a whole in chaos. The Russian Federation itself will crack open as Moscow's grip shatters. Regions, perhaps even the thinly populated Pacific region, will break away, its interests in the Pacific Basin far outweighing its interest in or connection to Russia proper. Chechnya and the other Muslim regions will break off. Karelia, with close ties to Scandinavia, will secede. Such disintegration will not be confined to Russia. Other countries of the former Soviet Union will fragment as well. The burdens imposed by Moscow will be entirely unsustainable. Where previously the collapse of the Soviet Union led to oligarchs controlling the Russian economy, the collapse of the 2020s will lead to regional leaders going their own way.

This disintegration will take place during a period of Chinese regionalism. China's economic crisis will kick off a regional phase in Chinese history that, during the 2020s, will intensify. The Eurasian landmass east of the Carpathians will become disorganized and chaotic as regions struggle for local political and economic advantage, with uncertain borders and shifting alliances. In fact, fragmentation on both sides of the Chinese border, from Kazakhstan to the Pacific, will start to render the boundaries meaningless.

From the United States' point of view, this will represent a superb outcome. The fifth geopolitical imperative for the United States was that no power be in a position to dominate all of Eurasia. With both China and Russia in chaos, the possibility is more distant than ever. There is, in fact, little need for the United States to even involve itself in maintaining the balance of power inside the region. In the coming decades the balance of power will maintain itself.

Eurasia will become a "poacher's paradise." For the countries around the periphery of the region, there will be extraordinary opportunities to poach. The vast region is rich in resources, labor, and expertise. The collapse of central authority will be an opportunity for countries on its periphery to take advantage of the situation. Fear, need, and avarice are the perfect combination of factors that would allow the periphery to try to exploit the center.

Three nations will be in particularly opportune positions for taking advantage of this. First, Japan will be in a position to exploit opportunities in the Russian maritime region and in eastern China. Second, Turkey will be in a position to press northward into the Caucasus and potentially beyond. Finally, an alliance of Eastern European countries, led by Poland, and in-

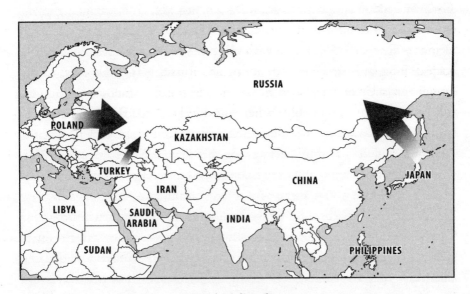

Poacher's Paradise

cluding the Baltic states, Hungary, and Romania, together will regard this as
an opportunity not only to return to older borders but also to protect themselves against any future Russian state. A powerful secondary benefit for
these countries is this: by increasing their strength, they will be further protecting themselves against their traditional Western enemy, Germany. These
Eastern European countries will be looking at this as an opportunity for redefining the balance of power in the region. India, for all its size, will not be
in this game. Geographically isolated by the Himalayas, India will not be
able to take serious advantage of the situation.

The American view of this activity in the 2020s will be supportive. Eastern Europe, Turkey, and Japan will be allies of the United States. Turkey and
Japan will have been its allies for seventy-five years by that point, Eastern
Europe for thirty years. During the confrontation with Russia, each will,
more or less, and for its own reasons, work with the United States, which
will regard them, as it did other allies, as extensions of the American will.

The events of the 2020s will have much broader implications beyond
Russia and China, however. The first will be the changing status of Asia in
relation to the Pacific, and therefore in relation to the United States. The
second will be the state of the Muslim world following the U.S.–jihadist
war. The third will be the internal order of Europe in an age of Franco-
German decline and Eastern European emergence. The fragmentation of
NATO is a given once the Germans and the French opt out of defending the
Baltic countries. NATO is based entirely on collective defense, the idea that
an attack on one member is an attack on all members. Embedded in this
idea is the understanding that NATO is prepared, in advance, to go to the
defense of any member country that is at risk. Since the Baltic states will be
at risk, a force will need to be forward deployed there as well as in Poland.
The unwillingness of some of the members to participate in collective defense means that action will need to be taken outside the context of NATO.
NATO, therefore, will cease to exist in any meaningful form.

All of these issues will be on the table in the 2010s as the confrontation
with Russia develops. They will be suspended—or at the very least not be
high on the global agenda—during the conflict. But eventually these questions are going to reemerge. Once the Russian threat has passed, each of
these regions must come to terms with its own geopolitics.

ASIA

Japanese involvement in China goes back to the nineteenth century. During the period of turmoil between Europe's interventions in China in the mid-nineteenth century and the end of World War II, Japan was continually exerting its influence in China, usually seeking some kind of economic advantage. The Chinese have bitter memories of Japanese behavior in China in the 1930s and 1940s, but not so bitter as to block the Japanese from returning to invest in post-Maoist China.

In the 1930s, Japan looked to China for markets, and to a lesser extent for labor. In the 2020s, the emphasis will be, as we have pointed out, on labor. With China regionalizing and to some extent fragmenting, Japan will have faced its old Chinese temptation in the 2010s and 2020s. Establishing some form of dominance over a Chinese region could rapidly contribute to solving Japan's demographic problems without forcing the Japanese to pay the social and cultural price of immigration. But Japan will need to foster deep ties to whatever region it dominates in China.

Various Chinese regions will be looking for protection from the central government as well as for investment capital and technology. Thus, the late-nineteenth- and early-twentieth-century symbiotic relationship, based on coastal China's need for investment and technology and Japan's need for labor, will reassert itself.

Historically, Japan has another interest besides a need for labor—access to raw materials. As I have stated, Japan is the world's second-largest economy, but it must import almost all of its raw materials. This has been a historical challenge for Japan and was the main reason that it went to war with the United States in 1941. Many people forget that Japan was divided internally before the decision was finally made to attack Pearl Harbor. Some Japanese leaders argued that an invasion of Siberia would provide Japan with the raw materials it needed and was less risky than taking on the United States. Either way, the seriousness with which the Japanese pursued (and will continue to pursue) raw materials must not be underestimated.

Pacific Russia is extremely rich in all sorts of minerals, including hydrocarbons. By the 2020s, Japan will be facing energy problems and a continued dependence on the Persian Gulf, which in turn would mean being entangled with the United States. Given American hubris after the second fall of Russia, Japan, like the rest of the world, will be increasingly uneasy about America's next move. Therefore, with Russia fragmenting, it would seem to make a great deal of sense for the Japanese to seek, at the very least, economic control over Pacific Russia. Japan will respond whenever its access to raw materials is threatened.

Japan will have a direct interest, then, in both northeast China and Pacific Russia, but it will have no appetite for military adventure. At the same time, Japan will be facing economic disaster by mid-century unless it starts

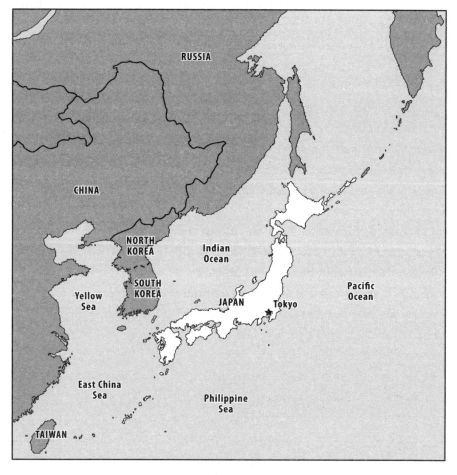

Japan

making some decisive moves in the 2020s. By 2050 Japan's population could drop to as low as 107 million from the current 128 million, with 40 million of those over the age of sixty-five and 15 million under the age of fourteen. With 55 million people out of the workforce, Japan will be hard pressed to maintain its economy at manageable levels. Between labor and energy concerns, Japan will have no choice but to attempt to become a regional power.

Let us look more closely at Japan and its history. It is currently the world's second-largest economic power, and will continue to be well into the twenty-first century. In many ways, the Japanese social structure that persisted through industrialization, through World War II, and during its economic miracle in the 1980s is the same structure that was in place before industrialization.

Japan is notable for internal stability that persists through major shifts in economic and political policy. Following its initial encounter with the West and the realization that industrial powers could squash countries like Japan, it began industrializing at a dizzying pace. After World War II, Japan reversed a deeply embedded militaristic tradition and suddenly became one of the most pacifist nations in the world. It then grew at an extraordinary rate until 1990, when its economic expansion halted due to financial failures, at which time the Japanese accepted their reversal of fortune with equanimity.

The mixture of continuity in culture and social discipline has allowed Japan to preserve its core values while changing its ways of doing things. Other societies frequently cannot change course suddenly and in an orderly fashion. Japan can and does. Its geographical isolation protects it from divisive social and cultural forces. In addition, Japan has a capable ruling elite that recruits new members based on merit, and a highly disciplined population prepared to follow that elite. This is a strength that makes Japan not necessarily unpredictable, but simply capable of executing policy shifts that would tear other countries apart.

We cannot assume that Japan will continue its reticence and pacifism in the 2020s. It will hold on as long as possible; the Japanese have no desire for military conflict, because of their long national memory of the horrors of World War II. At the same time, the current pacifism is an adaptive tool for the Japanese, not an eternal principle. Given its industrial and technological base, moving to a more assertive military stance is simply a question of a shift in policy. And given the pressures it will experience demographically and economically in the coming years, such a change is almost inevitable.

Japan will at first try to get what it needs through economic means. But Japan will not be alone in seeking to augment its labor force without immigration, nor will it be the only country looking to control foreign energy sources. The Europeans will also be interested in creating regional economic relationships. The fragmented regions of China and Russia will gladly play the Europeans and Japanese off each other.

Japan's challenge is that it can't afford to lose this game. For Japan, given its needs and geographic location, exerting its influence in East Asia is the only game in town. Japanese power in the region will encounter resistance in a number of ways. First, the Chinese central government, which has been waging anti-Japanese campaigns for years, will see Japan as deliberately undermining the integrity of the Chinese nation. Chinese regions themselves, allied with other foreign powers, will seek to dominate their counterparts. A complex struggle will emerge, potentially threatening Japan's interests and compelling it to intervene more directly than it might wish. Japan's last resort will be an increased militarism, which, even if it's a long way off, will eventually assert itself. By the 2020s and 2030s, as Chinese and Russian instability increases and as foreign presences rise, the Japanese, like others, will have to defend their interests.

By about 2030, the United States will have to reevaluate its view of Japan, as that country becomes more assertive. Japan, like the United States, is inherently a maritime power. It survives by importing raw materials and exporting manufactured products. Access to sea lanes is essential to its existence. As Japan begins to move from large-scale economic involvement to small-scale military presence in East Asia, it will be particularly interested in protecting its regional sea lanes.

Southern Japan is about five hundred miles from Shanghai. Five hundred miles also brings you from Japan to Vladivostok, Sakhalin Island, and the Chinese coast north of Shanghai. That radius will represent the outer limit of Japanese military interests. But even to protect such a small area, Japan will need a capable navy, air force, and space surveillance system. The truth is, Japan has these already, but by 2030 they will be explicitly oriented toward excluding unwelcome intruders in Japan's sphere of influence.

It is at this point that Japan's newfound assertiveness will begin to challenge American strategic interests. The United States wants to dominate all oceans. The reemergence of Japanese regional power not only threatens this interest but sets the stage for increased Japanese power globally. As Japan's interests in mainland Asia increase, its air and naval capabilities will need to improve as well. And as these improve, there is no guarantee that its range of action won't increase as well. It is, from the American point of view, a dangerous cycle.

The situation is likely to play out as follows: As the United States begins to react to increased Japanese power, the Japanese will become increasingly insecure, resulting in a downward spiral in U.S.–Japanese relations. Japan, pursuing its fundamental national interests in Asia, must control its sea lanes. Conversely, the Americans, viewing global sea lane control as an absolute requirement for their own national security, will press back on the Japanese, trying to contain what the United States will perceive as increased Japanese aggressiveness.

Right in the middle of the growing Japanese sphere of influence is Korea, which we expect will be united well before 2030. A united Korea will have a population of about seventy million, not much less than Japan. South Korea currently ranks twelfth economically in the world, and will rank higher in 2030 after unification. Korea historically fears Japanese domination. As Japan increases its power in China and Russia, Korea will be trapped in the middle, and it will be afraid. Korea will not be a trivial power in its own right, but its real importance will come from the United States seeing Korea as a counterbalance to Japanese power and as a base for asserting its own power in the Sea of Japan. Korea will want U.S. support against a rising Japan, and an anti-Japanese coalition will start to emerge.

In the meantime, changes will be taking place inside China. In recent centuries, China has run on a thirty- to forty-year cycle. China ceded Hong Kong to the British in 1842. In about 1875 the Europeans began taking control of China's tributary states. In 1911 the Manchu dynasty was overthrown by Sun Yat-sen. In 1949 the Communists took control of China. Mao died in 1976 and the period of economic expansion began. By 2010

China will be struggling with internal disruption and economic decline. This means that another reversal is likely sometime in the 2040s.

This reversal will be a reassertion of political control by Beijing and a campaign to limit the foreign presence in China. But obviously, this process won't begin in the 2040s. It will culminate there. It will be emerging in the 2030s as foreign encroachment, particularly by the Japanese, gets more intense. This will be another lever the United States will use to control the situation. It will support Beijing's efforts to reunify China and control Japan, a reversion of U.S. policy to the pre–World War II model.

By the 2040s, the United States and Japan will have reached a profound divergence of interests. The United States will be allied with Seoul and Beijing, all of them concerned about increased Japanese power. The Japanese, fearing American interference in their sphere of influence, will necessarily increase their military power. But Japan will be profoundly isolated, facing the regional coalition the United States will have created as well as American military power. There will be no way the Japanese can cope with the pressure alone, yet there will be no one nearby to help. However, technological shifts will create geopolitical shifts, and opportunities for Japan to form its own coalition will emerge at the other end of Asia.

TURKEY

During the Russo–American confrontation in Europe leading up to 2020, there is going to be a subsidiary confrontation in the Caucasus. The Russians will press south into the region, reabsorbing Georgia and linking up with their Armenian allies. The return of the Russian army to Turkey's borders, however, will create a massive crisis in Turkey. A century after the fall of the Ottoman Empire and the rise of modern Turkey, the Turks will have to face again the same threat they faced in the Cold War.

As Russia later crumbles, the Turks will make an unavoidable strategic decision around 2020. Relying on a chaotic buffer zone to protect themselves from the Russians is a bet they will not make again. This time, they will move north into the Caucasus, as deeply as they need to in order to guarantee their national security in that direction.

There is a deeper issue. By 2020, Turkey will have emerged as one of the top ten economies in the world. Already ranked seventeenth in 2007, and growing steadily, Turkey is not only an economically viable country but a strategically crucial one. In fact, Turkey enjoys one of the strongest geographic locations of any Eurasian country. Turkey has easy access to the Arab world, Iran, Europe, the former Soviet Union, and above all the Mediterranean. The Turkish economy grows in part because Turkey is a center of regional trade as well as a productive economic power in its own right.

By 2020 Turkey will be a surging, fairly stable economic and military power in a sea of chaos. Apart from the instability to its north, it will face challenges in every other direction as well. Iran, which has not been economically or militarily significant for centuries but whose internal affairs are historically unpredictable, lies to the southeast. To the south, there is the permanent instability and lack of economic development of the Arab world. To the northwest, there is the perpetual chaos of the Balkan Peninsula, which includes Turkey's historic enemy, Greece.

None of these regions will be doing particularly well in the 2020s, for several reasons. The Arabian Peninsula to Turkey's south will, in particular, be confronting an existential crisis. Except for oil, the Arabian Peninsula has few resources, little industry, and minimal population. Its importance has rested on oil, and historically the wealth produced by oil has helped stabilize the region. But by 2020 the Arabian Peninsula will be declining. Though it will not yet be out of oil, and far from improverished, the handwriting will be on the wall and crisis will loom. Struggles between factions in the House of Saud will be endemic, along with instability in the other sheikhdoms of the Persian Gulf.

The broader issue, though, will be the extreme fragmentation of the entire Islamic world. Historically divided, it has been badly destabilized by the U.S.–jihadist war. During the U.S.–Russian confrontation of the late 2010s, the Middle East will be further destabilized by Russian attempts to create problems for the United States to the south of Turkey. The Islamic world in general, and the Arab world in particular, will be divided along every line imaginable in the 2020s.

The Balkans, to Turkey's northwest, will also be unstable. Unlike the Cold War in the twentieth century, when U.S. and Soviet power locked Yugoslavia into place, the second round of the U.S.–Russian confrontation will destabilize the region. Russia will be much less powerful than it was the first time around and will confront a hostile Hungary and Romania. Just as the Russians will work to contain Turkey (through the Arab countries to Turkey's south), so they will attempt to contain Hungary and Romania by trying to turn Bulgaria, Serbia, and Croatia against them. They will cast a broad net, knowing that they will fail in some cases but hoping for enough success to divert Turkey's attention. As Greece, Macedonia, Bosnia, and Montenegro are drawn into the Balkan conflicts, the region will once again become a shambles. The immediate periphery of Turkey is going to be unstable, to say the least.

The Islamic world is incapable of uniting voluntarily. It is, however, capable of being dominated by a Muslim power. Throughout history, Turkey has been the Muslim power most often able to create an empire out of part of the Islamic world—certainly since the Mongol invasions of the thirteenth century. The century between 1917 and 2020 has been an anomaly, because Turkey has ruled only over Asia Minor. But Turkish power—the Ottoman Empire or a Turkic power ruling out of Iran—has been a long-term reality in the Islamic world. In fact, Turkey once dominated the Balkans, the Caucasus, the Arabian Peninsula, and North Africa (see map on page 84).

During the 2020s, that power will begin to reemerge. Even more than Japan, Turkey will be critical in the confrontation with the Russians. The Bosporus, the strait connecting the Aegean and the Black Sea, blocks Russian access to the Mediterranean. Turkey historically controlled the Bosporus, and therefore Russia historically saw Turkey as a power that was blocking its interests. It will be no different in the 2010s or early 2020s. The Russians will need access to the Bosporus to counter the Americans in the Balkans. The Turks know that if the Russians are given such access and succeed in achieving their geopolitical goals, Turkish autonomy will be threatened. The Turks, therefore, will be committed to their alliance with the United States against Russia.

As a result, the Turks will be instrumental in America's anti-Russian strategy. The United States will encourage Turkey to press north in the Caucasus and will want Turkish influence in Muslim areas of the Balkans, as well as in the Arab states to the south, to increase. It will help Turkey increase its maritime capabilities—naval, air, and space—to challenge the Russians in the Black Sea. It will ask the Turkish navy to share the naval burden in the Mediterranean and use its power to block Russian adventures in North Africa. The United States also will do everything it can to encourage Turkish economic development, which will further stimulate its already surging economy.

When the Russians finally collapse, the Turks will be left in a position they haven't been in for a century. Surrounded by chaos and weakness, the Turks will have an economic presence throughout the region. They also will have a substantial military presence. When the Russians collapse, the regional geopolitics will reorganize—without real effort on their part—around the Turks, who will become the dominant power in the region, projecting influence in all directions. Turkey will not be a formal empire yet, but it will be, without a doubt, the center of gravity in the Islamic world.

Of course the Arab world will have severe problems with Turkey's reemerging power. Turkish mistreatment of Arabs under the old Ottoman Empire has not been forgotten. But the only other regional players that could exert as much power will be Israel and Iran, and Turkey will be much less objectionable to the Arabs. With the Arabian Peninsula beginning its decline, the security and economic development of the Arab countries will depend on close ties to Turkey.

The Americans will see this development as a positive step. First, it will reward a close ally. Second, it will stabilize an unstable region. Third, it will bring the still significant hydrocarbon supplies of the Persian Gulf under the influence of the Turks. Finally, the Turks will block Iranian ambitions in the region.

But while the immediate response will be positive, the longer-term geopolitical outcome will run counter to American grand strategy. As we have seen, the United States creates regional powers to block greater threats in Eurasia. However, the United States also fears regional hegemons. They can evolve into not only regional challengers but global ones. That is precisely how the United States will begin to view Turkey. As the 2020s come to an end, U.S.–Turkish relations will become increasingly uncomfortable.

The Turkish perception of the United States will change as well. In the 2030s the United States will be seen as a threat to Turkish regional interests.

In addition, there might well be an ideological shift in Turkey, which has been a secular state since the fall of the Ottoman Empire. Historically, the Turks have taken a flexible approach to religion, using it as a tool as much as a system of belief. As it faces U.S. opposition to the spread of its influence, Turkey may find it useful to harness Islamist energies by portraying itself as being not only Muslim but also an Islamic power (as opposed to a faction like al Qaeda) attempting to create an Islamic superstate. This would shift Arab Muslims in the region from a position of reluctant alignment to energetic participation in Turkey's expansion, regardless of the history and cynicism of the move. We will see, as a result, the United States confronting a potentially powerful Islamic state that is organizing the Arab world and the eastern Mediterranean. The United States will be existentially threatened by the combination of Turkey's political power and the vibrancy of its economy, even as challenges continue to arise on other fronts.

POLAND

The most enthusiastic participants in the American confrontation with the Russians will be the former Soviet satellites, particularly Poland. In a sense, they will be leading the Americans as much as being led. Poland has everything to lose from Russia's reemergence and little to protect it from the Russians. As the Russians come back to its frontier, Poland will look to the rest of Europe to support it through NATO. There will be little enthusiasm in Germany or France for any confrontation, so Poland will do what it historically did when confronted by Russia or Germany—it will seek an outside power to protect it. Historically this did not work. The guarantees made by France and Britain in 1939 did nothing to protect Poland against Germany or Russia. The United States will be different. It is not a power in decline, but a young, vigorous risk taker. To Poland's pleasant surprise, the United States will be strong enough to block the Russians.

The rest of Europe, particularly France and Germany, will have extremely mixed feelings about America's superiority over the Russians. Having lived through one cold war in the twentieth century, they will have little desire to live through another one. At a time of declining populations in all of these countries, the Germans and the French might be relieved to see Russia—also with a declining population but still enormous—broken up. However, they will not be happy to see the United States in a strong position in Europe outside of institutions like NATO, which the Europeans actually used to control and contain the United States.

Nor will Germany, France, and the rest of Western Europe be used to the sudden self-confidence of Poland or of the Czech Republic, Slovakia, Hungary, and Romania. The confrontation with Russia will paradoxically make these countries feel more secure because of the strong bilateral ties with the United States through which they seek to block Russian power. Freed from their primordial fear of the Russians and increasingly unconcerned about a weakening Germany, these countries will see themselves as relatively safe for the first time in several centuries. Indeed, the Franco-German decline will be felt all around the European periphery, driven partly by population decline, partly by moribund economies, and partly by the geopolitical miscalculation of opting out of the confrontation with Russia (and therefore disrupting NATO). The net result will be an intensification of the crisis of confidence that has undermined France and Germany since World War I.

As a result, there will be a general redefinition of the European power structure. The collapse of the Russians will give the Eastern Europeans both the opportunity and the need to adopt a more aggressive foreign policy in the east. Eastern Europe will become the most dynamic region of Europe. As Russia collapses, the Eastern European countries will extend their influence and power to the east. The Slovaks, Hungarians, and Romanians have been the least vulnerable to the Russians because the Carpathians formed a natural barrier. The Poles, on the northern European plain, will be the most vulnerable, yet at the same time the largest and most important Eastern European nation.

As the Russians fall apart, the Poles will be the first to want to press eastward, trying to create a buffer zone in Belarus and Ukraine. As the Poles assert their power, the Carpathian countries will also project power east of the mountains, into Ukraine. For five hundred years, Eastern Europe has been a backwater, trapped between the great Atlantic European powers and Germany on the one side, and Russia on the other. In the wake of the collapse of Russian power, the European order will shift to the east, to an Eastern Europe with deep ties to the United States.

A political confederation among the Baltic countries, Poland, Slovakia, Hungary, and Romania will be impossible. They will have too many cultural and historical differences between them. But an alliance between at least some of them is easy to imagine, especially when they share the common interest of moving to the east.

That is precisely what they will do in the 2030s. Using their growing economic power—and military force as well, left over from their close collaboration with the Americans—they will form an alliance and face no significant resistance to any eastern move. On the contrary, given the chaos, many in the region will actually welcome them as a stabilizing force. The difficulty will be coordinating the movement and avoiding major conflicts over particular areas. The region is naturally fractious; however, in the late 2020s and 2030s, that will be the last thing on the Eastern European mind. Making certain that Russia never returns and increasing their labor force will be the major considerations.

The precise lines of an Eastern European advance are impossible to predict. However, seeing an occupation of St. Petersburg from Estonia, or a Polish occupation of Minsk, or a Hungarian occupation of Kiev is no more difficult to imagine than a Russian occupation of Warsaw, Budapest, or Berlin. What goes west can go east, and if the Russians crumble, then an eastward movement out of Eastern Europe is inevitable. In this scenario, Poland becomes a major and dynamic European power, leading a coalition of Eastern European countries.

The balance of power within Europe by 2040 will therefore shift to the east. All of Europe will be experiencing a demographic problem, but Eastern Europe will be able to compensate for it through the kind of complex financial relations that the United States traditionally maintains with allies. Eastern European countries might not surpass Western European countries in the absolute size of their economies, but certainly Eastern Europe will surpass Western Europe in terms of dynamism.

So what does all this mean for France and Germany? It was one thing to live in a Europe that was disorganized but in which France and Germany were the decisive powers. It is quite another thing to live in a Europe that is reorganizing itself and leaving them behind. With Britain drawn deeply into the American economic orbit and the Iberian Peninsula similarly attracted to the opportunities of an American relationship, the French and the Germans will face a profound dilemma.

Decadence means that you no longer have an appetite for great adventures, but it does not mean that you no longer want to survive. By 2040, France and Germany are going to be has-beens, historically. Between population crises and the redefinition of the geopolitics of Europe, the French and Germans will be facing a decisive moment. If they do not assert themselves, their futures will be dictated by others and they will move from decadence to powerlessness. And with powerlessness would come a geopolitical spiral from which they would not recover.

The key problem for France and Germany in their existential difficulties will be the United States. Although Eastern Europe will be surging as we approach the middle of the century, this surge will not be sustainable without support from the United States. If the United States could be forced to abandon its influence in Europe, Eastern Europe would not have the ability or confidence to pursue its strategic interests in the east. The old order would therefore be able to reassert itself, and some level of security could be retained by France and Germany.

Obviously, the French and Germans won't be in any position to confront the Americans directly, or to force them out alone. But with the end of the U.S.–Russian conflict, the immediate American interest in the region will decline. Inasmuch as U.S. power will still be in a state of constant flux, and its attention span short, the possibility of a reduced American presence will be real. There still may be an opportunity for the French and Germans to overawe the Eastern Europeans—particularly if American attention is diverted elsewhere in the world, such as toward the Pacific.

U.S. interest in Europe may wane in the immediate wake of Russia's collapse, seemingly opening the door to increased Franco-German power. But this will be transitory. As the U.S. crisis with Japan and Turkey emerges and intensifies, the U.S. interest in Europe, as we shall see, will reemerge. The United States will have a very real interest in Eastern Europe once the Turks start to make their move in the 2020s. And that will likely be enough to block the reemergence of German and French power.

SUMMING UP

The fragmentation of China in the 2010s and the breakup of Russia in the 2020s will create a vast vacuum from the Pacific to the Carpathians. All around the periphery there will be opportunities for nibbles, bites, and then entire mouthfuls by minor countries. Finland will take back Karelia, Romania will take back Moldova, India will help Tibet break free, and Taiwan will extend its power across the Taiwan Strait while Europeans and Americans create regional spheres of influence in China as well. There will be many opportunities for poaching.

But three nations will have both the power and the need to do something dramatic. Japan will expand its power to include both maritime Russia and areas of China. Turkey will expand its power not only into the Caucasus but also throughout the areas to its northwest and south. Poland, leading a coalition of Eastern European powers, will push eastward and deep into Belarus and Ukraine.

The United States will look at all of this benignly for the first decade or so, much as it viewed the world in the 1990s. Poland, Turkey, and Japan will be U.S. allies. Increasing their strength will in turn strengthen the United States. And if moralism is needed, it could be argued that these countries actually will be helping bring prosperity to their neighbors.

By the mid-2030s, however, as all three continue to increase their power, the United States will begin to feel uneasy. By the 2040s, it will be downright hostile. The fifth geopolitical principle for the United States is to oppose any power controlling all of Eurasia. Suddenly there will be three regional hegemons emerging simultaneously, and two of them (Japan and Turkey) will be significant maritime powers—one in the northwest Pacific and one in the eastern Mediterranean. Both will also have developed significant capabilities in space, and we will see in the next chapter how that becomes relevant by mid-century. The bottom line is as follows: In the 2040s, the United States will do what it does when it becomes uneasy. It will begin to act.

CHAPTER 9

THE 2040s

PRELUDE TO WAR

The years around 2040 will be a flush time in the United States, comparable to the 1990s, 1950s, or 1890s. About ten to twenty years after a fifty-year cyclical shift in the United States, the changes introduced start powering the economy. Economic, technological, and immigration shifts introduced in the 2030s will take effect by the end of the decade. Productivity gains from robotics and the surge in health care opportunities presented by genetic science will fuel growth. As in the 1990s, the internal processes of American research and development (particularly those ramped up during the second cold war) will bear fruit.

As we have seen countless times in history, however, flush times are not necessarily peaceful or stable times internationally. The question that will come to the fore in 2040 will be this: What will be the relationship between the United States and the rest of the world? On one level, the United States will be so powerful that virtually any action it takes will affect someone in the world. On the other hand, the United States will have such power, particularly after the Russian retreat and Chinese instability, that it can afford to be careless. The United States is dangerous in its most benign state, but when it focuses down on a problem it can be devastatingly relentless. The global impulse will be to block the United States, but in practical terms that will be easier said than done. Those who can avoid confronting the United States will choose that path because the risks of confrontation will be too high. Simultaneously, the rewards of collaboration will be substantial. These crosscurrents will be settled in different ways by different powers.

Around 2040, the most contentious issue on the table will be the question of the future of the Pacific Basin. It will be addressed more narrowly as a question of the northwest Pacific, and more narrowly still as Japanese policy toward China and Siberia. The surface issue will be Japan's increasingly aggressive role on the mainland of Asia as it pursues its own economic interests and interferes with other powers, including the United States. Additionally, there will be the question of Japanese respect for Chinese sovereignty and the question of self-determination for maritime Russia.

On a deeper level, the United States will be alarmed by Japan's rapidly growing maritime power, including sea-based and space-based military systems. Japan, still importing oil from the Persian Gulf, will be increasing its power in the South China Sea and in the Strait of Malacca. In the early 2040s, the Japanese will be concerned with the stability of the Gulf and will begin to probe and patrol in the Indian Ocean in order to protect their interests. Japan will have well-established, close economic ties with many of the island chains of the Pacific, and will begin to enter into agreements with them for satellite tracking and control stations. U.S. intelligence will suspect that these will also serve as bases for Japanese hypersonic anti-ship missiles. Hypersonic missiles move faster than five times the speed of sound—by the mid-twenty-first century, they will travel in excess of ten times the speed of sound, eight thousand miles an hour and faster. Hypersonics can be missiles, crashing directly into targets, or unmanned aircraft, releasing munitions on targets and then returning home.

The Japanese will share waters with the American Seventh Fleet and space with the U.S. Space Command—by now an increasingly independent service of the American military. Neither side will be provoking incidents at sea or in space, and both nations will be maintaining formally cordial relations. But the Japanese will be exquisitely aware of America's concern—that its private lake, the Pacific, contains a power that it does not fully control.

Japan will be deeply concerned with protecting its sea lanes against potential threats in the south, particularly in the waters of Indonesia, which are the paths between the Pacific and Indian oceans. Indonesia is an archipelago consisting of many islands and many ethnic groups. It is inherently fragmented, and it has—and will continue to have—many separatist movements. Japan will play a complex game in backing some of these movements versus others in order to secure the various straits in Indonesian waters.

Japan will also want to be able to keep the U.S. Navy out of the western Pacific. Toward this end, it will do three things. First, it will build and deploy hypersonic anti-ship missiles in its home islands, able to strike deep into the Pacific. Second, it will enter into agreements to allow sensors and missiles to be based on Pacific islands it already dominates economically, like the Bonin Islands (which include Iwo Jima), the Marshalls, and Nauru. The strategy here will be to create choke points that would potentially interdict U.S. transpacific trade and military transport. This, in turn, will create predictability in American routing, making it easier for Japanese satellites to monitor the movement of American ships. The most disturbing thing for the Americans, however, will be the degree of Japanese activity in space, where not only military but commercial and industrial facilities will be under construction.

American policy will be complex, as always, and influenced by different factors. The idea of a strong China threatening the Russian rear will become an obsession in the U.S. intelligence and military communities in the 2010s and 2020s. In the 2030s this fear will become an idée fixe in the State Department, where old policies never change or die. The United States will therefore continue its commitment to a secure and stable China. But this will become a major irritant in U.S.–Japanese relations by 2040. Obviously, Japanese behavior in China will be incompatible with the American idea of a stable China. By 2040 the relationship between Washington and Beijing will grow closer, irritating the Japanese no end.

TURKEY

Turkey, meanwhile, will move decisively northward into the Caucasus as Russia crumbles. Part of this move will consist of military intervention, and part will occur in the way of political alliances. Equally important, much of Turkey's influence will be economic—the rest of the region will need to align itself with the new economic power. Turkish influence inevitably will spread northward, beyond the Caucasus into Russia and Ukraine, asserting itself in the politically uncertain Don and Volga river valleys, and eastward toward the agricultural heartland of Russia. Muslim Turkey will influence Muslim Kazakhstan, spreading Turkish power into Central Asia. The Black Sea will be a Turkish lake, and Crimea and Odessa will trade heavily with Turkey. There will be massive Turkish investment throughout this region.

Russia will have created a system of alliances to the south of Turkey before its collapse, much as it did during the Cold War. As Russia weakens and withdraws, it will leave behind a belt of instability from the Levant to Afghanistan. Turkey will have no appetite for engaging Iran and will be quite content to leave it isolated and alone. But the instability in Syria and Iraq will directly affect Turkish interests, particularly as the Kurds become free to start thinking about setting up their own state again. Syria and Iraq will be weak without Russian support, torn apart by traditional internal conflicts. Between the danger of instability spreading north and the threat of other powers filling the vacuum, the Turks will move south. Certainly the Turks won't want the Americans moving into Iraq: they will have had enough of that in the 2000s.

The Balkans will be in chaos during this time as well. As the Russians weaken, their allies in the Balkans will also weaken, creating regional imbalances. The Hungarians and Romanians will try to fill some of these voids, as will the Greeks (Turkey's historic enemies). As the new regional power, Turkey will be drawn into the Balkans as a result of this widespread instability. Turkey will already have had close relations with Muslim countries in the Balkans—Bosnia and Albania—and they will seek to expand their sphere of influence not so much out of aggressive appetite, but out of the fear of the intentions of other countries.

Geographically speaking, there is only one essential goal for any power in this region: control of the eastern Mediterranean and Black seas. It is important to remember that Turkey has been historically both a land and naval power. The closer any European powers come to the Bosporus, the strait connecting the Black Sea to the Aegean Sea, the more dangerous it is for

Turkey. Turkish control of the Bosporus means pushing European powers out of the Balkans, or at least blocking them decisively. Therefore, involvement in the Balkans is essential in order for Turkey to become a major regional power.

And, by the mid-2040s, the Turks will indeed be a major regional power. They will create systems of relationships deep into Russia that feed agricultural products and energy into Turkey. They will dominate Iraq and Syria, and therefore their sphere of influence will reach the Saudi Peninsula with its dwindling oil and natural gas reserves, which are fueling the American economy. The Turks will push their sphere of influence northwest, deep into the Balkans, where their power will clash with the interests of key American allies like Hungary and Romania, who will also be pressing their influence eastward into the Ukraine and encountering Turkish influence all along the northern shore of the Black Sea. There will be conflicts, from guerrilla resistance to local conventional war, all around the Turkish pivot.

Turkey will enhance an already substantial armed force suitable for its needs, including a sizeable ground force and formidable naval and air forces. Projecting its power into the Black Sea, protecting the Bosporus, and moving into the Adriatic to help shape events in the Balkans all will require a naval force. It also, in effect, will require a dominant position in the eastern Mediterranean as far as Sicily. It is not only the Bosporus that will have to be protected. The Straits of Otranto, the gateway to the Adriatic, will also need to be controlled.

Turkey will wind up pushing against U.S. allies in southeastern Europe and will make Italy feel extremely insecure with its growing power. The breaking point will come when Egypt, inherently unstable, faces an internal crisis and Turkey uses its position as the leading Muslim power to insert troops to stabilize it. Suddenly Turkish peacekeepers will be in Egypt, controlling the Suez Canal, and in a position to do what Turkey has traditionally done: push westward in North Africa. If Turkey seizes this opportunity, it will become the decisive power in Western Eurasia. Israel will remain a powerful nation, of course, but Turkey's ability to expand its power as a Muslim nation will both block Israel and force Israel into an accommodation with Turkey, already seen as a friendly power.

Control of the Suez Canal will open up other possibilities for Turkey. It

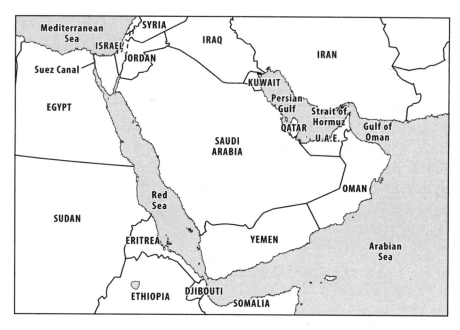

Middle East Sea Lanes

will have already pushed southward into the Arabian Peninsula and will be fighting Arab insurgents. Its overland supply lines will become strained, and with control of the Suez Canal, Turkey will be in a position to supply its forces through the Red Sea. This in turn will consolidate Turkish control over the Arabian Peninsula and place Turkey in a much more threatening position relative to Iran, enabling it to blockade Iran's ports as well as strike from the west. Neither of these will be things that Turkey wants to do. But just the threat of such actions will quiet Iran, which will serve Turkish interests.

It follows from this that Turkey will go beyond the Red Sea and enter the Indian Ocean basin. Its focus will be on the Persian Gulf, where it will consolidate its control over the Arabian Peninsula and the region's still valuable oil supplies. By doing so, it will also become an important factor in Japan's security calculations. Japan has historically depended on oil supplies from the Persian Gulf. With the Turks dominating that region, the Japanese will have an interest in reaching an understanding with Turkey. Both countries will be significant economic powers as well as emerging military powers.

Both countries also will have an interest in maintaining sea lanes from the Strait of Hormuz to the Strait of Malacca. So there will be a comfortable convergence of interests with few friction points.

Obviously the emergence of Turkey in the region and as a maritime power will be alarming to the United States, particularly as it will happen at the same time that Japan is surging. And the low-key cooperation between Turkey and Japan in the Indian Ocean will be particularly disconcerting. Turkish power will now be overwhelming in the Persian Gulf—as will be Japanese naval power in the northwest Pacific. The United States will still be the dominant power in the Indian Ocean, but as with the Pacific, the trend won't be moving in its direction.

Equally disturbing will be the way in which Turkey gathers up the remnants of the previous generation's Islamists, adding ideological and moral weight to its emerging preeminence in the region. As its influence spreads, it will be about more than military power. This obviously will be unsettling to the United States, as well as to India.

The United States will have had a long relationship with India, dating back to the U.S.–jihadist war of the early twenty-first century. While India, internally divided, will not have managed to become a global economic power, it will be a regional power of some importance. India will be disturbed by the entry of Muslim Turks into the Arabian Sea, and will fear further Turkish expansion into the Indian Ocean itself. India's interests will align with those of the Americans, and so the United States will find itself in the same position in the Indian Ocean as in the Pacific. It will be aligned with a vast, populated country on the mainland, against smaller, more dynamic maritime powers.

As this process intensifies, the power of Japan and Turkey—on opposite ends of Asia—will become substantial. Each will be expanding its interests in mainland Asia and therefore shifting its naval assets to support them. In addition, each will be enhancing its space-based operations, launching manned and unmanned systems. There will also be a degree of technical cooperation in space; Japan will be ahead of Turkey in technology, but access to Turkish launch facilities will give Japan added security against an American strike. This cooperation will be yet another source of discomfort for the United States.

By the middle of the century, Turkey's influence will extend deep into Russia and the Balkans, where it will collide with Poland and the rest of the Eastern European coalition. It will also become a major Mediterranean power, controlling the Suez Canal and projecting its strength into the Persian Gulf. Turkey will frighten the Poles, the Indians, the Israelis, and above all the United States.

POLAND

The Polish nightmare has always been to be simultaneously attacked by both Russia and Germany. When that happens, as it did in 1939, Poland has no hope. The collapse of Russia in the 2020s will therefore create an opportunity and necessity for Poland. Just as Russia will have no choice but to move its buffers as far west as possible, so Poland will want to move its border as far east.

Historically, Poland has rarely had this opportunity, having been squeezed and dominated by three empires—the Russian, the German, and the Austro-Hungarian. But in the seventeenth century, Poland had the opportunity to expand, faced with a fragmented Germany and a Russia that had not yet begun to be a powerful force in the West.

The Poles' problem had been an unsecured southern flank. In 2040, this will not be an issue since the rest of the Eastern European countries that will be facing the Russians will also be eagerly building buffers to the east, the lessons of the past still fresh in their minds. But there will be another dimension to this eastern bloc: an economic one. Since reunification in 1871, Germany has been the economic powerhouse of Europe. Even after World War II, when Germany had lost its political will and confidence, it remained the most dynamic economic power on the continent.

After 2020 that will no longer be the case. The German economy will be burdened by an aging population. The German proclivity for huge corporate megastructures will create long-term inefficiencies and will keep its economy enormous but sluggish. A host of problems, common to much of Central and Western Europe, will plague the Germans.

But the Eastern Europeans will have fought a second cold war (allied

Poland 1660

with the leading technological power in the world, the United States). A cold war is the best of all wars, as it stimulates your country dramatically but doesn't destroy it. Many of the technological capabilities from which the United States gains its massive advantage will be generated out of the second cold war, and Poland will be flooded with American technology and expertise.

By itself, Germany will have neither the appetite nor the power to challenge the Polish bloc, as we will refer to it. But the Germans will be painfully aware of the trajectory being followed. In due course, the Polish bloc will outstrip Central and Western Europe's power, and will achieve precisely what Germany had once dreamed of. It will assimilate and develop the western portion of the former Russian empire and, in so doing, build an economic bloc of substantial proportions.

The core weakness of the Polish bloc will be that it is relatively landlocked. It will have ports on the Baltic, but those could be readily blocked by any country with even minimal naval capabilities. The Skagerrak will be a dangerous choke point. If it is the only outlet Poland has, then Poland's maritime line of supply to the United States and the rest of the world will be strikingly vulnerable. The only other alternative will be to seek a port on the Adriatic. Croatia, historically close to the Hungarians, will control the port of Rijeka. Although it is limited, it certainly will be usable.

There will be two problems with using that port, both having to do with the Turks. First, the Turks will be deeply involved in the Balkans, as will the Hungarians and Romanians. As with all Balkan situations, this one will be a tangle, with religious ties complicated by national hostility. The Turks will not want to see the Polish bloc moving toward the Mediterranean, and will use Bosnian–Croatian tensions to maintain insecurity. But even if that is not an issue, the use of the Adriatic and Mediterranean will not be based on the Polish bloc simply having a merchant fleet there. It will depend on con-

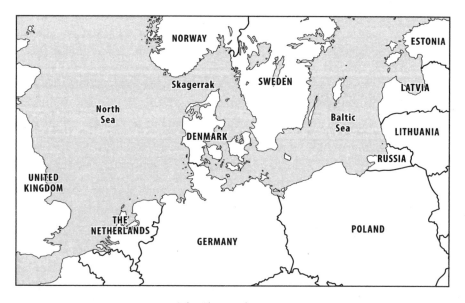

The Skagerrak Straits

trol of the Strait of Otranto. The only other alternatives will be for Denmark to seize the Skagerrak and Poland to invade Germany, and the Poles will not be in a position to do that.

The Polish bloc will collide with the Turks in two places. One will be in the Balkans, where the issue will be access to the Mediterranean. The other will be in Russia itself, where Turkish influence will spread westward through Ukraine while the bloc's influence spreads eastward. This will not be as explosive as the first issue, as there will be plenty of room, but it will be a secondary issue of some importance. No one will have defined the spheres of influence in Ukraine and southern Russia. And given Ukrainian hostility to Poles—with whom they had a historical antagonism going back to the sixteenth and seventeenth centuries—and to the Turks as well, each might manipulate the situation in ways uncomfortable to the other.

The Poles will need the Americans badly at this juncture. Only the Americans will have the weight to resist the Turks in the Mediterranean. And the Americans will be increasingly inclined to do so, as they will not want to see a new Eurasian power establish itself. While Turkey will be far from reaching that goal, it will be moving in that direction. America's strategies of disrupting Eurasian regional powers before they become too strong and preventing the emergence of any other naval power will dictate that the United States should try to block Turkey.

At the same time, U.S. policy will also require that, rather than take direct action, the United States should underwrite regional powers also interested in resisting the Turks. The Polish bloc won't be an immediate threat to any American interests, unlike the Turks. The American strategy, therefore, will be not to throw U.S. forces into the struggle, but to transfer technology to the Polish bloc so that it can pursue the strategy on its own.

By around 2045 the Polish bloc will have secured Rijeka, absorbing both Slovenia and Croatia. Both countries will seek protection from the bloc against Balkan rivals like Serbia and Bosnia. The Polish bloc will have heavily fortified the frontier with both of these countries. Serbia will be excluded from the bloc because the Poles and the others will not want to get bogged down in Serbian politics. And using American technological strength, Poland will proceed to rapidly integrate and develop naval and space capabilities needed to confront the Turks in the Adriatic and Mediterranean. The rate of the Polish bloc's development will be startling, and the Turks will begin to realize that they face a challenge not only from the Polish bloc but from the United States itself.

The Germans will watch this crisis anxiously from their nearby border, obviously supporting the Turks. They won't make a move on their own, but the Germans will be sufficiently aware of the consequences if the Polish bloc defeats Turkey. In that event, if they maintain their unity, the Polish bloc will essentially be the reincarnation of the former Soviet Union, with most of its European resources—added to which would be the Middle East. The Germans will understand the Americans well enough to know that they would move against the bloc in the event of victory of this magnitude, but the Germans will also know that they would bear the brunt of the new confrontation. If the Polish bloc were in this dominant position, the United States would have to keep it from also dominating Western Europe, and that would mean that Germany would, once again, become a potential battlefield. The success of the Polish bloc would present short- and long-range threats to Germany.

It will therefore be in the German interest to help the Turks in any way possible, short of war. But the help that the Turks will need would be help in strangling the Polish bloc. The key to this would be isolating it from the United States and global trade. If the Turks were to isolate the Polish bloc in the Adriatic, and the Germans could contrive a way to obstruct the Baltic, the Polish bloc would be in serious trouble. But for Germany to do this, it will have to be sure that the Turks will succeed—and for this it will need to be sure that the Americans won't come in with their full weight. Since Germany can't be sure of either, it will play a waiting game.

The Americans will also play a waiting game around the globe. They will arm the Polish bloc and encourage its confrontation with the Turks. They will help increase the strength of the Indians in the Indian Ocean. They will strengthen the Chinese and Koreans and build up American forces in the Pacific and the Mediterranean. They will do everything they can to strangle both Japan and Turkey without acting directly against them. And they will pursue the policy well—too well in fact. Both Turkey and Japan, well aware of the United States' historic ability to arm and support its allies, will be led to the conclusion that they are facing disaster at the hands of American proxies. And this will lead to massive escalation.

PRESSURES AND ALLIANCES

The United States faced crises on multiple fronts a century before when, in the 1940s, Germany and Japan simultaneously challenged American interests. In that case as well, the United States followed a strategy of strengthening regional allies, aiding Britain and Russia against Germany, and China against Japan. Now, a century later, it will again be prepared to play a long game. It will have no desire to occupy or destroy either Turkey or Japan, much less Germany. The United States is playing a defensive game, blocking emerging power. It is not engaged in an offensive strategy, however it might appear. American strategy will be to wear down any threats over an extended period of time, causing potential opponents to bog down in conflicts they cannot bring to a close and cannot easily abandon. In this strategy the United States will always invoke the principles of self-determination and democratic values, painting Japan and Turkey as aggressors undermining national sovereignty while violating human rights.

Alongside the public diplomacy, there will also be a series of more direct challenges.

The first will be economic. The American market, still huge, will be an enormous consumer of Japanese and, to a lesser extent, Turkish products, and the United States will also remain the major source of new technologies. Getting cut out of the American market or technologies would be painful, to say the least. The United States will use these levers against both countries. It will stop the exportation of some technologies, particularly those with potential military applications, and limit the importation of some products from these countries.

At the same time, the United States will support a range of nationalist movements in China, Korea, and India. Through the Polish bloc, the United States will also support nationalist Russian and Ukrainian movements within the Turkish sphere of influence. The major American focus in this strategy, however, will be in the Balkans and North Africa, particularly Egypt. In the Balkans, the Polish bloc (heavily dependent on Croatia) will steer clear of aligning with Serbia, Croatia's old enemy, thus creating something of a buffer with Turkey. The United States will begin an aggressive program of supporting Serbian resistance against the Turks, and extending it to Macedonia. The Greeks, historical enemies of the Turks, will become close allies of the United States and support this effort, although they will stay clear of formal alignment with the Polish bloc.

In many ways, from a geopolitical perspective, these alliances and maneuvers are not difficult to predict. As I have said, they follow well-established patterns that have been ingrained in history for many centuries. What I am doing is seeing how traditional patterns play themselves out in the context of the twenty-first century. In this particular region, after the United States begins to support targeted resistance to the Turks, the Balkans will become a tinderbox and the Turks will spend an inordinate amount of resources in an area where their primary interest is defensive. They will be trying to protect the Bosporus and little else. If they retreat, their credibility (in their still uncertain sphere of influence) will be badly hurt.

The United States also will try its hand at supporting Arab nationalism, both in Egypt and in the Arabian Peninsula. The Turks will be careful not to be excessively aggressive or greedy in asserting their power, but nevertheless anti-Turkish feeling will be prevalent. This type of nationalist feeling will be exploited by the United States, not because Americans genuinely want it to go anywhere but in order to sap the strength of the Turks. Turkey will be concerned about U.S. aid to the Polish bloc and northern Africa. The goal of the United States will be to reshape and limit the behavior of the Turks, but any meddling will be far short of what Turkey regards as challenging its fundamental national interest.

SPACE AND BATTLE STARS

The most threatening move the United States will make during this period is at sea—and those moves won't actually take place in the water, but in space. During the 2030s, the United States will have begun a fairly low-key program for the commercialization of space, focusing particularly on energy production. By the mid-2040s, this development will have proceeded to some extent but will still be heavily subsidized and in the research and development phase. In the course of commercializing space, the United States will increase its ability to work in space robotically, using humans only for the most complex and exacting work. Substantial infrastructure will have been created, giving the country even more of a head start.

Looking to leverage its advantage in space in order to improve its dominance of the earth's surface, the United States will begin building on that infrastructure. It will gradually abandon the costly and ineffective strategy of sending heavily armed troops in petroleum-burning vehicles thousands of miles away to exert its power. Instead, the United States will construct a system of hypersonic unmanned aircraft that will be based on U.S. soil but controlled from space-based command centers in geosynchronous orbit over potential target regions—platforms that I will call "Battle Stars," for no other reason than that it's a cool name. By mid-century, a hypersonic missile based in Hawaii could hit a ship off the coast of Japan or a tank in Manchuria in half an hour.

The United States will also create (quite secretly, since treaties from the last century will still be in place) missiles that can be fired from space with devastating effect, at very high speeds, at targets on the surface. If the platform were to be cut off from ground communication, it would be able to conduct the battle from space automatically—if what was called for was a quantity of explosives delivered to a precise point at an exact time based on superb, space-based intelligence.

Combat in the twenty-first century will require elegance of communication. Most important in the evolution of space warfare will be the transfer of primary command and control facilities into space. Land-based control is vulnerable. By the time an image is picked up in space and transmitted through a series of satellites to earth, and a command is sent out to hypersonic weapons systems, many seconds will have passed. Most important, the more links there are, the higher the number of possible failure points, and an enemy could disrupt that signal. An enemy could also attack the ground control center, the receivers, and transmitters. There will be many low-tech solutions for disruption, but placed in space, the command centers will be seen as more secure and survivable, with unimpeded ability to communicate with weapons and personnel.

Much of the science involved in these systems is in its infancy today. By the middle of the century, though, it will be online. Now stick with me here. I am telling you what the technological world is realistically going to look like . . . I'm not writing *Battlestar Galactica* here. These forecasts are based on real technology, reasonable extrapolations about future technology, and reasonable war planning. Space-based platforms will have superb sensing equipment as well as command and control systems. Battle Stars will control unmanned subsidiary platforms which will support the Battle Star system. They will see the surface of the earth with extraordinary precision, and will be able to order hypersonic aircraft strikes as needed—strikes that will be able to frequently hit their targets in a matter of minutes. They will be able to attack a group planting explosives by the roadside, or a fleet putting to sea. If they can see it, they will be able to hit it quickly.

Using lessons learned during space construction projects in the 2030s, I believe the United States' future plans will call for the creation of a system of three Battle Stars. The main Battle Star will be located in geosynchronous orbit over the equator near the coast of Peru. A second will be placed over Papua New Guinea, and a third over Uganda. The three will be arrayed at almost exact intervals, trisecting the earth.

Most countries won't be happy about the Battle Star system, but the Japanese and the Turks will be particularly alarmed. It just so happens that one Battle Star will be due south of Turkey and the other will be due south of Japan. Each will be able to use its onboard sensors, as well as remote sensors that orbit the earth but can stop and loiter for extended periods of time, to monitor those countries. They will be, essentially, guns pointed at the heads of both countries. And perhaps most important, they will be capable of imposing an unstoppable blockade on either country at a moment's notice. Battle Stars will not be able to occupy Turkey and Japan, but they will be able to strangle them.

Although the new space-based systems will have been planned for years, they will be put into place with breathtaking speed. With rapid deployment ordered around 2040, the systems will be fully operational in the second half of the decade . . . let's say by 2047, for argument's sake. This deployment will be based on the assumption that the Battle Star is invulnerable, that no other country has the ability to attack and destroy it. That assumption has been made by the United States before—about battleships, aircraft carriers, and stealth bombers. There is a built-in arrogance in American military planning built on the belief that other countries cannot match American technology. Assuming invulnerability, though, however risky, will make the system easier to deploy quickly.

ESCALATING TENSION

Deployment of the Battle Stars, the introduction of new generations of weapons managed from space, and aggressive political pressure coupled with economic policies will all be intended to contain Japan and Turkey. And from the Japanese and Turkish points of view, American demands will be so extreme as to seem unreasonable. The Americans will demand that both countries withdraw all forces to within their original borders, as well as guaranteeing rights of passage in the Black Sea, the Sea of Japan, and the Bosporus.

If the Japanese were to agree to these conditions, their entire economic structure would be imperiled. For the Turks, economic upheaval will be a consideration, but so will the political chaos that would then surround them. Moreover, the United States will make no equivalent demands on the Polish bloc. In effect, the United States will demand that Turkey turn over the Balkans and Ukraine, as well as part of southern Russia, to the Poles, and that it allow the Caucasus to fall back into chaos.

The United States will not actually expect Turkey or Japan to capitulate. That will not be the American intent. These demands will simply be the platform from which the Americans try to impose pressure on these countries, limiting their growth and increasing their insecurity. The Americans won't truly expect either country to return to its position of 2020, but it will want to discourage further expansion.

The Japanese and the Turks, however, will not see things this way. From their perspective, the best-case scenario will be that the United States is trying to divert their attention from pressing issues by creating insoluble inter-

national problems. Worst case will be that the United States is preparing the
way for their geopolitical collapse. In either case, both Turkey and Japan will
have no choice but to assume the worst, and prepare to resist.

Turkey and Japan won't have the extensive experience of the Americans
in space. They may be able to construct manned space systems, and will
have created their own reconnaissance systems by this point. But the military capabilities possessed by the United States will be outside their reach,
certainly within a time frame that might cause the United States to reconsider its policies. And neither the Japanese nor the Turks will be in a position to reconsider theirs.

The United States will not plan to go to war with either Japan or Turkey.
Its intention will simply be to squeeze them until they decrease their dynamism and become more malleable to American demands. As a result,
Turkey and Japan will have an interest in limiting American power and will
therefore form a natural coalition. By the 2040s, technological shifts in warfare will have made a close alliance remarkably easy. Space will change the
global geopolitical equation.

In more traditional terms as well, the Turks and the Japanese will be able
to support each other. The United States is a North American power. Japan
and Turkey will both be Eurasian powers.

This sets up a very natural alliance, as well as a goal for these countries.
Japanese power hugs the Pacific coast, but by 2045 it will have spread
throughout the Asian archipelago and on the mainland as well. The Turkish
sphere of influence will extend into Central Asia and even into Muslim
western China. The possibility will exist, therefore, that if Japan and Turkey
were to collaborate, they could create a pan-Eurasian power that would rival
the United States.

The fly in the ointment, of course, will be Poland, and the fact that
Turkish influence won't penetrate beyond the Balkans. But this won't prevent Turkey and Japan from seeking out an alliance. If just one European
power could be brought into the coalition, then Poland would have a serious problem. Its resources and attention would be diverted, giving Turkey a
freer hand in Ukraine and Russia, and giving the Turkish-Japanese alliance a
third leg. The European country they will have in mind is Germany. From
the Japanese and Turkish perspectives, if Germany could be persuaded that

the threat from a U.S.-backed Polish bloc would be sufficiently dangerous, and the creation of a tripartite pact sufficiently threatening to force the United States to act cautiously, then the possibility of securing Eurasia and exploiting its resources jointly would be viable.

Germany will not believe for a moment that the United States would be deterred. Indeed, it will fear that a tripartite coalition would trigger an immediate American military response. Germany also will reason that if the Polish bloc is eliminated, it will shortly be facing the Turks in the Danube basin and it will have no appetite for that game. So although I see the Germans as the most likely choice to form a coalition with Turkey and Japan, I also believe it will decline involvement—but with a caveat. If the United States winds up in a war with Turkey and Japan and is allied with Poland, Poland might well be severely weakened in that war. In that case, a later German intervention would hold lower risk and higher reward. If the United States won outright, Germany would be no worse off. If the United States and Poland were both defeated—the least likely outcome—then Germany would have an opportunity to move in quickly for the kill. Waiting to see what happens to Poland will make sense for Germany, and that is the game it will play in the middle of the twenty-first century.

The only other possible member of the coalition might be Mexico, however unlikely. Recall that Mexico was invited into an alliance by Germany in World War I, so this idea is hardly unprecedented. Mexico will be developing rapidly throughout the first fifty years of this new century and will be a major economic power by the late 2040s, although still living in the shadow of the United States. It will be experiencing a major outflow of Mexicans to the southwestern borderlands after the new American immigration policy of 2030. This will be troubling to the United States in a number of ways, but Mexico will hardly be in a position in the late 2040s to join an anti-American coalition.

U.S. intelligence, of course, will pick up the diplomatic discussions between Tokyo and Istanbul (the capital will shift there from Ankara, returning the capital of Turkey to its traditional city) and will be aware of the feelers to Germany and Mexico. The United States will realize that the situation has become quite serious. It also will have knowledge of the joint Japanese-Turkish strategic plans should war break out. No formal alliance will be in place, but the United States will no longer be certain it is facing two separate and manageable regional powers. It will start to appear that it is facing a single coalition that could, in fact, dominate Eurasia—the primordial American fear. This goes back to the grand strategies I discussed in the early sections of this book. If it controlled Eurasia, the Japanese–Turkish coalition would be secure from attack and able to concentrate on challenging the United States in space and at sea.

The American response will be a policy it has executed numerous times in history—it will squeeze each of the powers economically. Both countries will depend to some extent on exports, difficult in a world where populations will no longer be growing very fast. The United States will begin forming an economic bloc that will bestow most-favored-nation status on exports into the United States for countries that are prepared to shift their purchases away from Turkey and Japan and toward third countries—not even necessarily the United States—that could supply the same goods. In other words, the United States will organize a not particularly subtle boycott of Japanese and Turkish goods.

In addition, the United States will start limiting the export of technology to both of these countries. Given the American work being done in robotics and genetics, this will hurt Turkish and Japanese high-tech capabilities. Most important, there will be a surge in U.S. military aid to China, India, and Poland, as well as to forces resisting Turkey and Japan in Russia. American policy will be simple: to create as many problems as possible for these two countries in order to deter them from forming a coalition.

But the intense activity of the United States in space will be the most troubling to Japan and Turkey. The establishment of the Battle Star constellation will convince them that the United States will be prepared to wage an aggressive war if necessary. By the late 2040s, given all the actions of the Americans, the Japanese and Turks will have reached a conclusion about American intentions. The conclusion they will draw, however, is that the United States means to break them both. They will also conclude that only the formation of an alliance will protect them, by serving as a deterrent—or make it clear that the United States intends to go to war no matter what. A formal alliance will therefore be created, and with its formation Muslims throughout Asia will be energized at the thought of a coalition that will place them at the crossroads of power.

The resurgence of Islamist fervor built around Turkey's confrontation with the United States will spill over into Southeast Asia. This will give Japan, under the terms of the alliance treaty, access to Indonesia—which, together with its long-term presence in the Pacific Islands, will mean that U.S. control of the Pacific, and access to the Indian Ocean, can no longer be assured. But the United States will remain convinced of one thing—that although it might face challenges from the Japanese and the Turks within their region and in Eurasia, they will never challenge America's strategic power, which will be in space.

Having put the Japanese and Turks in an impossible position, the Americans will now simultaneously panic at the result and yet remain complacent about their ultimate capacity to manage the problem. The United States will not view the outcome as a shooting war, but as another cold war, like the one it had with Russia. The superpower will believe that no one would challenge it in a real war.

CHAPTER 10

PREPARING FOR WAR

The war in the mid-twenty-first century will have classic origins. One country, the United States, will place tremendous pressure on a coalition of two other countries. The United States will not intend to go to war, or even to seriously damage Japan or Turkey. It simply will want these two countries to change their behavior. The Japanese and Turks, to the contrary, will feel that the United States is trying to destroy them. They also will not want war, but fear will compel them to act. They will try to negotiate with the United States, but while the Americans will view their own demands as modest, the Turks and Japanese will see them as existential threats.

We will see the collision of three grand strategies. The Americans will want to prevent major regional powers from developing in Eurasia and will be concerned that these two regional powers would merge into a single Eurasian hegemon. Japan will need a presence in Asia in order to deal with its demographic problems and to get raw materials; for that it will have to control the northwest Pacific. And Turkey will be the pivot point of three continents that are all in various degrees of chaos; it will have to stabilize the region if it is to grow. While Japanese and Turkish actions will cause anxiety for the United States, Japan and Turkey will feel they cannot survive unless they act.

Accommodation will be impossible. Each concession made to the United States will bring new demands. Each refusal by Japan and Turkey will increase American fears. It will come down to submission or war, and war will appear to be the more prudent option. Japan and Turkey will have no illusion that they could destroy or occupy the United States. Rather, they will simply want to create a set of circumstances in which the United States would find it in its interests to reach a negotiated settlement guaranteeing Japan and Turkey their spheres of influence, which in their view will not affect fundamental American interests.

Since they won't be able to defeat the United States in a war, Turkey and Japan's goal will be to deal the United States a severe setback at the opening of the conflict in order to put the United States at a temporary disadvantage. This would be intended to generate a sense in the United States that the prosecution of the war would be more costly and risky than accommodation. It will be Turkey and Japan's hope that the Americans, enjoying a period of prosperity, and vaguely uneasy about Mexico's resurgence, will decide to decline extended combat and accept a reasonable negotiated settlement. Japan and Turkey will also understand the risks if the United States doesn't agree to settle, but will feel they have no choice.

It will be a replay of World War II in this sense: weaker countries trying to redefine the balance of power in the world will find it necessary to launch sudden, preemptive wars before the other side is ready. The war will be a combination of surprise attack and exploitation of that surprise. In many ways, war in the mid-twenty-first century will be similar to war in the mid-twentieth century. The principles will be the same. The practice, however, will differ dramatically—and that is why this conflict will mark the dawn of a new age in warfare.

A NEW KIND OF WAR

World War II was the last major war of the European Age. In that age there were two kinds of wars, which sometimes occurred simultaneously. One was global war, in which the world as a whole was the battlefield. Europeans waged wars on that scale as far back as the sixteenth century. The other was total war, in which entire societies were mobilized. In World War II, a nation's entire society was mobilized to field armies and to supply them. The distinction between soldiers and civilians, always tenuous, completely collapsed in the global and total wars of the twentieth century. War became an extraordinary display of carnage, unlike anything yet seen—both global and total.

The roots of total war are to be found in the nature of warfare since the emergence of ballistic weapons—weapons that delivered bullets, artillery shells, and bombs. A ballistic weapon is simply one that, once fired or released, can't change its course. That makes these weapons inherently inaccurate. A bullet fired from a rifle, or a bomb released by a bombardier, depends on the hand–eye coordination of a soldier or airman trying to concentrate while others try to kill him. In World War II, the probability of any one projectile hitting its target was startlingly low.

When accuracy is low, the only solution is to saturate the battlefield with bullets and shells and bombs. That means that there have to be masses of weapons, and that in turn requires masses of soldiers. Masses of soldiers require vast quantities of supplies, from food to munitions. That requires vast numbers of men to deliver supplies, and masses of workers to produce them. In World War II, gasoline was essential for virtually all weapons systems. Consider that the effort to drill oil, refine it, and deliver it to the battlefield—and to the factories that supplied the battlefield—was by itself an undertaking far larger than the total effort that went into warfare in previous centuries.

By the twentieth century, the outcome of wars required such a level of effort that nothing short of the total mobilization of society could achieve victory. War consisted of one society hurling itself against another. Victory depended on shattering the enemy's society, damaging its population and infrastructure so completely that it could no longer produce the masses of weapons or field the massive armies required.

But bombing a city with a thousand bombers is a vast and costly undertaking. Imagine if you could achieve the same outcome with a single plane and a single bomb. It would achieve the goal of total war at a fraction of the cost and danger to one's own nation. That was the logic behind the atomic bomb. It was designed to destroy an enemy society so quickly and efficiently that the enemy would capitulate rather than face the bomb. Technically the atomic bomb was radically new. Militarily, it was simply a continuation of a culture of war that had been developing in Europe for centuries.

The brute nature of nuclear weapons generated a technological revolution in warfare. Nuclear weapons were the reductio ad absurdum of global and total war. In order to fight nuclear wars, nations—the United States and the Soviet Union—had to be able to see globally. The only way to do that efficiently was to fly over enemy territory, and the safest and most effective way to do that was in space. While manned space projects were the public side of space programs, the primary motive—and funding—was driven by the need to know precisely where the other side had located its nuclear missiles. Spy satellites evolved into real-time systems that could pinpoint enemy launchers within meters, allowing them to be targeted precisely. And that created the need for weapons that could hit those targets.

THE AMERICAN AGE: PRECISION AND
THE END OF TOTAL WAR

The ability to see the target created the need for more accurate weapons. Precision-guided munitions (PGMs), which could be guided to their target after they were fired, were first deployed in the late 1960s and 1970s. This might appear to be a minor innovation, but its impact was huge. It transformed war. In the twentieth century, thousands of bombers and millions of rifles were needed to fight wars. In the twenty-first century, the numbers will be slashed to a small fraction—signaling an end to total war.

This change in scale will be of tremendous advantage to the United States, which has always been at a demographic disadvantage in fighting wars. The primary battlefields in the twentieth century were Europe and Asia. These were heavily populated areas. The United States was thousands of miles away. Its smaller population was needed not only to fight but to build supplies and transport them great distances, siphoning off manpower and limiting the size of the force available for direct combat.

The American way of war has thus always focused on multiplying the effectiveness of each soldier on the battlefield. Historically it did this by using both technology and masses of weapons. After World War II, however, the emphasis was increasingly on technological multipliers rather than mass. The United States had no choice in the matter. If it was going to be a global power, it would need to maximize the effectiveness of each soldier by wedding him to advanced weaponry. It has created a culture of war in which smaller forces can defeat larger ones. As the use of technology increases, the size of the force needed decreases until ultimately what is required is a remarkably small number of extremely well-trained and sophisticated warriors. It is important to see how the weapons culture created by the United States parallels its demographic shift. With an aging and contracting population, the maintenance of mass forces becomes difficult, if not impossible.

The key to warfare in the twenty-first century, then, will be precision. The more precise weapons are, the fewer have to be fired. That means fewer soldiers and fewer defense workers—but more scientists and technicians. What will be needed in the coming decades is a weapon that can be based in the United States, reach the other side of the world in under an hour, maneuver with incredible agility to avoid surface-to-air missiles, strike with absolute precision, and return to carry out another mission almost immediately. If the United States had such a system, it would never again need to deliver a tank eight thousand miles away.

Such a weapon is called an unmanned hypersonic aircraft. The United States is currently engaged in the development of hypersonic systems capable of traveling well in excess of five times the speed of sound. Powered by what are called scramjet engines, the craft have air-breathing, not rocket, engines. Their range currently is limited. But as scramjets develop during the twenty-first century—along with new materials that can withstand extremely high temperatures caused by friction with the air—both their range and speed will increase.

Imagine: Traveling at eight thousand miles per hour, or Mach 10, a missile fired from the east coast of the United States could hit a target in Europe in under half an hour. Increase this to Mach 20, and a strike could be completed in less than fifteen minutes. The American geopolitical need to intervene rapidly, with sufficient strength to destroy enemy forces, would be met in time to make a difference. Building enough hypersonic missiles to devastate a potential enemy would be extremely expensive. But considering the savings on the current force structure, it would be manageable. I would also note that this system would reduce the need for huge stockpiles of petroleum to fuel tanks, planes, and ships at a time when the hydrocarbon energy system will be in decline.

The result of deploying hypersonic systems will be to reverse the trend in warfare that has been under way since before Napoleon. The armies of the twenty-first century will be much smaller and more professional than previous forces, and highly technological. Precision will also allow the reintroduction of a separation between soldier and civilian: It will not be necessary to devastate entire cities to destroy one building. Soldiers will increasingly resemble highly trained medieval knights, rather than the GIs of World War II. Courage will still be necessary, but it will be the ability to manage extremely complex weapons systems that will matter the most.

Speed, range, and accuracy—and a lot of unmanned aircraft—will substitute for the massed forces that were required to deliver explosives to the battlefield in the twentieth century. Yet these talents will not solve a core problem of warfare, occupying hostile territory. Armies are designed to destroy armies, and precision weapons will do that more effectively than ever before. But the occupation of territory will remain a labor-intensive activity. It is, in many ways, more akin to police work than to soldiering. A soldier's job is to kill an enemy, whereas a policeman's job is to identify a lawbreaker and arrest him. The first requires courage, training, and weapons. The latter requires all of these plus an understanding of a culture that allows you to distinguish enemies from law-abiding civilians. That task will never become easier and will always be the Achilles' heel of any great power. Just as the Romans and British struggled with their occupation of Palestine, even as they easily defeated enemy armies, so too the Americans will win wars and then suffer through the aftermath.

SPACE WARFARE

Regardless of the changes taking place in warfare, there is one thing that remains unchanged: the commander on a battlefield must have knowledge of that battlefield. Even though the global battlefield may be radically different from the traditional battlefield, the principle of the commander's knowledge remains in place. On a global battlefield, command and control must be tied together with knowledge of what the enemy is doing and how your own forces are deployed. The only way to achieve this on a global battlefield, in real time, is from space. An essential principle of warfare has always been to hold the high ground, on the theory that it provides visibility. The same idea holds true in global war. The high ground permits visibility, and here the high ground is space—the area in which reconnaissance platforms can see the battlefield on a continuous, global basis.

Global war will therefore become space war. This is not by any means a radical change. Space is already filled with reconnaissance satellites designed to provide a large number of countries intelligence on what is happening around the world. For some, particularly the United States, space-based sensors are already creating a global battlefield, identifying tactical targets and calling in air strikes or cruise missiles. The weapons systems have not yet evolved, but the platforms are already there and moving into maturity.

Space provides line of sight and secure communications. It also provides clear tracking of hostile objects. Battle management will therefore move from earth to space as well. There will be space stations—command platforms—at various distances out from the earth's surface, tasked with commanding robotic and manned systems on land and at sea as they evade enemy attack, conduct operations, and attack enemy platforms.

Blinding one's enemy, then, would mean destroying the space-based systems that allow the enemy to select targets. In addition, there are navigational systems, communications systems, and other space-based systems that must be destroyed if an enemy's capability to wage war is to be crippled. Therefore, the destruction of enemy satellites will become an essential goal of twenty-first-century warfare.

It naturally follows, then, that defending one's own satellites will be critical. The simplest way to defend a satellite is to allow it to maneuver out of harm's way. But this is not as simple as it sounds. First, it requires fuel to maneuver a satellite, which is heavy and expensive to send into orbit. Second, maneuvering won't save a satellite from an anti-satellite (ASAT) system that can also maneuver, and certainly not from a laser beam. Finally, these are orbital platforms, placed in a certain orbit in order to cover the necessary terrain. Maneuvering shifts the orbit, degrading the satellites' usefulness.

Satellites must be protected, whether by deflecting the attack or destroying the attacker. By the middle of the twenty-first century this idea will have evolved in the mode of other weapons systems in history, and the result will be the satellite battle group. Like a carrier battle group, where the carrier is protected by other vessels, the reconnaissance satellite will be protected by auxiliary satellites with various capabilities and responsibilities, from blocking laser beams to attacking other satellites. The problem of defending space-based systems will escalate rapidly, as each side increases the threat and thereby increases defense measures.

Weapons will also be fired from space to earth eventually, but it is more complicated than it appears. A weapon in space is moving at many thousands of miles an hour, and the earth is rotating as well. Hitting a target on the surface of the earth from space is a capability that will develop more slowly than surveillance from space, but it will undoubtedly come to fruition eventually.

A satellite costs several billion dollars. A space-based battle group will cost even more. Currently, except for relatively rare instances, a damaged or failed satellite is a total loss—no part of it is ever recovered. The more extensively space is used, the more valuable platforms will become and the less this total loss model will work. Particularly as space becomes a battleground, the need to repair space platforms will become urgent. And, to repair complex, damaged systems, humans will have to go physically into space.

Launching them into space each time a repair has to be done is inherently inefficient, and launching spacecraft from earth will cost more than moving spacecraft already in orbit. At a certain point it will make more sense and become more economical to station personnel permanently in space to carry out repairs. Obviously, they will become targets themselves— and will have to have the capabilities to defend themselves. They will also be able to manage and oversee the space-based systems.

The task of efficiently managing warfare from space is not limited to repairing multibillion-dollar satellites quickly. The communications link from earth to space is complex, and subject to interference. Therefore, any enemy will try the most logical, and economical, attack first—disrupting communications between ground and space. This can be accomplished with low-tech maneuvers—the simplest method might be the destruction of earth-based transmitters with car bombs, for example. Launch facilities might also be attacked. Assume that the two major U.S. launch facilities, Kennedy Space Center and Vandenberg Air Force Base, came under attack by enemy missiles, causing enough damage to shut down operations for months. The United States would be unable to launch more equipment, and whatever was already in space at the time of the attack would be all that was available. Maintaining those systems could mean the difference between victory and defeat. Therefore, having repair teams deployed in space will be critical.

As we can see, space warfare is a tricky subject. The deeper we explore it, the greater the risk of sounding like science fiction, but there is no doubt that humans really will experience all this in the coming century. The technology is there—as are the strategic and tactical advantages.

Space warfare, like naval warfare in the sixteenth century, will spread outward. Geostationary orbit is strategic, and therefore it will be fought over. But orbits will be only one strategic point of conflict. Another will be the surface of the moon. As far-fetched as it sounds, bases on the moon will provide a stable platform—not encumbered by an atmosphere—for observing both the surface of the earth and any conflicts occurring in space. It would take too long for a weapon on the moon to reach earth—probably days. But a signal would be able to reach a hunter-killer satellite moving in to destroy a repair facility in seconds. Sustaining and defending a base on the moon will actually be easier than doing the same for orbiting systems.

Battles will be fought for control of low-orbit space, geostationary space, libration points (stable points between the earth and the moon), and the surface of the moon. The purpose of any battles, like all earthbound battles that preceded them, will be to deny an enemy the ability to utilize these areas, while guaranteeing a nation's own military access to them. Treaties or not, where humanity goes, war goes. And since humanity will be going into space, there will be war in space.

Controlling the world's oceans from space will be critical. Even today, the U.S. Navy depends heavily on space-based surveillance for making the fleet effective. Building fleets to challenge U.S. naval dominance is extraordinarily difficult, expensive, and time consuming. Mastering the technologies and operational principles of aircraft carriers can take generations. Most navies have abandoned any attempt to do so, and few will be in a position to attempt it in the future. But in the twenty-first century, control of the sea will be less dependent on oceangoing fleets than on space-based systems that can see enemy ships and target them. Therefore, whoever controls space will control the sea.

Let's turn our attention for a moment to robots. While I expect humans in space to maintain and command space-based warfighting systems, these will have to be augmented by robotic systems. Keeping a human being alive in space is a complex and expensive undertaking, and will remain so throughout the century. Autonomous systems, though, are already common, as are remotely controlled systems. Unmanned space flight is routine. In fact, space is where much of the pioneering work on robotics has been done, and will continue to be done. The technology is sufficiently developed that the U.S. Department of Defense already has fairly advanced projects in this area. We will see—or are already seeing—robotic aircraft, repair modules for satellites, intelligent torpedoes at sea. Toward the end of the century a robotic infantryman for relatively simple tasks, such as rushing fortified positions to avoid human casualties, is quite likely.

All of this leads to a vital change in warfare—actually, a reversion. Precision means there is no need to devastate.

WAR PLANS

By the middle of the century American power is going to rest in the global reach of its unmanned hypersonic aircraft and space-based missiles. With these systems the United States will be able to impose a naval blockade around both Turkey and Japan, if necessary. It could also strike at any land-based facilities it might want to destroy. And it could strike devastating blows against land forces.

American warfighting will consist of three stages. The first will be an assault on enemy aircraft that could strike at the United States, along with enemy air defenses, including space-based systems. The second will be a systematic attack on the rest of an enemy's military capability and key economic facilities. The final stage will be the insertion of limited ground forces, consisting of infantrymen in armored, powered suits with tremendous lethality, survivability, and mobility, accompanied by an array of robotic systems.

The United States will depend overwhelmingly not only on its satellites but on what I am calling its Battle Star management platforms. The Battle Stars are going to be the eyes, ears, and fists of the United States. They will command swarms of satellites and their own onboard systems, as well as orbiting pods that will be able to fire missiles at the ground and at other satellites. They will provide targeting information to ground-based unmanned hypersonic aircraft, and even be able to control such aircraft from space. If Battle Stars are destroyed or isolated, the entire warfighting system of the United States will be crippled. The country will be able to strike at unmovable facilities whose locations it knows, but as for anything mobile, it will be blind.

By mid-century, humans will have been in space on military missions for several decades. The pre-2020 process of launching multibillion-dollar satellites into orbit and simply hoping they work will make no sense. Critical systems that fail will have to be fixed. Today's space shuttle is capable of such repairs, but as space becomes more and more important, a permanent cadre of space repairmen will be needed. The most expensive part of space is the launch, and as I have said, constantly launching people into space will not be economical. Basing them in space and giving them the ability to intercept malfunctioning systems in orbit and repair them will become the norm. By mid-century orbiting repair stations at various altitudes will have been in space for twenty years, and over time they will take on more functions in relation to reconnaissance and warfighting operations—like the destruction of enemy satellites.

The Battle Star will be designed to be survivable. It will be a large platform, containing dozens or even hundreds of people to carry out its mission and to maintain it. It will be constructed from advanced materials, and with multiple hulls, so that laser and other high-energy beams will not be able to destroy the platform. It will also be loaded with sensor systems that will be able to see any approaching objects at extreme distances, and will be heavily armed with projectiles and energy beams that could destroy anything that might threaten it.

Security will be built around the assumption that anything launched into orbit with the purpose of destroying a Battle Star could not be large enough and robust enough to survive a Battle Star's weapons. A Battle Star itself will be constructed out of many components launched on thousands of missions. In addition, it will be assumed that U.S. sensors on the ground or in space will readily recognize any larger systems being constructed by other countries. The Battle Star will be able to see any danger and deal with any conceivable threat. The Americans will construct their systems first, increasing the risk to any other country trying to build one.

In light of this incredible advantage in the U.S. defense system, the Turkish–Japanese Coalition will have to devise a war plan that will simultaneously reduce U.S. warfighting capability dramatically, allow a period in which the Coalition can attack American interests worldwide without eliciting an effective counterattack, and set the stage for a negotiated settlement that the United States will be able to live with better than it can live with being hammered. Some approaches will be impractical, including invasion from the sea and naval surface warfare. Nuclear weapons, which the Japanese as well as the Turks will have, will be out of the question. By then the technology will be one hundred years old, and there won't be any mystery to how to build and deliver them. But as we have seen, nuclear weapons are more frightening before they are used than after. Turkey and Japan will be looking to secure their national interests, not commit national suicide. A nuclear strike against the United States would devastate it, but a counterstrike would devastate Turkey and Japan even more, and given their relative sizes, the risk would be greater for them than for the Americans.

The key will be to deny the United States its command of space. In order to do that, the Coalition will have to achieve what the Americans will believe is impossible—destroy the Battle Stars. Achieving that will open opportunities for the Coalition forces to redraw the map of the Pacific and East Asia, as well as of the vast region surrounding Turkey. It will all hinge on the small problem of doing the impossible.

Launching a projectile large enough to destroy a Battle Star (and not to be shot down by that Battle Star) will be an enormous challenge. It cannot be launched from earth, since the United States would detect the launch and destroy it immediately. But the Coalition will have one advantage: the Battle Star will not be capable of maneuvering. Parked in geostationary orbit, the Battle Star will have enough propellant on board to keep it in orbit, but it will not be able to execute substantial orbital shifts. That will require too much fuel. Moreover, once it maneuvers it will lose its geostationary orbit and therefore the stability it needs to carry out its mission. This is one of the corners that planners will cut. The U.S. Battle Star program will be a crash program in the 2040s. Creating an orbiting space station housing dozens of crewmen is one thing, but making it maneuverable will push the timeline far beyond what will be needed. So the planners will bow to technical reality and rationalize. The Battle Star will be indestructible, they will posit, so no capacity for maneuvering will be needed. Like the *Titanic*, it will be billed as unsinkable.

The Japanese will consider the problem of how to take out a Battle Star as early as the 2030s. They will develop a robust space program after 2020, substantially ahead of the Turks, whose attention will be focused on events closer to their border. Both will develop low earth-orbit reconnaissance satellites and geostationary communications systems, but the Japanese will be looking into the commercial uses of space as well and will be particularly interested in energy generation in space. Hungry for energy at a rate that new nuclear reactors would find difficult to keep up with, the Japanese will have been investing for a generation in all varieties of alternative energy, including space-based systems.

One of the research and development locations will be the surface of the moon. As with Antarctica in the 1950s, it is likely that several nations will have established research bases there, with the American and Japanese being the most ambitious. By 2040 the Japanese will have a substantial colony operating on the moon, and will have created large underground chambers for their work. Traffic back and forth to the moon will be common and unnoticed. The various nations working there will cooperate and will be constantly exchanging personnel. Nothing that could be done from the surface of the moon militarily could not be done more effectively from earth orbit, or so will go the thinking.

The Japanese will, of course, be planning solutions to potential warfare situations, as all militaries are supposed to do. The problem will be simple: how to destroy the center of gravity of the American warfighting system—the Battle Star. Launching an attack from earth, as noted, would be likely to fail and, if it failed, would thrust the Japanese into war with the United States under the worst possible circumstances.

The Japanese will have to come up with a new strategy. Think of 1941, when Japan sought to initiate war by crippling the American military center of gravity in the Pacific—the fleet at Pearl Harbor. Drawing out the American fleet while it was still intact was too dangerous, and the Americans regarded their battleships at Pearl Harbor as invulnerable. So the Japanese attacked using an unexpected means, an aircraft carrier–based attack with torpedoes in a harbor believed too shallow for them, and they attacked from an unexpected direction, the northwest, at a distance from home assumed to be too far for safety. This is not just a Japanese way of making war, but the application of universal principles of warfare by the Japanese.

In the mid-twenty-first century, the Japanese will face the same problem in a different context. They will need to destroy the Battle Stars. They must attack from an unexpected direction with unexpected means. The unexpected direction would be from the rear, the equivalent of the northwest Pacific. That would mean the moon. They would have to use unexpected means—weapons constructed in secret on the moon, since shipping weapons there for later use could be detected. The equivalent of Pearl Harbor in the twenty-first century would have to involve the principles of surprise in direction and means. There may well be alternatives to the scenario I am laying out, but this is certainly an extremely plausible scenario given the geometry of space.

There is an underlying geopolitical principle shaping my thinking. In World War II two emerging powers—Germany and Japan—wanted to redefine the global order. In the mid-twenty-first century, this continual cycle of geopolitics will repeat itself. In World War II, Japan had to strike unexpectedly to cripple U.S. power in the Pacific and, it hoped, open the door for a negotiated settlement on its own terms. The geography of Japan put it at a massive long-term disadvantage relative to the United States, so Japan had to create a window of opportunity through a surprise blow at the heart of American power. Japan will be in the same position relative to the United States in the mid-twenty-first century, only this time allied with Turkey instead of Germany. Therefore, whatever the details of Japan's military moves—and obviously we can only speculate on those details—the nature of the conflict is rooted in the same dynamics in both centuries, and therefore so is the general strategy.

Earlier in this book I talked about history as a chess game in which there are many fewer moves available than appears to be the case. The better a player you are, the more you see the weaknesses of moves, and the number of moves shrinks to a very few. We can apply this principle to the future. I have tried to lay out the logic of how Japan and Turkey will become major powers and how this will create friction with the United States. Looking at both history and the likely conditions at the time, I've tried to imagine how the Japanese will look at the board—what they will be worried about and how they might respond. The details are obviously unknown. But I am trying here to give a sense of how geopolitics, technology, and warfare might play out. I can't possibly know the details of this war, or even its timing. But I can lay out some of the principles and imagine some of the details.

The Japanese will already have established multiple lunar bases, but one of them will be designed for military uses with a civilian cover. In deep caverns secretly hollowed out, the Japanese will create a series of projectiles simply built out of lunar rock. Rocks are very heavy for their volume. Something the size of a compact car can weigh tons. At extremely high speeds, the kinetic energy of a rock can be fantastic, tearing apart large structures it might hit. In the airless moon, without friction or aerodynamic issues, it can be very roughly shaped. Rockets and fuel tanks can be readily attached to the rock and launched.

These projectiles will be designed to have two characteristics: heavy enough to destroy any Battle Star with kinetic energy but small enough to be boosted into orbit using rockets, taking advantage of the lower escape velocity of the moon relative to the earth. Given the speeds at which the mis-sile will impact the Battle Star, a few pounds will suffice. But it also will have to survive impacts with much smaller kinetic defensive missiles.

The Japanese will build another secret base, carefully camouflaged on the far side of the moon, which they will use to test the system, firing away from earth and shielded from its view. The system will be perfected over time, slowly so that traffic to the base, if noticed, will not raise undue con-cern. Underground launchers will be prepared and camouflaged. As the Bat-tle Stars become operational, so will the Japanese countermeasures. The Japanese know that any one missile could be destroyed, so they will prepare dozens of missiles to be fired at each Battle Star platform, in the hope that one will get through. And they will prepare to fire them in a wide range of orbits, hoping not to be noticed. No matter how advanced technology be-comes, there is never enough budget or personnel to keep watch on every-thing.

Not being noticed will be important. It will take about three days for the missiles launched from the moon to hit the Battle Stars. The time between the detection of the attack and the destruction of the Battle Star will be the period of greatest danger to Japanese plans. Once the missiles are detected, even though the Battle Star might not survive itself, it could order strikes against Japan with hypersonic systems and fire its own projectiles in a dev-astating attack on Japan and its space assets, while still leaving the Battle Star crew time to abandon ship in escape craft. The key will thus be to take out the Battle Star without any warning, blinding the United States.

That will not be something that can be guaranteed to succeed. The Japanese will have to have a Plan B. Once they fire their rockets successfully, the destruction of the Battle Stars will be assured. But between the time of discovery and destruction, disaster will be possible. The Japanese will have one advantage. The Battle Stars will be focused on the earth and the area be-tween the earth and geostationary orbit. Their primary mission will be of-fensive, and they won't see themselves in a defensive role. More important, the Battle Stars will not expect a threat from behind. If the Battle Stars think they are going to be hit, they will be expecting it from below. They won't conduct routine observations at higher altitudes.

The Americans will maintain a simple—and not particularly effective—

meteor watch, an obvious necessity for a manned space platform. Space is vast and, contrary to what you might imagine, complete coverage of space is impossible today and won't be possible in 2050. There will be gaps, in both technology and application. Knowing this, the Japanese will launch not a tight cluster of missiles, but rather a spread, coming from all directions. The watch radar might pick up one or two but would not interpret them as an attack. In fact, the Japanese will select orbits that will not be aimed at any of the Battle Stars; rather, the missiles will be equipped to do a terminal rocket burn to shift orbits in the last hours of their journeys in order to impact the stations—the fuel container and engine for the burn will be larger than the actual missile, really no more than a small, shaped rock. Any computer detecting a missile will read it as a meteorite that won't threaten anything—close but not a danger. The computerized systems might not even report the missiles they see to human monitors on the Battle Star. The system will be robotic, not given to subtlety.

There will be three dangers for the Japanese. The first will be that the United States will detect the launch from the lunar surface using technology the Japanese didn't know it had. Detection will also be possible in the period after launch and before terminal adjustment of orbit, which will last several days. And in the final few hours before impact, the United States could still retaliate. The later it detects the attack, the less time it will have to react, and the more devastating the strike.

The Japanese Plan B in case of detection will be to speed up phase two of the attack. If they take out the Battle Stars, the Japanese will then launch immediate hypersonic attacks against U.S. air and missile bases around the world, American submarines being tracked by the Japanese space-based system, as well as against all ground-based communications. In the event of detection, the Japanese would execute the follow-up plan before the Battle Stars are destroyed, in a desperate shot from the hip, hoping the Americans will be slow to respond. They will assume that they can tell if the Americans have detected the attack because detection will dramatically increase communication traffic between Battle Stars, ground command, and other platforms. The Japanese might not be able to break the codes, but they will see the surge in traffic. They will have orbited satellites for years with official reasons from navigation to weather but with another, secret purpose: intercepting and gauging the quantity of communications among U.S. space-based systems.

The Japanese will not share the details of their attack plans with the Turks. The secret lunar bases will represent the crown jewels of the Japanese military. The Turks will be allies, but not family. What they will be prepared to tell the Turks is that on a certain date the Japanese will commence hostilities, and that they will plan a devastating strike against the United States with which they will need no direct assistance. They will, however, need some indirect assistance.

The Japanese will want to tilt the table a bit more by giving U.S. intelligence and reconnaissance something to look at—something to keep them distracted. The Japanese will plan to attack over the American Thanksgiving holiday, when the American political leadership will be scattered around the country with family. This is in keeping with both the military principle of strategic surprise and Japan's application of this in prior wars: the attack at Pearl Harbor happened at dawn on a Sunday, when the fleet was in and the crews had been out partying on Saturday night. Obviously, it doesn't have to be Thanksgiving, but it has to be an unexpected time when U.S. leadership is not at its full strength. Just as North Korea attacked South Korea on a summer Sunday in 1950, causing massive confusion, the Japanese might attack on Thanksgiving, a very likely time to hit. The Japanese and Turks will do everything they can to keep the weeks prior calm, making sure that the American leadership disperses and the ground-based military is operating on minimal staffing.

The Japanese will know that the best way to accomplish this will be to stage a crisis and quickly settle it. Without giving away the nature of the Thanksgiving surprise, they will arrange for the Turks to generate a carefully planned crisis between their forces in Bosnia and Polish forces in Croatia. The crisis will begin in mid-October, with the claim that Croatian nationalists have carried out terrorist strikes in Turkey. The Turks will even hint that this was done with U.S. encouragement. Now, obviously we can't know that it will be this crisis in this place, but a system of deception is critical. The Japanese kept negotiations going with the United States until the last minute in 1941. The Vietnamese Tet Offensive occurred during a holiday cease-fire in 1968, and so on. Deception is the key.

A crisis will ensue, with the Polish bloc and the Turks coming to full alert. With U.S. forces in Serbia and the United States allied with the Polish bloc, the Balkan situation will directly impact the United States. The Turks will keep bringing their air and missile systems outside the region to full alert, just short of launch, and then bringing them down. They will deliberately try to trigger a Polish strike. Knowing that the Polish and U.S. defense networks are linked, and having mapped out American sensitivity to Turkish readiness over the years, the Turks will push just past what appears to be the point of no return in the first week of November. The Poles, receiving data indicating an imminent launch, suddenly will conduct a limited air strike against a Turkish base. The Turks will have succeeded in sucking in the Poles and will begin to cycle up their entire system. Realizing that a Balkan war is about to break out, the American president will call the Turkish and Polish prime ministers within moments of the strike and warn both to stand down. The Turks will be particularly belligerent, having lost an air base and some people, but will reluctantly agree to move back from the brink of war.

A peace conference will be organized in Geneva; where else would one hold a peace conference? No settlement will be reached, but all sides will agree to stand down and avoid provocative acts. The United States will commit itself to monitoring the situation—a commitment it will take seriously, as it won't want the Poles or Hungarians dragging it into a Balkan war. The national security advisor will order U.S. space surveillance to concentrate on the status of Turkish and Polish bloc forces. Things will calm down by mid-November, and the situation will seem to be returning to normal, but the Battle Star over Uganda will remain heavily focused on the Balkan situation, while the other two will be handling spillover work from its collectors. The Turks will continue to maneuver their forces well behind the lines, as will the Polish bloc. That will keep everyone busy.

The Japanese will have been cycling up their hypersonic forces and space capabilities at least once a quarter for several years. The United States will be watching these exercises regularly and therefore won't be particularly alarmed to see another exercise kicking off a few days before Thanksgiving. It will be nothing out of the ordinary to see the Japanese go to full battle alert. In fact, this time Japan will seem somewhat undermanned, with some units not even cycling to alert.

CHAPTER 11

WORLD WAR

A SCENARIO

Thus far I've been doing geopolitical forecasting. I've been working with the major themes that are unfolding in the twenty-first century and thinking about how they would affect international relations. In this chapter, I will change my approach a bit. I want to describe a war that I think will take place in the middle of the twenty-first century. Obviously I don't know when it will happen with any precision, but I can provide a sense of what a twenty-first-century war might look like. You can't imagine the twentieth century without some idea of what World Wars I and II were like, nor can you really get a sense of the twenty-first century until you've described war.

War is different from what I've been talking about so far because war is a matter of detail. Without this, you miss its essence. To understand war, you need to understand more than the reasons a war was fought. You need to think about technology, culture, and other matters, all of them in detail. So, for example, in talking about World War II we have to discuss Pearl Harbor. Pearl Harbor was, geopolitically, an attempt to buy time while Japan seized Southeast Asia and the Netherlands East Indies. But to really understand the reality of Pearl Harbor, you have to understand the details—the use of aircraft carriers, the invention of a torpedo that would work in the shallow waters of Pearl Harbor, and the decision to attack on Sunday morning.

What I've tried to show in previous chapters is how the United States, Poland, Turkey, and Japan will get entangled in the next century, and why the Japanese and the Turks will feel so threatened that they will have no choice but to launch a preemptive war. This is a book about my perception of the events of the next hundred years, so I now want to talk about the war itself. To do that, however, I have to pretend to know more than I do. I have to pretend to know the times and dates of the battles and precisely how they would be executed. I do think I understand the military technology that will be used in this war. I think I have a rough idea of when in the century the war will take place, and I think I have a good grasp of how it will play out. But I don't think you can grasp the nature of war in the mid-twenty-first century unless I go further and tell a story that in some sense I have no right to. But if you will indulge me on this, I think I can give you a *feel* for the warfare of the twenty-first century—and this particular war—if I take some license and give it real specificity.

OPENING SHOTS

The destruction of the three Battle Stars will be planned for November 24, 2050, at 5 p.m. At this time on Thanksgiving Day most people in the United States would be watching football and napping after digesting a massive meal. Some people will be driving home. No one in Washington will be expecting a problem. That is the moment that the Japanese will intend to strike. Final course corrections of the missiles targeting the Battle Stars will begin to be executed at about noon, on the theory that even if they were detected, getting hold of the Washington national security team would eat up an hour or two, and that if the missiles were detected by 3 or 4 p.m. it would be impossible to react in time. In order to do this, launches from Japan's lunar base will have to take place at various times on November 21, depending on orbit. Hence, the November 20 alert will be Plan B cycling up—the aforementioned shot from the hip.

The launches from the moon will go unnoticed. Many of the missiles will actually be detected by automated systems on board the Battle Stars, but none will have trajectories that indicate impact with the stations or represent a significant threat to earth. They will all be fired at different times in eccentric orbits. The data will not be passed on to human monitors. One technician reading the daily summary on the second day will note that there appears to be a large number of meteors in the area, with several passing close to his station, but since this is not an extraordinary event, he will ignore it.

On November 24 around noon, the rockets will reignite as planned, shifting the missiles' orbit. The collision-tracking radar on Battle Star–Uganda will pick up a single warning at about 2 p.m. The computer will be asked to reconfirm the trajectory. In the next hour all three stations will pick up multiple projectiles on trajectory to strike each of them. The commanding general of the three platforms, on board Battle Star–Peru, will recognize at about 3:15 that his platforms are under organized attack. He will then notify Space Command Headquarters in Colorado Springs, which in turn will notify the Joint Chiefs and the National Security Council.

Meanwhile, the commanding general on Battle Star–Peru will, on his own authority, begin firing lasers and kinetic missiles at the targets, hoping to intercept them. But the number of incoming missiles will strain his capacity to engage, as the system won't be designed to cope with fifteen simultaneous incoming missiles. He will quickly realize that there will be leakage, and that some of the missiles will hit.

The president will be notified, but, it being Thanksgiving Day, he won't be able to immediately gather most of his advisors. The questions the president will ask are the crucial ones: Who launched the attack? Where was it launched from? No one will be able to answer the questions immediately. The assumption will be that it is the Turks, since they will have been engaged in the most recent crisis, but U.S. intelligence will be certain that they won't have the ability to launch such an attack. The Japanese will be quiet—and no one would have expected such a strike by Japan. As more advisors gather, two things will be apparent: no one knows who launched the attack, and the Battle Stars are about to be destroyed.

The Japanese will inform the Turks as to what has happened at approximately 4:30 p.m. The Turks are Japan's allies, but the Japanese are not going to give them detailed information until the last moment, as they won't want the Turks to double-cross them. But the Turks will know that something is coming—the entire charade of early November will revolve around this, and they will be standing by to act as soon as the Japanese get around to alerting them.

Less than thirty minutes before impact, the president will authorize the evacuation of the Battle Stars. With so little time, the evacuation won't be able to be fully executed. Hundreds of people will be left behind. More important, even though no one will know who ordered the attack, the president's advisors will convince him to order a dispersal of all ground-based hypersonic aircraft from their primary bases to scattered locations. That order will go out at the same time the evacuation order goes out. There will be many glitches in the system. Controllers—skeleton staffs, really—will keep asking for confirmation. Some of the aircraft will disperse over the next hour. Most will not.

At 5 p.m., all three Battle Stars will explode, killing all of the remaining crew members and knocking out the rest of the U.S. space force—sensors and satellites that are mostly hooked into the Battle Star–Peru command center. They will be left uselessly orbiting in space. The Japanese will have launched satellites years earlier whose only job is to monitor the Battle Stars. They will note the disruption of communication from the stations, and Japanese radar will note the destruction of the stations themselves.

The Japanese will activate phase two as soon as destruction is confirmed. They will launch thousands of unmanned hypersonic aircraft—small, fast, and agile to evade interceptors—at the United States and its ships and bases in the Pacific. The targets will be U.S. hypersonic aircraft, ground-based anti-aircraft missiles, and command and control centers. They won't go after population centers. That would achieve nothing, plus the Japanese will want to negotiate a settlement, which would be inconceivable after massive civilian casualties. Nor will they want to destroy the president or his staff. They will need someone with whom to negotiate.

At the same time, the Turks will launch their own attacks against targets they will have been assigned in joint planning for war with the Japanese over the years. Joint contingency plans will already have been developed between the two countries. Given that the Turks are aware something is coming, and are in near-crisis mode already, they won't need extensive preparation to execute the war plan. The Japanese will communicate what they have done—and Turkish sensors will observe the events in geosynchronous orbit. They will move to quickly take advantage of the situation. Many targets will be in the United States, east of the Mississippi, but the Turks will also launch a massive attack against the Polish bloc and against India, not a major power but allied with the United States. The intention of the Coalition will be to leave the United States and its allies militarily helpless.

Within a few minutes, the missiles from the unmanned aircraft will begin to hit U.S. forces in Europe and Asia, but those targeted at the United States proper will take nearly an hour to reach their targets. That hour will bring the United States some valuable time. Most of its space-based sensors will be off-line, but an old system, used to detect the heat of ICBM launches and too old to be linked into the Battle Star system, will still be downloading to Colorado Springs. It will pick up a vast array of launches out of Japan and Turkey, but little additional information will be provided. There will be no way to tell where the planes and missiles are going. But the fact that the two countries lit up with launches minutes after the Battle Stars are killed will be relayed to the president, who now, at least, will know where the attack is coming from.

The United States will maintain a database of military targets in Japan and Turkey. The Japanese and Turkish aircraft will already have been launched, and therefore hitting those targets will make no sense. But there will be fixed targets in both countries, primarily command and control centers, airfields, fuel bunkers, and so on, that could be attacked. Plus the president will want his hypersonic fleet in the air and not on the tarmac. He will order a preset war plan to be activated. However, by the time the orders are transmitted and flight controllers are in place, there will be less than fifteen minutes until Japan and Turkey hit their targets. Some flights will take off and strike those two countries, but much of the force will be destroyed on the ground.

The devastation to the Polish bloc will be even more intense. The bloc command center in Warsaw won't be aware of the destruction of the Battle

Stars, so it won't have the warning the United States will have before missiles start hitting its bases. In fact, hypersonic aircraft will be dropping precision-guided munitions on bloc facilities with literally no warning at all. One moment they will be there, and suddenly the bloc's strike capability will be gone.

By 7 p.m., the U.S. space and hypersonic force will be devastated. The United States will have lost command of space and have only a few hundred aircraft left. Its allies in Europe will have had their forces overwhelmed. U.S. warships around the world will have been attacked and sunk. The Indians will have lost their assets as well. The American coalition will be militarily devastated.

COUNTERSTRIKE

At the same time, American society will be intact, as will be that of many U.S. allies. This is the underlying weakness of the Coalition strategy. The United States is a nuclear power—as, for that matter, will be Japan, Turkey, Poland, and India. Attacks on military targets will not trigger a nuclear response. However, if the Coalition would try to force capitulation by beginning to go beyond military targets and move to trying to attack the American population itself, the threshold at which the Americans, or their allies, might go nuclear could be reached. Since the Coalition will be looking not for mutual annihilation but for a political settlement that the Americans in particular could live with, and since the Americans are often profoundly unpredictable, using their hypersonic forces to start inflicting damage and casualties on American civilians would be incredibly dangerous. The possession of nuclear weapons will shape war to this extent. It circumscribes the degree of the conflict.

Nevertheless, the United States will be militarily damaged and won't know how far the Coalition will go. The Coalition's hope will be that when the degree of damage is recognized by the United States, together with the unpredictability of the Coalition, it will opt for a political settlement that would include accepting Turkish and Japanese spheres of influence, defining limits to America's sphere of influence, and introducing a workable, verifiable framework for limiting conflict in space. In other words, the Coalition will wager that the United States will realize that it is now one great power among several instead of the only superpower, and accept a generous and secure sphere of influence of its own. And it will hope that the suddenness and effectiveness of the assault in space will cause the United States to overestimate the Coalition's military power.

The United States will in fact overestimate the Coalition's military power, but that will generate the opposite response from what the Coalition hopes. The Americans won't see themselves as engaged in a limited war in which the enemy has limited and definable political goals that the United States can live with. Rather, the Americans will believe that the Coalition's forces are vastly greater than they really are, and that the United States faces the possibility, if not of annihilation, then of a massive reduction of power and heightened vulnerability to further attacks by the Coalition and other powers. The United States will see this as an existential threat.

The United States will react viscerally and emotionally to the attack. If it accepts the political settlement that has been transmitted to it on the evening of November 24, the country's long-term future becomes uncertain. Turkey and Japan—countries unlikely to fight each other—would between them dominate Eurasia. There would be two hegemons, not one, but if they were to cooperate, Eurasia would be united and exploited systematically. The ultimate nightmare of American grand strategy would be real, and over time the Coalition members—not easily manipulable into war with each other—would usurp command of space and the sea. Agreeing to the Coalition's offer would end the immediate war but would also initiate a long American decline. But this will not be carefully thought out that night. Just as it did after the sinking of the *Maine*, the attack on Pearl Harbor, and the shock of 9/11, the United States will go into a rage. It will reject the terms and go to war.

The United States won't make a move while Coalition reconnaissance spacecraft are in place. The Coalition won't have anything to equal the complex American Battle Star system that has been destroyed, but it will have an array of last-generation satellites that provide real-time intelligence on the United States. While they are operational, the Coalition will be able to see and counter any moves made by the Americans. The American reconnaissance system will quickly have to be re-architected so that remaining satellites—of which there will be many—will downlink to earth rather than to the destroyed Battle Stars. That will allow the United States to begin tracking enemy movements—and to strike back. When that happens, the first thing it will have to do is knock out any space launch facilities the Coalition might have, so as to keep it from launching any new space systems.

Japanese intelligence on U.S. assets, while not perfect, will be superb. The United States will have deliberately placed launch platforms for rockets in a variety of secret locations, carefully camouflaged. It will be one of the major black projects during the 2030s. By the time the Japanese begin surveillance on the United States, the sites will have been constructed—and hidden—for a long time. The secret launch facilities will not be manned during peacetime. Moving personnel to the sites without detection will take several days, during which time the United States will send diplomatic feelers through the Germans, who will be neutral, about negotiations. The United States will be trying to buy time. The negotiations will be a cover for planning and implementing a counterstrike.

The United States will be trying to even the playing field a bit with what assets it still has. To do that, it will need to blind the Coalition, taking out its space-based system (the United States will have stored hundreds of anti-satellite missiles and high-energy lasers at its secret reserve sites). Crews will move into place, carefully so as not to give away locations to reconnaissance satellites. While the Coalition will be eagerly engaged in negotiations with the United States, the sites will be readied. About seventy-two hours later, the United States will destroy the bulk of the Coalition's surveillance capability in a period of less than two hours. The Coalition won't be blind, but it will be close to it.

As soon as the satellites are destroyed, some of the United States' surviving hypersonic aircraft will initiate attacks on Japanese and Turkish launch facilities, hoping to make it impossible for them to launch new satellites or attack the remaining U.S. satellites. Unlike the Japanese, the Americans will have an excellent idea of the location of Japanese launches based on past reconnaissance. The United States, following the end of the second cold war, always had a massive advantage in reconnaissance capability. The United States' map of the Coalition will be much better than the Coalition's map of the United States. The aircraft will hit them all. Shortly thereafter, U.S. satellite controllers will begin capturing signals from surviving American satellites. The Coalition will now be the ones blinded. The Japanese intelligence failure about America's black anti-satellite capability will prove their undoing.

NEW TECHNOLOGIES, OLD WAR

The Coalition members will realize their original plan has failed. They will not be certain how well the United States can see, but they will know that it can't see all that well. Most disturbing, their belief that the entire U.S. air fleet was annihilated will be proven wrong, and they will know that the United States still has the capacity to strike them. They can't know that these are only the remnants of the force that was dispersed in the time between the detection of the attack on the Battle Stars and the Coalition air strike. They won't know how deep American reserves are, and they will have no way to find out. The fog of war will be as thick in the twenty-first century as in the past.

The United States will make one additional move. Engineers will analyze data to show the origination point of the missiles that took out the Battle Stars, and the military then will launch a missile at the site and the base will be destroyed. The United States will also order military forces it will have quietly built up at its own experimental stations on the moon to prepare and execute attacks on all Japanese bases on the moon. The United States will make sure it is not surprised again.

As frequently happens in war, once the initial attack, planned over years, is executed, everyone starts to improvise, working from uncertainty. And most war plans anticipate that a war will be over quickly. It rarely is. This war will continue, divided into three parts.

First, having reestablished a tenuous command of space, the United States will put in place a crash program to increase its hold and keep the Coalition out. The United States will gradually, over the next year, increase its surveillance capability until it equals preattack levels. The pace of research, development, and deployment in a time of war is extraordinary compared to peacetime. Within a year of Thanksgiving Day, the United States will have technologically exceeded the space-based capabilities that were destroyed.

Second, the United States will move to recover its hypersonic fleet in the face of continual air attacks on known fixed production facilities by Coalition aircraft. But the Coalition will not have the ability to maintain adequate surveillance over the United States, and despite some setbacks the plants will quickly be in operation, building new hypersonic aircraft.

Third, the Coalition will use the period before the United States reconstructs its forces to impose a new reality on the ground. The Japanese will try to seize other areas in China and Asia but will be far less aggressive than Turkey, which will see the period of U.S. preoccupation as a chance to deal with the Polish bloc and position itself as the decisive power in the region.

The war will have begun with a head fake toward the Polish bloc. Now it will become a concerted assault by Turkey on the ground, supported by its aerial capabilities. The elimination of the Polish bloc would give Turkey a free hand everywhere. Therefore, rather than dissipating its strength in North Africa or Russia, the Turks will bet it all on attacking north, out of Bosnia into the Balkans.

The key weapon will be the armored infantryman—a single soldier, encased in a powered suit that is able to lift substantial amounts of weight and protects the soldier from harm. The suit will also allow him to move rapidly. Think of him as a one-man tank, only more lethal. He will be supported by many armored systems, carrying supplies and power packs. The power pack will be critical. The systems will all be electrically powered and driven by advanced electrical storage units—batteries with a lot of power and life in them. But however advanced, they need to be recharged. That means that access to electrical grids will be the single most important thing in warfare—along with the electrical power plants pushing electricity through the grids. Electricity will be to war in the twenty-first century as petroleum was to war in the twentieth century.

Turkey's goal will be to draw the Polish bloc forces into a battle of annihilation. Unlike the fighting with the United States, this will be planned as a combined arms operation, including armored infantrymen, robotic logis-

Turkish Sphere of Influence 2050

tics and weapons platforms, and the now ubiquitous hypersonic aircraft serving as precision artillery.

Following the devastating opening strikes, the Polish bloc will seek to avoid concentrating its ground forces in order to evade air strikes. The Turks will want to pressure them to concentrate their forces by attacking in a way that will compel them to defend major targets or, alternatively, rip the bloc apart when the Poles refuse to commit their forces for such defense.

The Turks will attack north out of Bosnia into the Croatian plains, and into Hungary, where the country is open, flat, and lacking in natural barriers. They will drive on to Budapest, although their ultimate military goal will be the Carpathian Mountains in Slovakia, Ukraine, and Romania. If they take the Carpathians, Romania and Bulgaria will be isolated and collapse, turning the Black Sea into a Turkish lake. Hungary will be occupied, and Poland isolated and facing a threat from the south. If, however, the Poles decide to concentrate on the Hungarian plain to protect Budapest, and therefore attempt to hold the bloc together, Turkish airpower would likely destroy the bloc's forces.

The Poles will request American air support so they can engage Turkish forces as they advance into Croatia, but the United States will have no airpower to give them. The Turks, as a result, will capture Hungary in a matter of weeks and occupy the Carpathians soon after. The Romanians, isolated, will ask for and receive an armistice. Southeastern Europe, to the Polish border and Ukraine, will be in Turkish hands. All that will remain will be Poland.

Turkish forces will proceed toward Krakow, with air strikes ripping apart the Polish military. The United States will become concerned that the Poles will be unable to resist and may be forced to sue for peace. The U.S. strategy will be to buy time to rebuild its strategic assets and then launch a sudden global strike on Turkey and Japan. The United States will not want to dissipate its strength to support tactical combat in southern Poland. At the same time, it will not be able to risk losing its Polish ally, as that will end the game against Turkey. In order to get the Poles to carry on, the United States will have to seriously harm the Turks.

In February 2051, the United States will launch a substantial portion of its remaining air force, including some new aircraft with advanced capabilities, striking at Turkish forces everywhere from southern Poland to logistics centers back in Bosnia and farther south. It will take serious losses from the Turkish air force, but the Turkish army will suffer serious losses as hundreds of armored infantrymen are killed along with the destruction of large numbers of robotic systems and supplies. Turkey will be far from crippled, but it will be hurt.

The Turks will soon realize that there is no chance of their winning the war. Their inability to reenter space, plus the Americans' ability to create a new air force quickly, would, in time, defeat them. They also will realize that the Japanese won't be in a position to help them because they will be tied down with their own problems in China. The great gamble will fail, and with that failure it will be every man for himself. The United States will be clearly focusing on Turkey before Japan, so Turkey will need to knock Poland out of the war fast. But Turkish ground forces will by then be spread around a vast empire. Concentrating on Poland will mean stripping forces from elsewhere, and that will, in the long run, not be a viable option. The Turks would be deeply exposed to rebellion from Egypt to Central Asia.

Before the beginning of the war, the Coalition will have wanted Germany to join in the attack on Poland, but the Germans will have declined. This time when the Turks approach them, they will offer quite a prize. In return for helping Turkey in Poland, Turkey will retreat into the Balkans after the war, retaining only Romania and Ukraine. Turkey will build its power around the Black Sea, the Adriatic, and the Mediterranean, and the Germans will have a free hand from Hungary north, including Poland, the Baltics, and Belarus.

From the German point of view, what had been a Turkish pipe dream before 2050 will now be a very practical proposal. The Turks would be a Mediterranean and Black Sea power and would need the Balkans to secure their hold. The Turks would have no interest north of there, as such involvement would soak up forces needed in these areas. The Germans, like the Poles and Russians, will be exposed on the northern European plain, and this new arrangement would secure their eastern flank. Most important, this arrangement would reverse the trend that had been running against Germany and Western Europe since the collapse of Russia. The Eastern Europeans would finally be put back in their place.

The Germans will know that the Americans will eventually refocus on the region, but it will take the Americans a while to come back. There will be a genuine window of opportunity for the Germans to seize. Self-absorbed and risk averse, they won't be as adventurous as the Turks. But the alternative will be a Turkish force to their east or, worse, the defeat of the Turks and an even more powerful Polish and American force facing them. The Germans will not be risk takers in general, but this is a risk they will have to take. They will mobilize their forces, including their older but still capable air force, and strike the Poles from the west in late spring of 2051, while the Turks will relaunch their attack from the south. The Germans will recruit the French and a handful of other countries into the exercise, but their participation will be more political than military.

Britain, on the other hand, will be appalled at what is happening. Even though there will be a giant game of global power politics going on, the British will still be deeply concerned with the local balance of power. They will once again be facing the possibility of a German-dominated continent, however awkwardly achieved by Germany and however dependent on Turkish underpinnings. The British will recognize that if this happens, any neglect toward Europe on the part of the United States, any cyclical retreat into isolation, could mean catastrophe. Britain will have had no intention of getting involved in this war. But at this point it will have no choice, and it could bring something valuable to the table: a small, intact air force that, when coupled with U.S. intelligence, could seriously damage the Germans and the Turks. In addition, its advanced air defenses to protect against Turkish and German air strikes will make Britain a secure base of operations. Britain will appear to hold back, while stealthily redeploying a substantial portion of its air force to the United States, where air defenses and warning time will be even greater.

In the end, Poland will be attacked on two sides, from the west and south. The attacking forces will advance geographically as invaders have before, but the technology will be quite different. It won't be the massed infantry of Napoleon or the armored formations of Hitler; the force that will attack will be quite small in terms of actual troops. The human force will consist of armored infantrymen, fanned out as infantrymen usually are, but with clear and overlapping fields of fire—and these fields now will measure dozens of miles. Linked together by computer networks, they will command not only the weapons they carry but also robotic systems and hypersonic aircraft thousands of miles away that they can call on as needed.

The robotic systems will live on data and power. Cut off either, and they would be helpless. They need a constant stream of information and instructions. They also need a steady flow of power to keep them going. Since the space-based systems of the Turks are gone, the Turks will substitute unmanned aerial vehicles hovering, swooping, and flying around the battle space to give them information. The information will always be incomplete, as the UAVs will constantly be shot down. The United States will have much better data but will lack the air force to decimate the attackers.

Providing enough power for the infantrymen's armored suits and robots will also be a problem. These suits will be electrically driven and will need to be recharged or have their massive batteries swapped out every day or so. Tremendous advances will have been made in the storage of electrical power, but in the end the batteries will still run out. A key resource, therefore, will be the electrical power grid tied to electrical generation plants. Destroy the power generation plants, and the attackers will have to ship in massive, charged batteries from wherever there is power and then distribute them around the battlefield. The farther the troops advance, the longer the supply line will become. If the defenders are prepared to shut down their own power grid and, when necessary, destroy their power plants—a scorched-earth strategy—the attack would be slowed by lack of power. Everything will depend on the tactical delivery of electricity.

At a secret meeting of American, British, Chinese, and Polish commanders, a strategy will be worked out: the Poles will resist, and slowly retreat under the pressure of the Coalition forces. The two geographic thrusts, one from the west and one from the south, will converge on Warsaw. It will be agreed that the Poles will resist, fall back, and regroup endlessly, buying as much time as possible for the allies to rebuild their air forces. The Poles will be reinforced by several thousand American troops flown over the North Pole to St. Petersburg and deployed with the Polish troops in their delaying action. As the situation becomes more desperate, in late 2051, available airpower in Britain will begin to be released to further slow the advancing Turkish armies. The Herculean American industrial effort will be under way, as thousands of advanced hypersonic aircraft are built, capable of traveling twice as fast as prewar systems, and with a payload double in size. By mid-2052, the American force will be available for a massed and devastating strike that, when coupled with major improvements in space-based systems, will devastate Coalition forces worldwide. Until then, the rule will be hold, retreat, and buy time.

The Coalition will massively underestimate U.S. industrial capacity. It will think it has several years to battle the Polish forces. At first, the Coalition will choose not to attack Polish electrical generation systems, not wanting to have to rebuild them after the war and needing their power to fight after they've captured them. The Poles, on the other hand, will destroy their grids as they retreat, wanting to complicate the Coalition advance and forcing the Germans and the Turks to divert resources to shipping heavy electrical storage units to the battlefield. Those lines of supply are exactly what will be most vulnerable when the counterattack comes in the summer of 2052.

When the American armored infantrymen arrive on the battlefield, with their sophisticated, space-linked systems, the Coalition will realize that Poland is not going to fall quickly. The Coalition will also see that the electrical generation plants are the foundation of allied power and that unless they are taken out—and the Americans reduced to shipping electrical storage units to the battlefield from their own country—the United States will be victorious. Therefore, in the summer of 2051, the Coalition will begin to destroy the Polish electrical system, hitting plants as far east as Belarus. Poland will go black.

The Coalition will wait for two weeks, forcing the United States and its allies (the Alliance) into continual combat to make them use up available electricity. Then they will attack on all fronts simultaneously, expecting Polish and American troops to be out of power and out of luck. Instead, they will not only meet intense resistance but also find that the U.S. troops are calling in air strikes that are devastating Coalition lines. Allied command will send British air forces into combat, and the superbly coordinated space-based reconnaissance systems—coupled with a new, more sophisticated Battle Star management system—will identify, target, and destroy the German and Turkish armored infantry.

It will turn out the United States will have learned not to put all its eggs in one basket militarily, particularly in terms of space-based systems. Before the war begins, the United States will have another Battle Star—a next-generation system—built but not yet launched due to a lack of funds. Congressional inaction will for once be a godsend. The station will be secret, and on the ground. It will be launched into space just months after the surprise attack and the destruction of Japan's lunar base. The jury-rigged architecture created immediately after the war began will be replaced by one centered around the new Battle Star, stationed near Uganda but capable of rapid maneuver to new points along the equator as needed, as well as tactical maneuvering to avoid attacks such as those that destroyed its three predecessors. The United States will restore its command of space—to a degree that will far surpass its space dominance of several years before.

The Turks and Germans will be stunned by one thing. Having decided to destroy Polish electrical generation and distribution, they will expect resistance to weaken dramatically, as their own forces run out of juice. Yet the Polish and American armored infantry will be going full blast. It will seem impossible that the Americans are flying in enough batteries to maintain the troops. The question will be, where is the power coming from?

The Japanese won't be the only ones experimenting with the commercial uses of space. During the first half of the century, a consortium of American entrepreneurs will have spent a great deal of money both developing the inexpensive, plentiful launchers the Americans will be using and trying their hand at electrical generation in space, beaming energy to earth in microwave form, then reconverting it to usable electricity. As the U.S. military commanders game out the problem of defending Poland, they will understand from endless war games that the problem will be maintaining electrical power. When the Turks take only a few weeks to overrun southeastern Europe, the United States will realize that defeating them depends on the supply of electrical power to Alliance forces and the destruction of Coalition electrical supplies. The key to victory will be keeping Poland supplied with electricity.

The core technology will have been developed. The space launchers will be able to be built quickly, as will the solar panels and microwave beaming systems. The real challenge will be to get the receivers built and out to the field, but once again, with unlimited budget and motivation, the Americans will be able to perform miracles. Unknown to the Coalition, the new Battle Star will have been designed for two purposes: battle management and managing the construction and operation of enormous arrays of solar panels and their microwave radiation systems. Mobile receivers will have been delivered to the battlefield.

When the switch is flipped, thousands of receivers on the Polish side of the front will begin receiving microwave radiation from space and converting it to electricity. In a way this will be like cell phones replacing landlines. The entire architecture of power will change. That will be important later.

For now, it will mean that the resistance facing the Turks will not decline, as their enemies inexplicably will have far more electricity than Turkey expected.

The Coalition won't be able to take out the power generation system in space or identify the microwave receiving stations. There will be too many solar panels in too many different places, and they will be moving around. Even if they could be taken out, they would be replaced faster than they could be destroyed, given the Coalition's capabilities.

The Coalition won't be able to break the Polish-American force through logistics. The defenders will survive because the Coalition will have inadequate reconnaissance, having lost its satellites early. Now, its command of the air will slip as well, as the smaller Allied air forces will have enormously better intelligence—and will therefore be infinitely more effective.

END GAME

There will be a stalemate on the ground until the summer of 2052, when the United States finally will unleash its new, massive air forces. Combined with Battle Star intelligence and weapons, the U.S. air forces will devastate Coalition forces in Poland and smash their power generation system. The Americans will do the same against Japanese troops fighting in China. Further, they will target Japanese surface vessels.

The counterstrike will stagger the Japanese and the Turks and leave the Germans in a complete shambles. Their ground forces will nearly evaporate on the battlefield. But now the Americans will face the nuclear problem. If the Coalition powers are pushed to the point where they believe that their national sovereignty, let alone national survival, is at stake, they might well consider the use of nuclear weapons.

The United States will not demand unconditional surrender any more than it can give it. It will not threaten national survival, nor ultimately will it have intended to. The United States will have learned over the past fifty years that the devastation of the enemy, no matter how satisfying, is not the best strategy. Its goal will be to maintain the balance of power, to keep regional powers focused on each other and not the United States.

The United States won't want to destroy Japan. Rather, it will want to maintain a balance of power between Japan, Korea, and China. Similarly, it will want not to destroy Turkey or create chaos in the Islamic world, but only to maintain a balance of power between the Polish bloc and Turkey. The Poles and the Polish bloc will scream for Turkish blood, as will the Chinese and Koreans for that of the Japanese. But the United States will pull a Woodrow Wilson at Versailles. In the name of all that is humane, it will make certain that Eurasia remains chaotic.

At a hastily organized peace conference, Turkey will be forced to retreat south in the Balkans, leaving Croatia and Serbia as a buffer zone and pulling back toward, but not into, the Caucasus. In Central Asia, Turkey will have to accept a Chinese presence. The Japanese will have to pull all forces out of China, and the United States will transfer defense technology to the Chinese. The precise terms will be actually quite vague, which will be exactly how the Americans want it. Lots of new nations will be carved out. Lots of boundaries and spheres of influence will be ambiguous. The victors won't quite win and the losers won't quite lose. The United States will have taken a major step toward civilization.

In the meantime, the United States will have total command of space, an economy booming as a result of defense spending, and a new, advanced power generation system that will begin to transform the way humans receive power.

In the mid-twentieth century, World War II cost perhaps fifty million lives. A hundred years later, the first space war will take perhaps 50,000 lives, the majority of these in Europe during the Turkish-German ground offensive, and others in China. The United States itself will lose a few thousand people, many in space, some during the initial air strikes on the United States, and some in fighting to support the Poles. It will be a world war in the truest sense of the word, but given the technological advances in precision and speed, it won't be total war—societies trying to annihilate societies.

This war will, however, have one thing in common with World War II. In the end, the United States—having lost the least—will have gained the most. Just as it roared out of World War II with a tremendous leap in technology, a revived economy, and a more dominant geopolitical position, so too will it now emerge into what will be regarded as a golden age for America—and a new and growing maturity in handling its power.

CHAPTER 12

THE 2060s

A GOLDEN DECADE

The outcome of the war will unequivocally affirm the position of the United States as the world's leading international power and of North America as the center of gravity in the international system. It will allow the United States to consolidate its command of space, and with that, its control of international sea lanes. It also will begin to create a pattern of relationships the country will depend on in the coming decades.

The most important outcome of the war will be a treaty that formally will cede to the United States exclusive rights to militarize space. Other powers will be able to use space for nonmilitary purposes subject to U.S. inspection. This will be, simply, the treaty recognition of a military reality. The United States will have defeated Japan and Turkey in space, and it will not let that power slip away. The treaty will also limit the number and type of hypersonic aircraft that Turkey and Japan can have, though it will be well understood that this will be unenforceable—merely a gratuitous humiliation victors enjoy imposing on the vanquished. The treaty will serve American interests and remain in force only so long as American power can enforce it.

Poland will have been the great victor, expanding its reach enormously, although its losses will have been the most substantial of any major partici-pant. The Chinese and Koreans will feel well rid of the Japanese, who will have lost an empire but will retain their country, having suffered only a few thousand casualties. Japan will still be facing its population problems, but that will be the price of defeat. Turkey will remain the leader of the Islamic world, governing an empire made restive by defeat.

But Poland will feel embittered in spite of its victory. Its territory will have been directly invaded by Germany and Turkey, its allies occupied. Its casualties will be in the tens of thousands, the result of civilian battle casual-ties from ground combat—house-to-house fighting in which armored in-fantrymen are safer than civilians. Poland's infrastructure will have been shattered and, along with it, the nation's economy. Though Poland will be able to tilt the region's economic table in its favor, exploiting its conquests to quickly rebuild its economy, the victory will still be a painful one.

To the west, Poland's traditional enemy, Germany, will be weakened, subordinate, and sullen, while the Turks, beaten for the moment, will retain their influence a few hundred miles south in the Balkans and in southern Russia. The Poles will have taken the port of Rijeka and maintain bases in western Greece to prevent Turkish aggression at the entrance to the Adriatic. But the Turks will be still there, and Europeans have long memories. Per-haps most stinging, Poland will be included among nations banned from the military use of space. The United States will make no exception to that. In fact, the United States will be most uneasy about Poland after the war. Poland will have regained the empire it had in the seventeenth century, and added to it.

Poland will create a confederated system of governance for its former al-lies and will directly rule Belarus. It will be economically weak and badly hurt by the war, but it will have the territory and time to recover.

The defeat of France and Germany by Poland will decisively shift power in Europe to the east. In a sense, the eclipse of Atlantic Europe that began in 1945 will complete itself in the 2050s. The United States won't relish the long-term implications of a vigorous, self-confident Poland dominating Europe. It therefore will encourage its closest ally, Britain, which will have thrown its weight decisively into the war, to increase its own economic and political influence on the continent. With Western Europe in demographic and economic shambles, and fearing Polish power, England will willingly organize a bloc oddly resembling the twentieth-century NATO, whose task it will be to rehabilitate Western Europe and block Polish movement westward from Germany, Austria, or Italy. The United States won't join, but it will encourage the formation of this alliance.

Most interestingly, the Americans will move to improve their relations with the Turks. Given the old British adage that nations have no permanent friends and no permanent enemies but only permanent interests, the American interest will be to support the weaker power against the stronger, in order to maintain the balance of power. Turkey, understanding the long-term potential power of Poland, will happily accept closer ties with Washington as a guarantee of its long-term survival.

Needless to say, the Poles will feel utterly betrayed by the Americans. But the Americans will be learning. Rushing into battle may satisfy some urge, but managing the situation so that battles either won't occur or will be fought by others is a much better solution. In supporting Britain and Turkey, the United States will move to create a European balance of power matching the one in Asia. No other country will represent a coherent threat to the United States and, so long as it controls space, the United States will easily be able to deal with any other issues that rise to a level requiring its attention.

One interesting facet of geopolitics is this: there are no permanent solutions to geopolitical problems. But for the moment in the 2060s, as was the case in the 1920s and 1990s, there will appear to be no serious challenges facing the United States, or at least none that pose a direct threat. The United States will have learned that security is illusory but for the moment will luxuriate in that security nonetheless.

The American economic expansion of the 2040s won't be interrupted by the war. In fact, it will continue unchecked. As we have seen over the centuries, the United States has historically profited from major wars. It will be fairly untouched by the war, and increases in government spending will stimulate the economy. Since the United States fights its wars using technology, any war—or anticipation of war—against other nation-states will increase government expenditures on research and development. As a result, a range of new technologies will be available for commercial exploitation at the end of the war. So we will see in the postwar world, until about 2070, a period of dramatic economic growth, accompanied by social transformation.

The war will occur right in the middle of one of America's fifty-year cycles, about twenty years into it. That will mean that the war occurs at the point at which the country is its strongest internally. Its population problems, never as severe as the rest of the world's, will be well managed through immigration and the death of the boomers, relieving the pressure of a graying workforce. The balance between capital availability and demand for products will be intact, and both will grow. America will be moving into a period of dramatic economic, and therefore social, transformation. However, as with World War II, when a major war occurs in the early to middle stages of the cycle, the cycle is kicked into overdrive as the economy adjusts to the immediate aftereffects of war. That means that the mid- to late 2050s will be a jackpot period, similar to the 1950s. In every sense of the term, the fifteen years after the war will be an economic and technological golden age for the United States.

The United States will reduce its defense expenditures after the collapse of the Russians in the 2030s but will raise them again dramatically as the global cold war in the 2040s intensifies. Then, during the mid-century war, America will engage in extraordinary feats of research and development and will apply its discoveries immediately. What would have taken years to do in a peacetime economy will be done in months, and even weeks, due to the urgency of war (especially following the annihilation of U.S. space forces).

The United States will have developed an obsession with space. In 1941 Pearl Harbor created a national belief, especially among the military, that a devastating attack might come at any moment, and certainly when least expected. That mind-set governed U.S. nuclear strategy for the next fifty years. An unrelenting fear of surprise attack permeated military thinking and planning. That sensibility subsided after the fall of the Soviet Union, but the attack in the 2050s will revive the terror of Pearl Harbor, and fear of surprise attack will become a national obsession again, this time focused on space.

The threat will be very real. Control of space means the same thing strategically as control of the sea. Pearl Harbor nearly cost the United States control of the sea in 1941. Conversely, the war in the 2050s will almost cost the United States control of space. The resulting obsessive fear of the unexpected, combined with an obsessive focus on space, means that enormous amounts of both military and commercial money will be spent on space.

The United States is therefore going to construct a massive amount of infrastructure in space, ranging from satellites in low earth orbit to manned space stations in geostationary orbit, to installations on the moon and satellites orbiting the moon. Many of these systems will be robotically maintained, or will be robots themselves. The disparate advances in robotics in the previous half century will now come together—in space.

One key development is that there will now be a steady deployment of troops in space. Their job will be to oversee the systems, since robotics, no matter how good, are far from perfect, and in the 2050s and 2060s this effort will be a matter of national survival. U.S. Space Forces, a new branch of the military separate from the air force, will become the biggest service in terms of budget, if not troop size. A range of low-cost launch vehicles, many derived from commercial versions developed by entrepreneurs, will be constantly shuttling from earth to space and between the space-based platforms.

The goal of all this activity will be threefold. First, the United States will want to guarantee enough robustness, redundancy, and depth in defense so that no power will ever again be able to disrupt U.S. space capabilities. Second, it will want to be in a position where it can shut down any attempt by another country to gain a toehold in space against American wishes. Finally, it will want to have massive resources—including space-based weapons, from missiles to new high-energy beams—to control events on the surface of the earth. The United States will understand that it won't be able to control every threat (such as terrorism or the formation of coalitions) from space. But it will make sure that no other nation can mount an effective operation against it.

The cost of building this kind of capability will be enormous. It will have almost no political opposition, will generate huge deficits, and will stimulate the American economy dramatically. As with the end of World War II, fear will override caution. Critics, marginal and without influence, will say that this military spending is unnecessary and that it will bankrupt America, leading to a depression. In fact, it will cause the economy to surge dramatically, as deficits normally have in American history, particularly during the centers of the fifty-year cycles, when the economy is robust.

REVOLUTION IN ENERGY

The American obsession with space will intersect another intensifying problem: energy. During the war, the United States will invest huge amounts of money to solve the problem of delivering power to the battlefield from space. It will be uneconomical, primitive, and wasteful, but it will work. It will power Allied forces in Poland in the face of the Turkish-German invasion. The military will see space-based power generation as a solution to its massive logistical problem on the battlefield. In particular, the delivery of energy to power new weapons involving intense energy beams will be a critical problem. The military will be prepared, therefore, to underwrite the development of space-based power generation, as a military necessity, and Congress will be prepared to pay for it. It will be one of the lessons learned from the war—and it will instill a sense of urgency into the project.

There are two other episodes in American history that are instructive here. In 1956, the United States undertook to construct the interstate highway system. Dwight Eisenhower favored it for military reasons. As a junior officer he had tried to lead a convoy across the United States—it took months. In World War II he saw how the Germans had moved entire armies from the eastern front to the west to launch the Battle of the Bulge using their autobahns. He was struck by the contrast.

The military reasons for the interstate system were compelling. But the civilian impacts were both unexpected and unintended. With the time and cost of transportation reduced, land outside of cities became usable. A massive decentralization of cities took place, leading to suburbs and the distribution of industry outside of urban areas. The interstate system reshaped the United States, and without the military justifications it might not have been built or seen as economically feasible.

A second example can be drawn from the 1970s, when the military was heavily engaged in research. It needed the means to move information around among different research centers more quickly than it could by courier or the mails—there was no FedEx. The Defense Advanced Research Projects Agency (DARPA) funded an experiment designed to create a network of computers that could communicate data and files to each other at a distance. The creation was called ARPANET. It was developed at some cost and effort for a highly specialized use. ARPANET, of course, evolved into the Internet, and its essential architecture and protocols were designed and administered by the Department of Defense and its contractors until well into the 1990s.

As with the automobile superhighways, the information superhighway might have come about on its own, but it did not. The basic cost of creating it was a military undertaking designed to solve a problem the military was experiencing. To push this analogy a bit, the energy superhighway will have its origins in the same kinds of necessities. It will be built for the military, and therefore its economics will make it more competitive than other energy sources. Since the military will absorb the basic capital cost and will deploy the systems, the commercial cost of this energy will be enormously lower than it might be otherwise. Cheap energy in the civilian sector will be critical, particularly as robots become more and more prevalent in the economy.

Military space programs will, quite literally, reduce the cost of commercial endeavors by piggybacking them. Advances in commercial launches into space will reduce the cost of lifting payload but will never have the capacity to handle a massive project such as the development of space-based solar power generation. The military program of the 2050s and 2060s will solve this problem in two ways. First, one of the important parts of the project will be reducing the cost per pound of payloads. The United States will be putting a lot of stuff into space and will need to dramatically lower the price of a launch. Partly through new technology and partly through the sheer volume being launched, cost will begin to decline dramatically, even over that of commercial vehicles developed earlier.

Second, there will be surplus capacity built into the system. One of the lessons of the war will be that not having spare space-lift capacity left the

United States scrambling to deal with the initial attack. That will not be allowed to happen again. So the nation will have a huge surplus of usable lift capacity. Private sector utilization of the project will be essential to reduce costs.

The period when the interstate highway system and the Internet came into being was a period of explosive economic growth. The interstate highway system stimulated the economy by employing armies of construction crews and civil engineers, but it was the entrepreneurial spin-offs that really drove the boom. McDonald's was as much a creature of the interstate highway system as was the suburban mall. The Internet's construction involved a lot of Cisco servers and PC sales. But the real boom came with Amazon and iTunes. Both had massive entrepreneurial consequences.

NASA has been involved in research on space-based energy since the 1970s, in the form space solar power (SSP). In the war of the 2050s the United States will really start using this new system. And in the space-based energy project of the 2060s, it will become a feature of everyday life. Vast numbers of photovoltaic cells, designed to convert solar energy into electricity, will be placed in geostationary orbit or on the surface of the moon. The electricity will be converted into microwaves, transmitted to the earth, reconverted to electricity, and distributed through the existing and expanded electric grid. The number of cells needed could be reduced by concentrating sunlight using mirrors, thus reducing the cost of launching the photovoltaic arrays. Obviously, the receivers would have to be installed in isolated areas on earth, since the localized microwave radiation would be intense, but the risks would be far less than that from nuclear reactors or from the environmental effects of hydrocarbons. One thing that space has available is space. What would be unbearably intrusive on earth (say, covering an area the size of New Mexico with solar panels) is swallowed up by the limitlessness of space. Plus there are no clouds, and collectors can be positioned to receive continual sunlight.

These advances will lead to reduced energy costs on earth, and thus many more energy-intensive activities will become feasible. The entrepreneurial possibilities that emerge will be astounding. Who could have drawn a line between ARPANET and the iPod? All that can be said is that this second wave of innovations will transform things at least as much as the interstate highway and the Internet did—and bring as much prosperity in the 2060s as the interstate brought in the 1960s, and the Internet in the 2000s.

The United States will also have created another foundation for its geopolitical power—it will become the largest energy producer in the world, with its energy fields protected from attack. Japan and China and most other countries are going to be energy importers. As the economics of energy shifts, other sources of energy, including hydrocarbons, will become less attractive. Other countries will not be able to launch their own space-based systems. For one thing, they will not have a military making the down payment on the system. Nor will any country have the appetite to challenge the United States at that moment. An attack on American facilities will be unthinkable given the now vast imbalance of power. The ability of the United States to provide much cheaper solar energy will create an additional lever for the superpower to increase its international dominance.

We will see here a fundamental paradigm shift in geopolitical realities. Since the start of the industrial revolution, industry has guzzled energy, which was accidentally and haphazardly distributed around the world. The Arabian Peninsula, which otherwise had little importance, became crucially important because of its oil fields. With the shift to space-based systems, industry will produce energy instead of simply consuming it. Space travel will be the result of industrialization, and an industrialized nation will produce energy at the same time as it fuels its industry. Space will become more important than Saudi Arabia ever was, and the United States will control it.

A new wave of American-generated culture will sweep the world. Remember that we define culture not simply as art, but in the broader sense of how people live their lives. The computer was the most effective introduction to American culture, far more profound than movies or TV. The robot will represent the computer's logical and dramatic conclusion. In a world that needs economic growth but no longer has a surging population, robots will become the driver of productivity, and with space-based solar systems there will be ample electricity to power them. Robots, still primitive but developing rapidly, are going to sweep the world, and will be particularly embraced by the population-constrained advanced industrial world, and by countries that will be closing in on the first tier and nearing or passing population peaks.

Genetics science will continue to extend life expectancy, and will eradicate or bring under control a series of genetic diseases. This will lead to increasing social instability. The radical shifts that have wracked Europe and the United States, transforming the role of women and the structure of the family, will become a worldwide phenomenon. Deep tensions—between supporters of traditional values and new social realities—will become intense throughout the second-tier countries, and all major religions will be wracked by them. Catholicism, Confucianism, and Islam will all be arrayed with traditional understandings of family, sexuality, and the relations between generations. But the traditional values are going to collapse in Europe and the United States, and they will then collapse throughout most of the rest of the world.

Politically, this will mean intense internal tensions. The late twenty-first century will become a period in which tradition tries to contain a medically and technologically driven upheaval. And since the United States will be the originator of much of the controversial technology, and its model of internal social chaos will be becoming the norm, it will become the enemy of traditionalists everywhere. To the rest of the world, America will be seen as dangerous, brutish, and treacherous, but it will be treated with caution—and envied. It will be a time of international stability, regional stress, and internal unrest.

Outside the United States two powers will be thinking about space. One will be Poland, which will be busy consolidating its land empire and still smarting at its treatment under the peace treaty of the 2050s. But Poland will also still be recovering from the war and surrounded by American allies. It will not be ready for a challenge. The other country thinking about space will be Mexico, which into the late 2060s will be emerging as one of the top economic powers in the world. Mexico will see itself as a rival of the United States, and will be stepping onto the continental and world stage, but it will not yet have defined a coherent national strategy (and will be afraid of going too far in challenging American power).

There will be other emerging powers whose economies begin to surge as population growth pressures decline. Brazil will be a particularly important emerging power, a generation behind Mexico in population stability but moving rapidly in that direction. Brazil will be considering a regional economic alliance with Argentina, Chile, and Uruguay, all of whom will be making major strides. Brazil will be thinking in terms of peaceful confederation but, as is often the case, will in due course entertain more aggressive ideas. The Brazilians will certainly have a space program by the 2060s, but not a comprehensive one, and not one linked to immediate geopolitical need.

Countries like Israel, India, Korea, and Iran all will have limited space programs, but none of them is going to have the resources or the motivation to make a play for substantial space presence, let alone try to deny the United States space hegemony. Therefore, as happens at the end of global wars, the United States will have a wide-open shot—and will take it. The United States will be living in a golden moment, lasting at least until around 2070.

CHAPTER 13

2080

The United States, Mexico, and the Struggle for the Global Heartland

From the beginning of this book, I've talked about North America being the center of gravity of the international system. Until now I've basically equated North America with the United States, simply because U.S. power in North America is so overwhelming that no one is in a position to challenge it. The great global war of the twenty-first century will make clear that no Eurasian power is going to emerge to challenge the United States for quite a while. In addition, a crucial geopolitical principle will be tested, and modernized: whoever controls the Atlantic and Pacific oceans will control global trade—and whoever controls space will control the world's oceans. The United States will emerge in unchallenged control of space, and therefore in control of the world's oceans.

Reality, however, is more complex than appearances. The United States will have an underlying weakness in the second half of the twenty-first century, one that it will not have confronted for two hundred years. The first geopolitical imperative of the United States—the one that all others rest upon—is that the United States dominate North America. Since the Mexican-American War and the Treaty of Guadalupe Hidalgo that concluded it in 1848, the United States has been in practical control of the continent. It has simply seemed to be a foregone conclusion.

By the end of the twenty-first century, this will no longer be the case. The question of Mexico's power relative to the United States will be raised again in the most complex and difficult way imaginable. Mexico, after two hundred years, will be in a position to challenge the territorial integrity of the United States, and the entire balance of power of North America. If this sounds far-fetched, go back to my introductory chapter and think about the way the world changes in just twenty years, remembering that we are talking about nearly a century here.

The Mexican challenge will be rooted in the economic crisis of the 2020s, which will be solved by the immigration laws that will be passed in the early 2030s. These laws will aggressively encourage immigration to the United States in order to solve America's labor shortages. There will be a massive influx of immigrants from all countries, and this will obviously include Mexico. The other immigrant groups will behave much as previous immigrants did. But the Mexicans will behave differently for a single reason, having nothing to do with culture or character, but having to do with geography. And that, coupled with the growing strength of Mexico as a nation, will shift the North American balance of power.

Historically, other immigrant groups have had what we might call a lumpy distribution in the United States. They have lived in ethnic enclaves, and while they might have dominated in those neighborhoods and influenced surrounding politics, no one group simply overwhelmed any region or state since the late nineteenth century. As the second generation reached adulthood, they became culturally assimilated and distributed themselves around the country as they pursued economic opportunities. The life of the ethnic enclave was simply not as attractive as the opportunities available in the wider society. In the United States, minority populations were never an indigestible mass—with the major exceptions of the one ethnic group that did not come here voluntarily (African Americans) and those who were here when Europeans arrived (American Indians). The rest all came, clustered and dispersed, and added new cultural layers to the general society.

This has always been the strength of the United States. In much of Europe, for example, Muslims have retained religious and national identities distinct from the general population, and the general population has given them little encouragement to blend. The strength of their own culture has therefore been overwhelming. In the United States, Islamic immigrants, like other immigrant groups, were transformed over generations into a population that bought into basic American principles while retaining religiosity almost as a cultural link to the past. This both bound the immigrants to the United States and created a chasm between the first generation and later ones (as well as between the American Muslim community and Muslims elsewhere in the world). This has been a well-worn path for immigrants to the United States.

Immigrants from Mexico will behave differently starting in the 2030s. They will distribute themselves around the country, as they have in the past, and many will enter the mainstream of American society. But unlike other immigrant groups, Mexicans are not separated from their homelands by oceans and many thousands of miles. They can move across the border a few miles into the United States but still maintain their social and economic links to their homeland. Proximity to the homeland creates a very different dynamic. Rather than a diaspora, at least part of Mexican migration is simply a movement into a borderland between two nations, like Alsace-Lorraine between France and Germany—a place where two cultures intermingle even when the border is stable.

Consider the map on page 226, drawn from U.S. census bureau data, of Hispanic population concentration in the United States in 2000.

In 2000, looking at Hispanic residents as percentages of counties in the United States, we can already see the concentration. Along the border from the Pacific to the Gulf of Mexico there is an obvious concentration of people of Mexican origin. The counties range from about one-fifth Mexican (we will use that term to apply here to ethnicity, not citizenship) to over two-thirds Mexican. In Texas, this concentration goes deep into the state, as it does in California. But the border counties tend to be the most heavily Mexican, as would be expected.

I've superimposed the outline of the territory that used to be part of Mexico and became part of the United States: Texas and the Mexican Cession. Notice how the Mexican community in 2000 is concentrated in these formerly Mexican territories. There are pockets of Mexicans outside

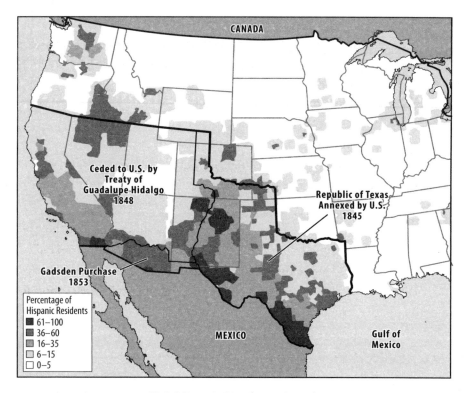

U.S. Hispanic Population (2000)

this area, of course, but they are just that, pockets, behaving more like
other ethnic groups. In the borderland, Mexicans are not isolated from
their homeland. In many ways they represent an extension of their homeland into the United States. The United States occupied Mexican territory in the nineteenth century, and the region maintained some of the
characteristics of occupied territory. As populations shift, the border is increasingly seen as arbitrary or illegitimate, and migration from the poorer
to the richer country takes place, but not the reverse. The cultural border
of Mexico shifts northward even though the political border remains
static.

That's the picture in 2000. By 2060, after thirty years of policies encouraging immigration, the map we saw in 2000 will have evolved so that areas
that had been around 50 percent Mexican will become almost completely
Mexican and areas that had been about 25 percent Mexican will move to

over half. The entire map will have turned one to two shades darker. The borderland, extending far into the United States, will become predominantly Mexican. Mexico will have solved its final phase of population growth by extending its nonpolitical boundaries into the Mexican Cession—with the encouragement of the United States.

POPULATION, TECHNOLOGY, AND
THE CRISIS OF 2080

Surging immigration into the United States and the aftereffects of the war will kick off an economic boom from about 2040 to 2060. The availability of land and capital in the United States, coupled with one of the most dynamic labor pools in the advanced industrial world, will stoke the economic fires. The relative ease with which the United States absorbs immigrants will give it a massive advantage over other industrialized countries. But there will be another dimension to this boom that we must acknowledge: technology. Let's consider this and then return to our discussion of Mexico.

During the crisis of 2030, the United States will look for ways to compensate for labor shortages, particularly in developing technologies that can take the place of humans.

One of the dominant patterns in technology development in the United States has been:

1. Basic science or designs are developed at universities or by individual inventors, frequently resulting in conceptual breakthroughs, modest implementations, and some commercial exploitation.
2. In the context of a military need, the United States infuses large amounts of money into the project to speed development toward specific, military ends.
3. The private sector takes advantage of commercial applications of this technology to build entire industries.

The same is happening with robotics. At end of the twentieth century basic development in robotics had already been undertaken. Core theoreti-

cal breakthroughs had taken place and there were some commercial applications, but robots have not become staples of the American economy.

The military, however, has been pumping money into both basic robotics theory and its applications for years. The U.S. military, through DARPA
and other sources, has been actively funding robotics development. Building a robotic mule to carry infantry equipment and creating a robotic aircraft that would not need a pilot are but two examples of work in robotics.
Deploying in space intelligent robotic systems that don't need to be controlled from earth is another goal. Ultimately, it is a matter of demographics. Fewer young people means fewer soldiers. However, U.S. strategic
commitments will increase, not decrease. The United States, more than any
other nation, will need robotic support for soldiers as a matter of national
interest.

By the time the social and political crisis of 2030 occurs, robotics applications will have been field-tested and proven by the military and thus ready
for commercial application. Obviously, robots won't be ready for mass deployment by 2030. And in no way will robots eliminate the need for immigration. This situation will sound familiar to many of us, as we've been here
before. Computing was at this stage in 1975; the military had paid for the
development of the silicon microchip, and many military applications could
be found. Commercialization processes were just beginning, and it would
take several decades to transform the civilian economy. So the mass deployment of robotics technologies will not be taking place until the 2040s, and
the full transformative power of robotics will not be felt until about 2060.

Ironically, immigrant technologists will be critical in developing robotics
technology, a technology that will undercut the need for mass immigration.
In fact, as robotics enters the mainstream of society, it will undercut the economic position of those migrants engaged in unskilled labor at the bottom
of the economic pyramid.

Once again, the solution to one problem will be the catalyst for the next
one. This situation will set the stage for the crisis of 2080. The system for
encouraging immigration will be embedded into American culture and politics. Recruiters will continue offering incentives for immigrants to come to
the United States. An emergency measure will have become a routine part of
government. The problem is that by 2060 or so, the crisis will have passed,

both because of migration and due to new technologies like robotics. The last boomers will be gone and buried, and America's demographic structure will look more like a pyramid—which is what it should look like. Advances in robotics will eliminate the need for an entire segment of immigrants.

Technology has frequently promised to eliminate jobs. The exact opposite has always happened. More jobs have been created in order to maintain the technology. What has happened is a shift from unskilled to skilled labor. That will certainly be one result of robotics. Someone will have to design and maintain the systems. But robotics differs from all prior technologies in a fundamental way. Prior technologies have had labor displacement as a by-product. Robotics is designed explicitly *for* labor displacement. The entire point of this class of technology is replacing scarce human labor with cheaper technology. The first goal will be replacing labor that is no longer available. The second will be to shift available labor to support robotics. The third—and this is where the problem starts—will be the direct displacement of workers. In other words, while robotics will be designed to replace disappearing workers, it will also create unemployment among workers who are displaced but don't have the skills to move into robotics.

As a result, unemployment will begin rising, beginning around 2060 and accelerating throughout the next two decades. There will be a temporary but painful population surplus. Whereas the problem of 2030 will be coping with a population shortage, the problem by the 2060s to the 2080s will be coping with a surplus population driven by excessive immigration and structural unemployment. This will be compounded by advances in genetics. Human life may not be extended dramatically, but Americans will remain productive longer. We shouldn't discount, either, the possibility of massive increases in longevity as a wild card.

Robotics, coupled with genetics and attendant technologies, will simultaneously replace labor and increase the labor pool by making humans more efficient. It will be a time of increasing turmoil. It will also be a time of turmoil in terms of energy use. Robots, which will both move and process information, will be even more ubiquitous energy hogs than automobiles. This will kick off the energy crisis discussed in previous chapters and the end of hydrocarbon technology rooted in the European Age. The United States will be forced to look to space for energy.

Developments in space-sourced energy systems will have been under way well before 2080. In fact, the Defense Department is already thinking about such a system. The National Security Space Office released a study in October 2007 entitled "Space-Based Solar Power as an Opportunity for Strategic Security." It states:

> The magnitude of the looming energy and environmental problems is significant enough to warrant consideration of all options, to revisit a concept called Space Based Solar Power (SBSP) first invented in the United States almost 40 years ago. The basic idea is very straightforward: place very large solar arrays into continuously and intensely sunlit Earth orbit, collect gigawatts of electrical energy, electromagnetically beam it to Earth, and receive it on the surface for use either as baseload power via direct connection to the existing electrical grid, conversion into manufactured synthetic hydrocarbon fuels or as low-intensity broadcast power beamed directly to consumers. A single kilometer-wide band of geosynchronous earth orbit experiences enough solar flux in one year to nearly equal the amount of energy contained within all known recoverable conventional oil resources on earth today.

By 2050 early installations of this new solar technology should be in place, and the crisis of 2080 will propel development forward. A significant drop in energy costs will be essential to the implementation of the robotics strategy, which is, in turn, essential to maintaining economic productivity during a period of long-term population constraints. When population doesn't grow, technology must compensate, and for this technology to work, energy costs must come down.

So in the United States after 2080 we will see a massive effort to extract energy from space-based systems. Obviously, this will have begun decades before, but not with the intensity required to make it the primary source of power. The intensifying crisis of 2070 will move the project forward dramatically. As with any government effort, the cost will be high, but by the end of the twenty-first century, when private industry starts taking advantage of the vast public investment in space, the cost of energy will drop substantially. Robotics will be evolving quickly and dramatically. Think of the evolution of home computers between 1990, when most homes and offices still did not even have e-mail, and 2005, when literally billions of e-mails were sent daily around the planet.

The United States will be one of the few advanced industrial countries experiencing a temporary surplus in its population. The economic imperative of the previous fifty years—encouraging immigration by all means possible—will have run its course, and it will have become the problem rather than the solution. So the first step toward solving the crisis will be limiting immigration, a massive and traumatizing reversal that will cause a crisis, just as the shift toward attracting and increasing immigration had fifty years before.

Once immigration has been halted, the United States will have to manage the economic imbalance caused by its population surplus. Layoffs and unemployment will strike disproportionately at the working poor—and particularly the Mexican population in the borderlands. Serious foreign policy issues will then arise. Add to this picture soaring energy prices, and all of the catalysts for the crisis of the 2080s are in place.

MEXICO'S ECONOMIC DEVELOPMENT

Mexico's economy is currently ranked fifteenth in the world. Since its economic meltdown in 1994, it has recovered dramatically. Mexico's per capita GDP, measured in terms of purchasing power, is a little over $12,000 a year, which makes it the wealthiest major country in Latin America, and places Mexico in the ranks of developed, if not advanced, economies. And we have to remember that Mexico is not a small country. It has a population of about 110 million, making it larger than most European nations.

Will Mexico's economic strength increase substantially over the next sixty or seventy years? If it does, considering its starting point, Mexico would then become one of the world's leading economies. Given Mexico's internal political instability, outflows of population, and history of economic problems, it is difficult to imagine Mexico in the top tier of nations. But it is equally difficult for most people to understand how it has already risen as high as it has.

There are several things working in Mexico's favor economically. The first is oil. Mexico has been a major oil producer and exporter over the last century. For many, that is an argument against Mexico becoming a major power. Oil exports frequently undermine the ability—or appetite—of a nation to develop other industries. It's therefore important to understand one other fact about Mexico: despite the surge in global oil prices since 2003, its energy sector actually represents a declining portion of Mexico's overall economy. Oil constituted about 60 percent of Mexico's exports in 1980, but by 2000 it was only about 7 percent. Mexico has oil reserves, but it doesn't depend on oil exports to grow.

The second factor in Mexico's economic growth has to do with its proximity to the United States—the same thing that will later pose a geopolitical challenge. Mexico—with or without NAFTA—will be able to export efficiently into the world's largest and most dynamic market. While NAFTA cut the cost of exports and increased the institutional efficiency of the relationship, the fundamental reality is that Mexico's proximity to the United States has always given it an economic advantage, despite the geopolitical disadvantage that goes with it.

Third, there are massive amounts of cash flowing back to Mexico from the United States in the form of remittances from legal and illegal immigrants. Remittances to Mexico have surged and are now its second-largest source of foreign income. In most countries, foreign investment is the primary means for developing the economy. In Mexico, investment by foreigners is being matched by foreign remittances. This remittance system has two effects. It leverages other sources of investment when it is banked. And it serves as a social safety net for the lower classes, to whom most remittances flow.

The inflow of money into Mexico has meant a growth in technologically based industry and services. Services now account for 70 percent of Mexico's GDP, and agriculture for only about 4 percent. The rest is made up of industry, oil, and mining. The proportion of services centered around tourism is relatively high, but the mix as a whole is not typical of a developing country.

There is an interesting measure, created by the United Nations, called the human development index (HDI), which charts global standards of living, including factors like life expectancy and literacy rates. The HDI divides the world into three classes. On the map that follows, black represents the advanced industrial world, medium gray indicates the middle-tier and developed countries, and light gray shows the developing world. As the map shows, Mexico already ranks with Europe and the United States on the human development scale. That doesn't mean it is the equal of the United States, but it does mean that Mexico cannot simply be viewed as a developing country.

When we drill deeper into the HDI, we see something else interesting about Mexico. Mexico as a whole has an index of 0.70, which puts it in the same class as the United States or Europe. But there are enormous regional inequalities within Mexico. The darker areas on the map below have rankings equal to some European countries, while the lightest areas are the equivalent of poorer, North African countries.

This tremendous inequality is exactly what you would expect to see in a country in the process of rapid development. Consider the descriptions of Europe written by Charles Dickens or Victor Hugo. They captured the essence of nineteenth-century Europe—tremendous growth amid inten-

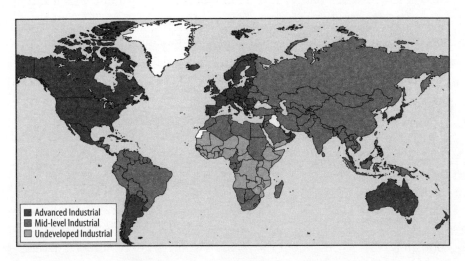

Levels of Economic and Social Development

sifying inequality. In Mexico, one can find that contrast in Mexico City or Guadalajara. But one can also see it regionally, contrasting the relative wealth of Mexico's north with the poverty of the south. Inequality does not mean lack of development. Instead, it is the inevitable by-product of development.

It is interesting to note in this map, of course, that the areas bordering the United States and the tourist regions in the south—as well as Mexico City—are at the highest levels of development. As one moves away from the U.S. frontier, the HDI declines. This indicates the importance of the United States in Mexican development. It also reveals the real danger facing Mexico—which is an insurgency in the south fueled by its inequality. This inequality will intensify as Mexico develops.

There is one other important factor driving Mexico's growth: organized crime and the drug trade. In general, there are two types of crime. One is simply distributive and consumptive—someone steals your television and sells it. The other creates large pools of capital. The American Mafia that

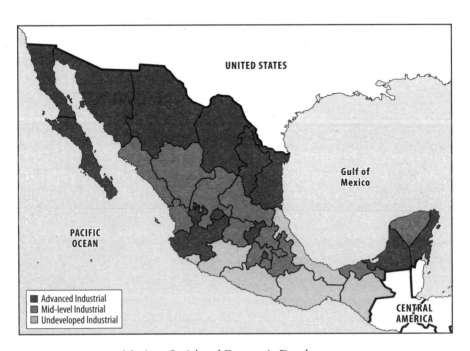

Mexican Social and Economic Development

dominated bootlegging used that money to move into legitimate business, until, at a certain point, the original money had been merged into the general flow of capital such that its origin in criminality was no longer relevant. When this happens inside a country, it stimulates growth. When the transfer is between two countries, it really stimulates growth. The key is that the cost of the product is artificially inflated by its illegality. This encourages the emergence of cartels that suppress competition, maintain high prices, and facilitate the transfer of funds.

In the case of the contemporary drug trade, the sale of drugs at artificially high prices to American drug consumers creates huge pools of money available for investment in Mexico. The amount of money is so large that it must be invested. Complex money-laundering operations are designed to allocate the funds legally. The next generation becomes heir to a fairly legitimate pool of money. The third generation becomes economic aristocrats.

This obviously oversimplifies the situation. It also neglects the fact that in many cases, dealers located in Mexico will not repatriate the money to Mexico but will instead invest it in the United States or elsewhere. But if Mexico is becoming increasingly productive, and if the government can be corrupted to provide a degree of protection while the money is being laundered, then reinvesting drug money in Mexico makes a great deal of sense. Listen closely: the giant sucking sound you hear is investment capital leaving the United States and going to Mexico via the drug cartels.

The problem with this process is that it is politically destabilizing. Because the authorities are complicit in the process, and the courts and police ineffective, the situation creates instability from the street to the highest reaches of government. A society can rip itself apart when this much money is involved. Yet societies that are sufficiently large and complex, and in which the amount of money represents a relatively small fraction of available capital, can eventually stabilize themselves. The United States, where organized crime has played a critical role since the 1920s and did destabilize entire regions, ultimately rechanneled criminal money into legal activities. It is my view that this is the most likely path for Mexico and that this activity will ultimately contribute to Mexican economic growth.

This is not to say that there will not be a fearsome period of instability in Mexico. During the coming years, the ability of the state to control the cartels will be challenged and Mexico will face extensive internal crises. But in the long term, viewed in terms of the century, Mexico will both weather the crises and benefit from the massive inflows of money from the United States.

Finally, when we look at Mexico's population, we see not only continued growth during a time when labor will be needed to fuel it but also a soft landing in population growth by mid-century, indicating social stabilization as well as easing demographic pressures on society. The population pattern also allows for increased migration to the United States during the 2030s, resulting in increased remittances and therefore enhanced capital formation without the burden of the overpopulation within Mexico's boundaries. Although not critical for Mexico's development, this migration will certainly be something that supports it.

Thus, we can see Mexico, which has joined Europe in some measures of its standard of living, passing through an inevitable period of turbulence and growth on the way to order and stability. Then, around the middle of the twenty-first century, while the world is at war, Mexico will emerge as a mature, balanced economy with a stable population—and will rank among the top six or seven economic powers in the world, with a growing military power to boot. Mexico will be the leading economic power of Latin America and, perhaps allied loosely with Brazil, will pose a challenge to U.S. domination of North America.

MEXICO'S GEOPOLITICS

During the 1830s and 1840s, Mexico lost its northern regions to the United States, following the Texas rebellion and the Mexican-American War. Essentially, all of the lands north of the Rio Grande and the Sonoran Desert were taken by the United States. The United States did not carry out ethnic cleansing: the existing population remained in place, gradually being overlain by the arrival of non-Hispanic American settlers. The border was historically porous, and both U.S. and Mexican citizens were able to move readily across it. As I said before, a classic borderland was created, with clear political boundaries but complex and murky cultural boundaries.

Mexico has never been in a position to attempt to reverse the American conquests. It adopted the view that it had no choice but to live with the loss of its northern land. Even during the American Civil War, when the Southwest was relatively unprotected, the Mexicans made no move. Under the emperor Maximilian, Mexico remained weak and divided. It couldn't generate the will or power to act. When Mexico was approached by the Germans in World War I with the offer of an alliance against the United States and the return of northern Mexico, the Mexicans declined the offer. When the Soviets and Cubans tried to generate a pro-communist movement in Mexico to threaten America's southern frontier, they failed completely. Mexico couldn't move against the United States, nor could it be manipulated by foreign powers to do so, because Mexico couldn't mobilize.

This was not because anti-American sentiment wasn't present in Mexico. Such sentiment is in fact deeply rooted, as one might expect given the history of Mexican–American relations. However, as we have seen, sentiment has little to do with power. The Mexicans were absorbed by their own fractious regionalism and complex politics. They also understood the futility of challenging the United States.

Mexico's grand strategy was simple after 1848. First, it needed to maintain its own internal cohesion against regionalism and insurrection. Second, it needed to secure itself against any foreign intervention, particularly by the United States. Third, it needed to reclaim the lands lost to the United States in the 1840s. Finally, it needed to supplant the United States as the dominant power in North America.

Mexico never really got past the first rung in its geopolitical goals. It has, since the Mexican-American War, simply been trying to maintain internal cohesion. Mexico lost its balance after its defeat by the United States and never regained it. In part this was due to American policies that helped destabilize it, but mostly Mexico was weakened by living next to a dynamic giant. The force field created by the United States always shaped Mexican realities more than Mexico City did.

In the twenty-first century, the destabilizing proximity of the United States will instead become a stabilizing force. Mexico will still be affected by the United States, but the relationship will be managed to increase Mexican power. By the middle of the twenty-first century, as Mexican economic power rises, there will inevitably be a rise in Mexican nationalism, which, given geo-political reality, will manifest itself not only in pride but in anti-Americanism. Given U.S. programs designed to entice Mexicans to immigrate to the United States at a time when the Mexican birthrate is falling, the United States will be blamed for pursuing policies designed to harm Mexican economic interests.

U.S.–Mexican tensions are permanent. The difference in the 2040s will be a rise in Mexican power and therefore a greater confidence and assertiveness on its part. The relative power of the two countries, however, will remain staggeringly in favor of the United States—just not as staggeringly as fifty years earlier. But even that will change between 2040 and 2070. Mexico will cease being a national basket case and become a major regional power. For its part, the United States will not notice. During the mid-century war, Washington will think of Mexico only as a potential ally of the Coalition. Having maneuvered Mexico out of any such considerations, Washington will lose interest. In the euphoria and economic expansion following the war, the United States will maintain its traditional indifference to Mexican concerns.

Once the United States realizes that Mexico has become a threat, it will at once be extremely alarmed at what is happening in Mexico and among Mexicans, and calmly certain that it can impose any solution it wants on the situation. U.S.–Mexican tensions, always present under the surface, will fester as Mexico becomes stronger. The United States will view the strengthening of the Mexican economy as a benign stabilizing force for both Mexico and its relations with the United States, and will therefore further support the rapid rate of Mexican economic development. The American view of Mexico as ultimately a client state will remain unchanged.

By 2080, the United States will still be the most overwhelmingly powerful nation-state in North America. But as Americans will learn repeatedly, enormously powerful does not mean omnipotent, and behaving as if it does can readily sap a nation's power. By 2080, the Americans will again face a challenge—but this one will be much more complex and subtle than what they faced in the war of the 2050s.

The confrontation will not be planned, since the United States will not have ambitions in Mexico and the Mexicans will be under no illusion about their power relative to the United States. It will be a confrontation that grows organically out of the geopolitical reality of the two countries. But unlike most such regional conflicts, this will involve a confrontation between the world hegemon and an upstart neighbor, and the prize will be the center of gravity of the international system, North America. Three factors will drive the confrontation:

1. Mexico will emerge as a major global economic power. Ranked fourteenth or fifteenth early in the century, it will be firmly within the top ten by 2080. With a population of 100 million, it will be a power to be reckoned with anywhere in the world—except on the southern border of the United States.

2. The United States will face a cyclical crisis in the 2070s, culminating in the 2080 elections. New technology coupled with the rationalization of the demographic curve will reduce the need for new immigrants. Indeed, pressure will grow to return temporary immigrants, even those here for fifty years with children and grandchildren born here, to Mexico. Many of these will still be menial laborers. The United States will begin forcing long-term residents back across the border, loading down the Mexican economy with the least desirable workers, workers who had been American residents for many decades.

3. In spite of this, the massive shift in the population of the borderlands cannot be reversed. The basic predominance of Mexicans—both U.S. citizens and not—will be permanent. The parts of Mexico occupied by the United States in the 1840s will again become Mexican culturally, socially, and in many senses, politically. The policy of repatriating temporary workers will appear to be a legal process from the American point of view, but will look like ethnic cleansing to the Mexicans.

In the past, Mexico would have been fairly passive in the face of these shifts in American policy. However, as immigration becomes the dominant issue in the United States during the 2070s and the pivot around which the 2080 elections will turn, Mexico will begin to behave in unprecedented ways. The crisis in the United States and the maturation of the Mexican economy and society will coincide, creating unique tensions. A major social and economic shift in the United States (that will disproportionately hurt Mexicans living here) and a dramatic redefinition of the population of the American Southwest will combine to create a crisis that will not be easily solved by American technology and power.

The crisis will begin as an internal American matter. The United States is a democratic society, and in large regions of the country, the English-speaking culture will no longer be dominant. The United States will have become a bicultural country, like Canada or Belgium. The second culture will not be formally recognized, but it will be real and it will be not merely a cultural phenomenon but a clearly defined geographic reality.

Biculturalism tends to become a problem when it is simply ignored—when the dominant culture rejects the idea of formalizing it and instead attempts to maintain the status quo. It particularly becomes a problem when the dominant culture begins to take steps that appear designed to destroy the minority culture. And if this minority culture is essentially an extension of a neighboring country that sees its citizens as inhabiting territory stolen from it, the situation can become explosive.

By the 2070s, Mexicans and those of Mexican origin will constitute the dominant population along a line running at least two hundred miles from the U.S.–Mexican border through California, Arizona, New Mexico, and Texas and throughout vast areas of the Mexican Cession. The region will not behave as other immigrant-heavy areas have. Rather, as happens in border-lands, it will be culturally—and in many ways economically—a northward extension of Mexico. In every sense but legally, the border will have moved north.

These immigrants won't be disenfranchised peons. The economic expansion in Mexico, coupled with the surging American economy in the 2050s and 2060s, will make these settlers relatively well-to-do. In fact, they will be the facilitators of U.S.–Mexican trade, one of the most lucrative activities in the world in the late twenty-first century. This group will dominate not only local politics but the politics of two whole states—Arizona and New Mexico—and much of the politics of California and Texas. Only the sheer size of the latter two will prevent immigrants from controlling them outright as well. A subnational bloc, on the order of Quebec in Canada, will be in place in the United States.

At a certain critical mass, a geographically contiguous group becomes conscious of itself as a distinct entity within a country. More exactly, it begins to see the region it dominates as distinct, and begins to ask for a range of special concessions based on its status. When it has a natural affinity to a neighboring country, a portion of the group will see itself as native to that country but living under foreign domination. And across the border, in the neighboring country, an annexation movement can arise.

This issue will divide the Mexican-American bloc. Some inhabitants will see themselves as primarily Americans. Others will accept that Americanism but see themselves as having a unique relationship to America and ask for legal recognition of that status. A third group, the smallest, will be secessionist. There will be an equal division within Mexico. One thing to remember is that illegal immigration will have generally disappeared after 2030, when migration to the United States will be encouraged as American national policy. Some on each side of the border will see the problem as solely American and will want to have nothing to do with it lest it interfere with peaceful economic relations with Mexico. Others, though, will see the demographic problems in the United States as a means for redefining Mexico's relations with the United States. In exchange for a hands-off policy regarding migration, some will want the United States to make concessions to Mexico on other issues. And a minority will advocate annexation. A complex political battle will develop between Washington and Mexico City, each manipulating the situation on the other side of the border.

Large numbers of senators and representatives of Mexican origin will be elected to serve in Washington. Many will not see themselves as legislators who just happen to be of Mexican origin, representing their states. Rather, they will see themselves as representatives of the Mexican community living in the United States. As with the Parti Québécois in Canada, their regional representation will also be seen as the representation of a distinct nation living in the United States. The regional political process will be beginning to reflect this new reality. A Partido Mexicano will come into existence and send representatives to Washington as a separate bloc.

This state of affairs will help drive the reversal on immigration policy that is going to define the 2070s and the election of 2080. Beyond the demographic need to redefine the immigration policies of the 2030s, the very process of redefining them will radicalize the Southwest. That radicalization will, in turn, frighten the rest of the American public. Anti-Mexican feeling will be growing. A primal fear that the outcome of the Texan Revolution and the Mexican-American War, in place for more than two centuries, could be reversed will whip up hostility toward Mexican Americans and Mexico in the United States.

This fear will not be irrational. The American Southwest is occupied territory into which American settlers streamed from the mid-1800s to the early twenty-first century. Starting in the early twenty-first century, Mexican settlers will be streaming back in, joining others who never left. Population movement will thus reverse the social reality that was imposed militarily in the nineteenth century. Americans imposed a politico-military reality and then created a demographic reality to match it. Mexicans, more through American policy than anything else, will create a new demographic reality, and will be discussing several options: whether to attempt to reverse the politico-military reality created by the Americans; create a new, unique reality; or just accept the existing realities. Americans will be discussing whether to reverse the demographic shift and realign population with borders.

However, any discussion will take place in a context of immobility of borders. The borders are not going to change simply because Mexicans on both sides are discussing it, nor will the demographic reality change because Americans want it to. The border will have an overwhelming political and military force enforcing it—the United States Army. The Mexican population in the Mexican Cession will be deeply embedded in the economic life of the United States. Removing the Mexicans would create massive instability. There will be powerful forces maintaining the status quo and powerful forces resisting it.

A major backlash in the rest of the United States will lock down the border and exacerbate tensions. As Mexican rhetoric becomes more heated, so will American. Splits in the Mexican American community will become less and less visible in the rest of the country, and the most radical figures will dominate the American perception of the community and of Mexico. More radical figures in Washington will dominate the Mexican perception of the United States. Attempts will be made at moderate compromise, many of them quite reasonable and well intentioned, but all will be seen as a betrayal of the fundamental interests of one side or the other and sometimes both. Fundamental geopolitical disputes are rarely amenable to reasonable compromise—simply consider the Arab–Israeli conflict.

While all of this is going on, Mexican citizens who are living in the United States on temporary visas granted decades before will be forced to return to Mexico, regardless of how long they have been in America. The United States will have placed increased controls on the Mexican border, not to keep out immigrants—no one at this point will be clamoring to get in—but to drive a wedge between Mexico and ethnic Mexicans in the United States. It will be portrayed as a security measure, but what it will really be is an effort to reinforce the reality created in 1848. These and similar actions will be merely irritating to most Mexicans on either side of the border, but will provide fuel for the radicals and pose a threat to the vital trade between the two countries.

Within Mexico political pressure will grow for the Mexican government to assert itself. One faction will emerge that will want to annex the occupied region, reversing the American conquest of 1848. This won't be a marginal group but a substantial, if not yet dominant, faction. Others will be demanding that the United States retain control of the regions within the Mexican Cession and protect the rights of its residents—especially by halting the expulsion of Mexicans regardless of visa status. The group that simply wants to maintain the status quo, driven by businesses that want stability, not conflict, will become weaker and weaker. Calls for annexation will compete with demands for regional autonomy.

Anti-Mexican elements in the United States will use the radicalization of Mexican politics to argue that Mexico intends to interfere with internal American affairs, and even to invade the Southwest—something the most radical Mexicans will, in fact, be calling for. This, in turn, will justify the American extremists' demand for even more draconian measures, including the deportation of all ethnic Mexicans, regardless of citizenship status, and the invasion of Mexico if the Mexican government resists. The rhetoric on the fringes will feed on itself, driving the process.

Let's play this forward, imagining what the conflict might look like, bearing in mind that we can't possibly do more than imagine the details.

In the 2080s, anti-American demonstrations will begin taking place in Mexico City—and in Los Angeles, San Diego, Houston, San Antonio, Phoenix, and other cities in the borderland that will have become predominantly Mexican. The dominant theme will be ethnic Mexicans' rights as American citizens. But some will demonstrate for annexation by Mexico. A small radical faction of Mexicans in the United States will begin carrying out acts of sabotage and minor terrorism against federal government facilities in the region. While not supported by either the Mexican government, the state governments dominated by Mexicans, or most Mexicans on either side of the border, the terrorist acts will be seen as the first steps in a planned insurrection and secession by the region. The American president, under intense pressure to bring the situation under control, will move to federalize the National Guard in these states to protect federal property.

In New Mexico and Arizona, the governors will argue that the National Guard reports to them—and will refuse the order to nationalize. Instead they will order the Guard to protect federal facilities but will insist that the forces remain under state control. The Guard units, predominantly Mexican in these states, will obey the governor. Some in Congress will argue that a state of insurrection be declared. The president will resist but will instead ask Congress to permit the mobilization of U.S. troops in these states, leading to a direct confrontation between National Guard and U.S. Army units.

As the situation gets out of hand, the problem will be compounded when the Mexican president, unable to resist pressure to do something decisive, mobilizes the Mexican army and sends it north to the border. His justification will be that the U.S. Army has mobilized along the Mexican frontier and he wants to prevent any incursions and to coordinate with Washington. In reality, there will be a deeper reason. The Mexican president will be afraid that the U.S. Army will uproot Mexicans in this area—citizens, green card holders, and visa holders alike—and force them back over the Mexican border. Mexico will not want a surge of refugees. Moreover, the Mexican president will not want to see Mexicans in the United States stripped of their valuable property.

When the Mexican army mobilizes, the U.S. military will be placed on full alert. The U.S. military is not very good at policing hostile populations, particularly not those that include U.S. citizens. On the other hand, it is very good at attacking and destroying enemy armies. U.S. space forces and

ground troops will therefore begin focusing on the possibility of confrontation with the massed forces along the Mexican border.

A meeting between the two presidents will defuse the situation, as it will
be clear that no one really wants a war. In fact, no one in power will have
wanted the crisis in the Southwest. But the problem is this: during these negotiations, however much both sides want a return to the status quo ante,
the Mexican president will, in effect, be negotiating on behalf of American
citizens of Mexican origin who are living in the United States. To the extent
the crisis is defused, the status of Mexicans in the Mexican Cession is being
discussed. From the moment the discussion turns to defusing the crisis, the
question of who speaks for the Mexicans in the Mexican Cession will be decided: it is the president of Mexico.

While the crisis of the 2080s will subside, the underlying issue will not.
The borderland will be in play, and while the Mexicans will not have the
power to impose a military solution, the American government will not
have the ability to impose a social and political solution. The insertion of
American troops into the region, patrolling it as if it were a foreign country,
will have changed the status of the region in the mind of the public. Mexican negotiations on behalf of the people of the region will have extended
that change. A radical secessionist movement in the region, heavily funded
by Mexican nationalists, will continually irritate the situation, especially
when splinter terrorist groups begin carrying out occasional bombings and
kidnappings—not only within the Mexican Cession but throughout the
United States. The question of the Mexican conquest will be opened up yet
again. The region will still be part of the United States, but its loyalty will be
loudly questioned by many.

Expelling tens of millions of people will not be an option, as it would be
logistically impossible and would have devastating consequences for the
United States. At the same time, however, the idea that in the region those
who are of Mexican origin are simply citizens of the United States will break
down. Many will no longer see themselves that way, and neither will the rest
of the United States. The political situation will become increasingly radi-
calized.

By about 2090, radicals in Mexico will have created a new crisis. In a
change to the Mexican constitution, Mexicans (defined by parentage and

culture) who live outside of Mexico, regardless of citizenship, will be now permitted to vote in Mexican elections. More important, Mexican congressional districts will be established outside of Mexico, so that Mexicans living in Argentina, for example, can vote for a representative in the Mexican congress, representing Mexicans living in Argentina.

Since so many voters will qualify in the United States—the whole point of the change after all—the Mexican Cession will be divided into Mexican congressional districts, so that there might be twenty congressmen from Los Angeles and five from San Antonio elected to Congress in Mexico City. Since the Mexican communities will pay for the elections out of private funds, it is unclear whether this will violate any American law. Certainly, while there will be rage in the rest of the country, the federal government will be afraid to interfere. So the election to Congress will go forward in 2090—with Mexicans in the United States voting for both the Congress in Washington and the Congress in Mexico City. In a few cases, the same person will be elected to both congresses. It will be a clever move, putting the United States on the defensive, with no equivalent countermeasure available.

By the 2090s, the United States will be facing a difficult internal situation, as well as a confrontation with a Mexico that will be arming itself furiously, afraid that the United States will try to solve the problem by taking military measures against it. The Americans will have a tremendous advantage in space, but the Mexicans will have an advantage on the ground. The United States Army won't be particularly large, and controlling a city like Los Angeles still will require the basic grunt infantryman.

Groups of Mexican paramilitaries will spring up throughout the region in response to the U.S. occupation, and will remain in place after the troops withdraw. With the border heavily militarized on both sides, the possibility of lines of supply being cut by these paramilitaries, isolating U.S. forces along the border, won't be a trivial matter. The United States will be able to destroy the Mexican army, but that doesn't mean it could pacify its own Southwest, or Mexico for that matter. And at the same time, Mexico will begin to launch its own satellites and build its own unmanned aircraft.

As for the international reaction to this situation, the world will stand aside and watch. The Mexicans will hope for foreign support, and the

Brazilians, who will have become a substantial power in their own right, will make some gestures of solidarity with Mexico. But, while the rest of the world will secretly hope that Mexico will bloody its neighbor's nose, no one is going to get involved in a matter so fundamentally critical to the United States. Mexico will be alone. Its strategic solution will be to pose a problem on the American border while other powers challenge the United States elsewhere. The Poles will have developed serious grievances against the Americans, while emerging powers like Brazil will be stifled by the limits placed on them by the United States in space.

The Mexicans won't be able to fight the United States until they can reach military parity. Mexico will need a coalition—and building a coalition will take time. But Mexico will have one enormous advantage: the United States will be facing internal unrest, which, while not rising to the level of insurrection, will certainly focus U.S. energies and limit U.S. options. Invading and defeating Mexico would not solve this problem. It might actually exacerbate it. America's inability to solve this problem will be Mexico's major advantage, and the one that will buy it time.

The U.S. border with Mexico will now run through Mexico itself; its real, social border will be hundreds of miles north of the legal border. Indeed, even if the United States could defeat Mexico in war, it would not solve the basic dilemma. The situation will settle into a giant stalemate.

Underneath all of this will be the question that the United States has had to address almost since its founding: what should be the capital of North America—Washington or Mexico City? It had appeared likely at first that it would be the latter. Then centuries later it appeared obvious that it would be the former. The question will be on the table once again. It can be postponed, but it can't be avoided.

It is the same question that faced Spain and France in the seventeenth century. Spain had reigned supreme for a hundred years, dominating Atlantic Europe and the world until a new power challenged it. Would Spain or France be supreme? Five hundred years later, at the end of the twenty-first century, the United States will have dominated for a hundred years. Now Mexico will be rising. Who will be supreme? The United States will rule the skies and the seas, but the challenge from Mexico will be on the ground, and—a challenge only Mexico will be positioned to make—inside the borders of the United States. It is the kind of challenge that U.S. military power will be least suited to fight. Therefore, as the twenty-first century draws to a close, the question will be: North America is the center of gravity of the international system, but who will control North America?

That is a question that will have to wait until the twenty-second century.

EPILOGUE

It might seem far-fetched to speculate that a rising Mexico will ultimately challenge American power, but I suspect that the world we are living in today would have seemed far-fetched to someone living at the beginning of the twentieth century. As I said in the introduction to this book, when we try to predict the future, common sense almost always betrays us—just look at the startling changes that took place throughout the twentieth century and try to imagine using common sense to anticipate those things. The most practical way to imagine the future is to question the expected.

There are people being born today who will live in the twenty-second century. When I was growing up in the 1950s, the twenty-first century was an idea associated with science fiction, not a reality in which I would live. Practical people focus on the next moment and leave the centuries to dreamers. But the truth is that the twenty-first century has turned out to be a very practical concern to me. I will spend a good deal of my life in it. And on the way here, history—its wars, its technological changes, its social trans-formations—has reshaped my life in startling ways. I did not die in a nuclear war with the Soviets, though I did witness many wars, most of them unforeseen. *The Jetsons* did not define life in 1999, but I write these words on a computer that I can hold in one hand and that can access information on a global basis in seconds—and without wires connecting it to anything. The United Nations did not solve the problems of mankind, yet the status of blacks and women underwent breathtaking changes. What I expected and what happened were two very different things.

In looking back on the twentieth century, there were things we could be certain of, things that were likely, and things that were unknown. We could be certain that nation-states would continue to be the way in which humans organized the world. We could know that wars would become more deadly. Alfred Nobel knew that his invention would turn warfare into endless horror, and it did. We could see the revolutions in communications and travel—radio, automobiles, airplanes already existed. It took only imagination, and a will to believe, to see what they would mean to the world. It took the suspension of common sense.

Knowing that wars were inevitable and that they would grow worse, it did not take a great leap to imagine who would fight whom. The newly united European powers—Germany and Italy—and newly industrialized Japan would try to redefine the international system, controlled by the Atlantic European powers, Britain and France chief among them. And as these wars ripped apart Europe and Asia, it was not hard to forecast—indeed many did forecast—that Russia and America would emerge as the great global powers. What followed was murkier, but not beyond imagination.

Early in the century H. G. Wells, the science fiction writer, described the weapons that would fight wars in the coming generations. All that was required was that he look at what was already being imagined and what could already be built, and tie it to the warfare of the future. But it was not only the technology that could be imagined. War gamers at the U.S. Naval War College and on the Japanese defense staff both could describe the outlines of a U.S.–Japanese war. The German general staff, before the two world wars, laid out the likely course of the wars and the risks. Winston Churchill could see the consequences of the war, both the loss of Britain's empire and the future cold war. No one could imagine the precise details, but the general outline of the twentieth century could be sensed.

That is what I have tried to do in this book—to sense the twenty-first century with geopolitics as my primary guide. I began with the permanent: the persistence of the human condition, suspended between heaven and hell. I then looked for the long-term trend, which I found in the decline and fall of Europe as the centerpiece of global civilization and its replacement by North America and the dominant North American power, the United States. With that profound shift of the international system, it was easy to discern both the character of the United States—headstrong, immature, and brilliant—and the world's response to it: fear, envy, and resistance.

I then focused on two issues. First, who would resist; second, how the United States would respond to their resistance. The resistance would come in waves, continuing the short, shifting eras of the twentieth century. First there is Islam, then Russia, and then a coalition of new powers (Turkey, Poland, and Japan), and finally Mexico. To understand American responses, I looked at what seemed to me a fifty-year cycle in American society over the past several hundred years and tried to imagine what 2030 and 2080 would look like. That allowed me to think of the dramatic social change that is already under way—the end of the population explosion—and consider what it would mean for the future. I could also think about how technologies that already exist will respond to social crises, charting a path between robots and space-based solar power.

The closer one gets to details, the more likely one is to be wrong. Obviously I know that. But my mission, as I see it, is to provide you with a sense of what the twenty-first century will look and feel like. I will be wrong about many details. Indeed, I may be wrong about which countries will be great powers and how they will resist the United States. But what I am confident about is that the position of the United States in the international system will be the key issue of the twenty-first century and that other countries will be grappling with its rise. In the end, if there is a single point I have to make in this book, it is that the United States—far from being on the verge of decline—has actually just begun its ascent.

This book is emphatically not meant to be a celebration of the United States. I am a partisan of the American regime, but it is not the Constitution or the Federalist Papers that gave the United States its power. It was Jackson's stand at New Orleans, the defeat of Santa Anna at San Jacinto, the annexation of Hawaii, and the surrender of British naval bases in the Western Hemisphere to the United States in 1940—along with the unique geographical traits I have spent much time analyzing in these pages.

There is one point I have not touched upon. Any reader will have noticed that I do not deal with the question of global warming in this book. This should be a glaring omission. I do believe the environment is warming, and since we have been told by scientists that the debate is over, I easily concede that global warming was caused by human beings. As Karl Marx, of all people, put it: "Mankind does not pose problems for itself for which it does not already have a solution." I don't know if this is universally true, but it does seem to be true in this case.

Two forces are emerging that will moot global warming. First, the end of the population explosion will, over the decades, reduce the increases in demand for just about everything. Second, the increase in the cost of both finding and using hydrocarbons will increase the hunger for alternatives. The obvious alternative is solar energy, but it is clear to me that earth-based solar collection has too many hurdles to overcome, most of which are not present in space-based solar energy generation. By the second half of the twenty-first century, we will be seeing demographic and technological transformations that, together, will deal with the issue. In other words, population decline and the domination of space for global power will combine to solve the problem. The solution is already imaginable, and it will be the unintended consequence of other processes.

The unintended consequence is what this book is all about. If human beings can simply decide on what they want to do and then do it, then forecasting is impossible. Free will is beyond forecasting. But what is most interesting about humans is how unfree they are. It is possible for people today to have ten children, but hardly anyone does. We are deeply constrained in what we do by the time and place in which we live. And those actions we do take are filled with consequences we didn't intend. When NASA engineers used a microchip to build an onboard computer on a spacecraft, they did not intend to create the iPod.

The core of the method I have used in this book has been to look at the constraints placed on individuals and nations, to see how they are generally forced to behave because of these constraints, and then to try to understand the unintended consequences those actions will have. There are endless unknowns, and no forecast of a century can be either complete or utterly correct. But if I have provided here an understanding of some of the most important constraints, the likely responses to those constraints, and the outcome of those actions on the broadest level, I will be content.

As for me, it is extraordinarily odd to write a book whose general truth or falsehood I will never be in a position to know. I therefore write this book for my children, but even more for my grandchildren, who will be in a position to know. If this book can guide them in any way, I will have been of service.

ACKNOWLEDGMENTS

This book could not have been even imagined, let alone attempted, without my colleagues at Stratfor. My friend Don Kuykendall has been steadfast and supportive throughout. Scott Stringer has been patient and imaginative with the maps. All at Stratfor have tried to make me and this a better book. I particularly want to thank Rodger Baker, Reva Bhalla, Lauren Goodrich, Nate Hughes, Aaric Eisenstein, and Colin Chapman. In particular, I want to thank Peter Zeihan, whose meticulous and withering critiques helped me, and irritated me, immeasurably. Outside the Stratfor family, I want to thank John Mauldin and Gusztav Molnar, who taught me other ways to look at things. Susan Copeland made sure that this, and many other things, got done.

Finally, I want to thank my literary agent, Jim Hornfischer, and Jason Kaufman, my editor at Doubleday, both of whom made great efforts to try to lift me beyond the impenetrable. Rob Bloom made sure it all came together.

This book had many parents, but I am responsible for all its defects.